The Final Odyssey of the Sweet Ride

Bill "Spaceman" Lee's Epic Journey Through America

In Search of Heat-Moon's Banana Slug

Scott Russell

Visit our website at
www.StillwaterPress.com
for more information.

First Stillwater River Publications Edition

ISBN 978-1-955123-72-3

Library of Congress Control Number: 2021925600

1 2 3 4 5 6 7 8 9 10
Written by Scott Russell
Images courtesy of Bill Lee & Scott Russell
Published by Stillwater River Publications,
Pawtucket, Rhode Island, USA

Publisher's Cataloging-In-Publication Data
(Prepared by The Donohue Group, Inc.)

Names: Russell, Scott D., 1945- author.
Title: The final odyssey of the sweet ride : Bill "Spaceman" Lee's epic journey
through America in search of Heat-Moon's banana slug / Scott Russell.
Description: First Stillwater River Publications edition. |
Pawtucket, RI, USA : Stillwater River Publications, [2022] | Book two of a trilogy.
Identifiers: ISBN 9781955123723
Subjects: LCSH: Lee, Bill, 1946---Anecdotes. | Pitchers (Baseball)--
United States--Biography. | LCGFT: Anecdotes. | Biographies.
Classification: LCC GV865.L36 R872 2022 |
DDC 796.357092--dc23

The views and opinions expressed
in this book are solely those of the author
and do not necessarily reflect the views
and opinions of the publisher.

FOR BETHANY,
    THE SECOND OF OUR BLASPHEMOUS
TRILOGY.

Love,
Scott D. Russell
2022

For Drexel Twitty

DISCLAIMERS

"Scott Russell's novel Prophet's End should be required reading."
—David McCaine, San Jose Christian Perspective

"Loved every page in this thoroughly entertaining masterpiece ♥.
I highly recommend for any avid reader, baseball fan or not! An
inside peek at a unique man, beautifully written by Scott Russell!"
—Lela Tsinopoulos

"If the second part of the trilogy is half as good as the first, it is a big
winner. Spaceman was a tremendous read."
—Hal McCoy, Hall of Fame writer of the Dayton Daily News

"Scott Russell is a gem!"
—Jane Leavy, Author of The Big Fella, The Last Boy,
and Sandy Koufax: A Lefty's Legacy

"I believe Jane Leavy meant 'germ.'" —Peg Russell, wife of the author

Contents

INTRODUCTION

"When the going gets weird, the weird turn pro."
—*Dr. Hunter S. Thompson*

"Remember your humanity and forget the rest." —*Bertrand Russell*

"Our job is to put all of this in order so that the readers can find the meaning of life."—*Bill "Spaceman" Lee to the author, "Scott Russell?" or perhaps Kilgore Trout*

You hold in your hands a truly extraordinary book. Now I suggest you put it down and read this one. This is the second of our trilogy, "The Final Odyssey of the Sweet Ride," a collaboration between author Scott Russell and Bill "Spaceman" Lee. Our initial foray into the abyss of abject insanity was titled *The Spaceman Chronicles*. Bill Lee and yours truly were looking forward to an actual book tour; however, that possibility was precluded by a global pandemic. It is likely you have heard about it.

Bill had planned to visit numerous Native American reservations across the United States and Canada to spread the word that he and a nitwit—that would be me, Scott Russell—had written a controversial, funny, poignant, and perhaps even occasionally blasphemous biography about his life. Covid-19, or Covid Freddie Lynn as the Spaceman often referred to it, prevented such a tour. Billy Shakespeare no doubt was also faced with numerous obstacles as he weaved his magic.

Since the Spaceman and I were prevented from traveling across our vast country, we chose a more practical method in "getting the word out," still another of the countless silly idioms in our vocabulary. We resorted to various other means of promoting our work, including "virtual" book appearances and radio interviews whenever provided with the opportunity. What more effective way, thought Bill Lee, than calling NPR (National Public Radio) and informing the masses that he and his brilliant literary partner (that would be me) had collaborated on an instant classic, his astoundingly great biography, *The Spaceman Chronicles*. Therefore, one bright morning—or was it evening? we forget—Bill Lee decided to call a program hosted by a young woman named Jane Lindholm and provide her with a once-in-a-lifetime opportunity to thrill her listening audience by hearing the Spaceman's dulcet tones describing his venture into the world of literary immortality.

I should note that Ms. Lindholm has an extensive and impressive background. For quite some time she hosted the award-winning Vermont public radio program, "Vermont Edition." The erudite young woman earned a BA from prestigious Harvard University and her father, Karl Lindholm, served as the dean of students at Middlebury College in Vermont, perhaps the most eminent language university on the entire planet. The fact that Karl Lindholm is a good friend of Bill Lee also served as a good omen that the Spaceman would have an eager and perhaps even elated audience. Alas, the plans of left-handed space travelers and former Vermont gubernatorial candidates often go awry. As the Spaceman described his ill-fated attempt to join the program:

"I called in early and since Jane Lindholm's dad is a good friend, I didn't anticipate not getting on the program. During the time I was placed on hold, I listened to the other callers as they discussed "extremely important" issues. Jane Lindholm spoke with a hermaphrodite fraud salesman and some Potawatomi Indian who lectured about frogs in the Northeast Kingdom. Finally, I was bumped by a transexual who recently had undergone a sex-change operation and offered a story about traveling to Ireland to become a Druid priest or priestess, I don't remember which."

The Spaceman had me spellbound, as he continued:

"The woman who had me on hold had no intention whatsoever of allowing me on the air to discuss something as 'mundane' as my biography. This woman sounded like Erin Andrews multiplied by forty. She was speaking at 78 RPM and I'm on 33. She sounded like Bart Simpson. I didn't stand a chance of getting on the air. Finally, the woman—I guess she was the engineer—told me, 'Sorry, but we don't have time for you, Mr. Lee.'"

Bill Lee concluded with:

"Let me ask you a question: If a seventy-four-year-old man calls to ask a question on a talk show hosted by two women, is he always wrong?"

The Spaceman laughed as he offered:

"Jane Lindholm doesn't allow her own father to call in and speak. He disguises his voice and says, 'Hi, it's Earl from Cornwall.' Jane responds, 'Oh, Dad, I know it's you,' and she hangs up on him."

Despite these daunting obstacles, the Spaceman and the author (and there is some confusion as to his identity) plan to "soldier on," as it were. After all, we have "Earl from Cornwall" leading the charge.

The Noble Bards,
Bill "Spaceman" Lee &
Scott Russell?
Kilgore Trout?

FOREWORD

"Earth provides enough to satisfy every man's needs, but not every man's greeds." —*Mahatma Gandhi*

It is somewhat ironic that the earthling known as Bill "Spaceman" Lee resides in virtual isolation atop the highest point overlooking rural Northeast Kingdom in northern Vermont, hard by the Canadian border. The Spaceman and his beautiful Canadian wife, Diana, dwell among the creatures of the wild they both love, and make frequent forays to the places below to acquire food and other means of sustenance that are required to continue to exist in their pastoral environment, albeit one that other members of their too often bothersome species have, in their self-destructive ways, continued to endanger.

Peering down at the world below which includes the beautiful city of Burlington, Vermont, Bill Lee manages to observe mankind, and can easily forecast its inevitable demise. Make no mistake, though, the Spaceman is not one of those nutcases holed up in one of those remote cabins in the north of Montana or Wyoming, armed with a sawed-off pogo stick or whatever, planning to overthrow our government while not paying his taxes. On the contrary, the Spaceman is a nutcase who is perhaps chronicling the end of civilization as we know it, or what passes for civilization these days.

During those times that the Spaceman descends from the rural road upon which he built his home a few decades ago, he is not Andrew Lloyd Webber's "Phantom of the Opera," who in his lust, killed other members of his questionable species and retreated to his perch in the rafters above his most recent carnage. In Bill Lee's actual world, the lone bodies below are the results of "friendly fire," as it were. Homo sapiens, as the Spaceman has observed, are well into the process of committing mass suicides, as well as murder.

The irony, of course, is that Bill Lee, who made his living throwing baseballs in anger at his opponents, is an extremely sociable member of our species. In fact, the Spaceman, much like the author of this tome, either "Scott Russell" or Kilgore Trout, is wont to have lengthy conversations with complete strangers he has just met. There is no anti-social part of Lee's behavior.

Bill Lee majored in geography and baseball at the University of Southern California, although he is also quite knowledgeable regarding geology, and in recent years, has taken a deep interest in meteorology. As an environmentalist, the Spaceman closely studies weather patterns, many of which have been "created" by lesser members of his fellow human race in their quest to destroy what is left of our planet and the creatures that inhabit it. Upon concluding his daily conversation(s) with the author of this tome, Bill Lee nearly invariably reports on current cloud formations, wind direction, and other pertinent information that may be helpful in forecasting impending meteorological events. The Spaceman then plans his day's activities accordingly. I can state this unequivocally: I live approximately 242 miles south of Craftsbury, Vermont and Bill Lee's weather forecasts are generally far more accurate than those Peg and yours truly view on our television screens.

In their infinite wisdom, the keepers of the keys on our endangered planet are determined to make further inroads leading to its destruction. Bill Lee's rustic home in its bucolic setting has a three-tenths of a mile driveway up a steep hill. The nitwit legislators—and that is, of course, redundant—recently requested that since the Spaceman resides at the top of the driveway, that he should name the road. No, really. The reason is apparently to direct emergency vehicles in the event of a crisis. Bill Lee, of course, adamantly refused. After all, he merely comes down from atop the hill, visits his post office and library, and every friggin' postman in the area knows where to drop off his mail. Therefore, Bill Lee was given an ultimatum. Either he named the short road, or they would name it for him. It became apparent, however, that the town did not approve of the southpaw's choice of "The Ted Kaczynski Memorial Thruway."

If the name Ted Kaczynski sounds familiar, perhaps you may recall the man referred to as "The Unabomber." As for the subject of this enormously great book, the earthling known as Bill "Spaceman" Lee, one might believe that his thoughts are often disjointed (keep in mind, however, that Lee is quite the expert on "joints"), and perhaps they are, but there is a method to his madness. One must only know how to crack the code, despite the decalogue, and I promised myself I would include that word in this testament to insanity, being as indecipherable as the Code of Hammurabi. One must pick up the pieces, so to speak.

"The Ted Kaczynski Memorial Thruway." The name seems to roll off the tongue. For those not aware of Mr. Kaczynski, who is still living, incidentally, he is currently serving eight concurrent life sentences in a federal penitentiary. Kaczynski, the aforementioned infamous "Unabomber," has quite a diversified portfolio. If Kaczynski had a business card, it might read, "American domestic terrorist, anarchist, mathematics professor, author, and environmentalist."

Ted Kaczynski abandoned his academic career in 1969 (the Space-man surmises that the Mets becoming a winning team might have driven him over the edge) to pursue "a more primitive life," and in truth, he may have succeeded in that endeavor. Proving that he was indeed a concerned environmentalist, after moving to a remote cabin near Lincoln, Montana in 1971, a shack sans electricity or running water, he began in earnest to end the lives of folks he believed to be advancing the modern technology which would eventually destroy our environment. Between 1978 and 1995, Kaczynski's strategically placed bombs killed three people and injured another twenty-three in a nationwide bombing campaign. Much like Clay Allison, a character in Lee Child's *New York Times* best-selling Jack Reacher novels, who was once quoted, "I never killed a man who didn't need killing," Ted Kaczynski's calling was, at least according to him, a noble and praise-worthy cause. Hell, someone must protect our rivers and streams.

Ted Kaczynski was indeed a brilliant, if not an overly sensitive, individual. He earned a BA in mathematics from prestigious Harvard University in 1962 and his fraternity of three years is still renowned as one of the most educationally advanced associations in western civilization: "Eliot House." *

Kaczynski was described by his fellow students as "very intelligent, but socially reserved."

* It should be noted that the author of this tome, "Scott Russell," whose existence is circumspect at best, was somewhat affiliated with Eliot House for many years, through a figure skating exhibition called "An Evening with Champions," an event which raised hundreds of thousands of dollars for the "Jimmy Fund," a part of the Dana-Farber Children's Cancer Institute, and that Bill "Spaceman" Lee had attended the affair. Both men, however, deny knowing anyone named Ted Kaczynski.

In 1995, Ted Kaczynski, having eluded capture by the authorities, forwarded a letter to the *New York Times*, promising to desist from terrorism if either the *Times* or the *Washington Post* published his essay, "Industrial Society and its Future." A manifesto, as it were.

In 1996, Kaczynski was taken into custody by the FBI and sentenced to eight life sentences, ones that he is still serving. As for the three-tenths of a mile "Ted Kaczynski Memorial Thruway" leading up to "Spaceman" Lee's humble abode near the Canadian border, at last report, the "road" remains unnamed, and our planet remains besieged by those determined to destroy it.

Clay Allison, the character in Lee Child's great books, which included *The Killing Floor* and *Echo Burning*, Allison, the Texan who exclaimed, "I never killed a man who didn't need killing," he REALLY existed. Ironically, the author, "Lee Child" is merely a pseudonym. Lee Child's name is really Jim Grant (James Dover Grant), not to be confused with Jim "Mudcat" Grant, a pitching opponent of the earthling known as Bill "Spaceman" Lee. As the Spaceman recalled, "Mudcat" Grant, a colorful character, once teed off some golf balls and proudly exclaimed, "That ball landed like a butterfly with sneakers on." A majestic shot, I am sure.

To learn more about the Spaceman's "Ted Kaczynski Memorial Thruway," we suggest turning to chapter nine in this tome.

PREFACE

"A masterpiece may be unwelcome, but it is never dull."
—*Gertrude Stein*

"Bill 'Spaceman' Lee qualifies as a "masterpiece." —*Kilgore Trout*

One might wonder how exactly we arrived at the title, *The Final Odyssey of the Sweet Ride: Bill "Spaceman" Lee's Epic Journey Across America*. The answer is not as complicated as it may seem. The "sweet ride" is a turbo-charged 1998 four-door Buick Park Avenue Ultra with a gold leather interior and reclining seats. The earthling known as "Spaceman" Lee had driven it cross-country from California to Vermont following his dad's death some twenty years ago. The vehicle had rested in Bill and Diana Lee's garage until the year 2021. It was then, or now as it were, that the Spaceman decided to spruce it up and once more drive it back to California, and in the process, "take it home, where it belonged."

As the earthling named Bill Lee has often stated, "Life is a journey," and *The Final Odyssey* describes many journeys he has taken during his illustrious and often controversial lifetime, expeditions that he continues to embrace. In so many ways, *The Final Odyssey* pays homage to great wanderers such as William Least Heat-Moon, John Steinbeck, Jack Kerouac, and perhaps the most unusual of all wanderers, a Frenchman named Alexis de Tocqueville, known colloquially as "Tocqueville," who traveled the expanse of the United States and was likely the king of restless souls of that persuasion; the ephemeral thinkers of any generation. Transient souls are often restless, many with differing reasons and backgrounds for their meanderings, but all with a common insatiable desire to see what is beyond the next ridge. Having known "Spaceman" Lee for forty-eight years, I can state unequivocally that he is of the transmigratory species. This then, is a sort of travelogue.

Note: While traveling, Bill frequently asks, "I wonder what's beyond the next ridge?" Diana, his ball-busting beautiful Canadian wife invariably answers, "A Walmart." Diana is, of course, practical.

These types of travelers are often motivated for vastly different reasons. Upon reading William Least Heat-Moon's epic *Blue Highways* and his other extraordinary writings, I came away with the impression that the remarkable Native American's greatest goal was to observe people up close and personal, but rather anonymously, and that is not necessarily a contradiction. On the other hand, upon rereading John Steinbeck's *Travels with Charley*, I arrived at the conclusion that Steinbeck was more of a voyeur. Having known Bill Lee since 1973, I can honestly say that Bill is not only one of the most affable, outgoing, and gregarious human beings I have ever met, but one that comes by his congeniality naturally. There exists little, if any, false pretense.

Make no mistake: Bill Lee is no male version of a Pollyanna. The Spaceman is fully aware that the human species is flawed, and in fact, most likely doomed. He half-kiddingly describes himself as a "compassionate misanthrope." As hilarious as it sounds, it is not that far from the truth. Upon getting to know this truly remarkable character, one will learn that Bill does two things as quickly, if not faster, than his earthly brethren. Those two things are laughing and crying, and often they are affected nearly simultaneously. Bill Lee is often devastated by injustice, and there is an overabundance of iniquities being doled out to those less fortunate souls in our society, especially during these dark days of intolerance. And despite this, Bill also sees what he perceives as hope; from those saints in our questionable civilization that still believe in humanity and in its salvation.

In these pages, as many of you did in our initial collaboration, *The Spaceman Chronicles,* you will get to know the earthling known as Bill "Spaceman" Lee, even more closely. Bill Lee will make you laugh. Bill Lee will make you cry. Bill Lee will make you wonder how the hell he has managed to survive his stay on Planet Earth for all these years. Oh, and there is also little doubt that Bill Lee will please a lot of folks with these tales, as well as infuriate just as many. Just know the following, however: As the great Kurt Vonnegut stated, "All this happened, more or less."

Sincerely,
Scott D. Russell?
Kilgore Trout?

A LETTER FROM THE AUTHOR

I write novels. Novels are largely fiction with various elements of truth interspersed. This is not a novel, although a definition of novel is "not known or experienced before." The subject of this second of a planned trilogy, the earthling known as Bill "Spaceman" Lee, can be described accurately as "novel." Bill Lee, and I've known the man for forty-eight years, is a paradigm unto himself.

Bill Lee is as unique as any character, real or imagined, in American history. He is a conservative with a liberal heart, or perhaps a liberal with a traditional heart. As a self-described "compassionate misanthrope," contradiction be damned, Bill Lee refuses to be stereotyped or pigeon-holed by those that desire to categorize others. He is his own classification, and that category is not determined by partisanship, but by his own moral consciousness.

Much of what is written between the covers of this volume certainly appears to be fiction. I can assure you, however, but implausibly, it is not. When the great Jim Grant, aka "Lee Child," penned his Jack Reacher novels, he mentioned being interested in "dislocation and alienation." Those two terms are indeed part of Bill Lee's persona, but so are the polar opposites: method affection and endearment.

Following Bill Lee around for any length of time is akin to vigilantly tracking a puppy who refuses to be restrained. Pity poor Diana, Bill's long-suffering bride, but also envy her: each day is a new adventure in improbability, perhaps even peril, but never lacking some form of indefinable hilarity. Bill Lee has witnessed the inequities of life for nearly his entire existence, but unlike most of his fellow questionable species, his sensitivity to injustice often manifests itself into an overwhelming empathy, and yes, anger at the establishment.

The aforementioned great author, James Grant, aka "Lee Child," perhaps put it best when he stated: "Character is king. There are probably fewer than six books each century remembered specifically for their plots. People remember characters. Same with television. Who remembers the Lone Ranger? Everybody. Who remembers any actual Lone Ranger storylines? Nobody."

It is ironic that James Grant, aka Lee Child, is British, since he pens the greatest American novels around these days. As for the subject of the second of my trilogy with "Spaceman" Lee, there are no plots in this book. However, just as in Lee Child's Jack Reacher novels, you will remember the character, the earthling known as Bill "Spaceman" Lee. Except Bill Lee, unlike Jack Reacher, is real.

It should be noted that also unlike Jack Reacher, the protagonist in Lee Child's masterpieces, Bill Lee has had no issues to resolve. You see, he is the issue. Bill Lee not only gets caught up in maelstroms, but he is, in fact, often the maelstrom.

Bill Lee is a lot of things, but none of them is indifferent. If Bill Lee had a calling card, it would read, "There is no inequity too small. It must be addressed." Bill Lee is generally the first to laugh. He is ebullient and sees humor in nearly everything. However, Bill will also cry at the drop of a hat. Even motion pictures and books set him off, and no athlete on this planet immerses himself in books more than the Spaceman. Here is hoping that you will immerse yourself in our book(s).

Sincerely,
Scott D. Russell
North Attleboro, Massachusetts
Planet Earth, 2021

THE FINAL ODYSSEY
OF THE SWEET RIDE

Bill "Spaceman" Lee's
Epic Journey Through America

In Search of Heat-Moon's Banana Slug

CHAPTER ONE

Finding Lefty

"Life is the interruption of an otherwise peaceful nonexistence."
—*Anonymous*

"I'm not addicted to cocaine. I just like how it smells."—*Richard Pryor*

Armed only with an outdated map of the Scottish Highlands and his pet three-legged Norwegian rat, "Guido," a defrocked Bulgarian midget priest and his trusty companion, Sylvia, a Romanian strip tease aerialist with a harelip, take off in search of their hero, a former iconoclastic pitcher named Bill "Spaceman" Lee…………Wait a minute, that's our next book. This one revolves around the life of the earthling named William Francis Lee III, the subject of our earlier collaboration, *The Spaceman Chronicles*.

The earthling known as Bill "Spaceman" Lee much like Napoleon, who had been banished to Elba centuries before, found himself exiled to the city of Montreal in the province of Quebec, in a country called "Canada." The year was 1979. Bill Lee, as was his wont, refused to adhere to the archaic rules of major league baseball, and therefore was "punished" for not kissing the ample behinds of the establishment at large, and in particular, those rear ends of Boston Red Sox "management." The Spaceman, however, was determined to continue earning a living by throwing a baseball in anger, and therefore doggedly joined his new ball club, a formerly floundering organization known as the Montreal Expos.

Rather than prove his former "superiors" correct in their assessment that he was no longer capable of dominating major league batsmen, the Spaceman arrived at Olympic Stadium in Montreal and proceeded not only to win 16 games with a stellar ERA of 3.04 but was named "National League Left-Handed Pitcher of the Year" by the wire services. Gee, who knew? Don Zimmer, "manager" and Haywood Sullivan, "general manager" were not the geniuses they pretended to be. Of course, in any endeavor, employees of any organization are afforded "downtime," and during those welcomed respites from gainful employment, boys will be boys.

Upon his arrival in Montreal, Bill Lee was not above indulging in the medicinal benefits derived from the usage of certain consciousness-altering substances. Many in our society enjoy "euphoriants" as they offer an alternative to what others often refer to as grim reality. To each his own. Of course, it is generally forbidden to acquire such psychoactive entities, and since their inherent illegalities are frowned upon by the authorities, one must not be careless when acquiring such beneficial and psychological enhancements. Of course, during his time in Montreal, having "Gustavo" as a trustworthy friend was certainly an advantage for the fun-loving Spaceman.

Recently, Bill Lee was reminded about his illustrious friend, "Gustavo." As the Spaceman recalled:

"I would nearly always listen to Bill Littlefield's show on NPR (National Public Radio) every morning between 7:00 and 8:00 a.m. The show was amazing. It was called *Only a Game*. Then one morning I tuned in and found out that they dropped the show and replaced it with a *Latin American Hour*. I was pissed! I'm livid and I wanted to drop my donations to NPR, but I listened to the first show. It's not that bad. Then I listened to it again and it was really good. By the third week, I was thinking, 'Who the fuck is Bill Littlefield?'"

The Spaceman continued:

"They just did a show, and they interviewed some forty-year-old named 'Gustavo.' The guy is a Venezuelan sub-runner* who ships cocaine out of Venezuela. The guy had seen me pitch when I played for La Guaira, which is a port town. Get this: When he was a kid, he was the head of the LA Symphony Orchestra. He's at the Rose Bowl doing virtual shit (interview), the guy was just in Madrid and I'm getting chills just listening to him because my drug dealer's name in Montreal was also named Gustavo!"

Which brings us to:

One evening before a game in Venezuela, Bill was approached by a youngster approximately twelve years his junior. Gustavo, as the Spaceman would learn, was a former shoeshine boy from the streets of Caracas, Venezuela. As the Spaceman explained:

"Gustavo soon had advanced his career to the extent that he was working for the head of a major clothing company in Caracas, and he was shipping clothing to Montreal. Gustavo was, as I would also learn, shipping cocaine to Montreal. Since I would be now pitching for the Expos once the season would begin, Gustavo approached me at the ballpark and informed me that he had a broken kilo of coke and asked if I would ship the cocaine to Montreal in hollowed out bats. I looked at Gustavo and replied, 'Are you fucking nuts?! I'm a pitcher, what would I be doing with bats?!'"

The Spaceman laughed and added, "Who knows? I could've been the 'El Chapo' of Montreal!"

Not surprisingly, the Spaceman and Gustavo became tight friends in Montreal, Gustavo becoming Bill Lee's "drug dealer."

> * A "sub-runner" transports homemade narco-submarines that are twenty-five to sixty-five feet long. These vessels can carry three to five tons of cocaine and are designed solely for smuggling drugs.

As we detailed in our initial collaboration, *The Spaceman Chronicles*, Bill Lee's closest friend for decades has been Michael Mulkern, an equally brilliant and colorful character. Mike and his lovely wife, Deirdre, have shared countless experiences with the Spaceman and Diana throughout the years, and there is no one on Planet Earth with more knowledge of Bill's history and eccentricities. Therefore, in researching the legend of "Gustavo" and other members of our questionable species, Mike Mulkern shared one of the most hilarious, but true, tales of Bill Lee's early days in Montreal. It should also be noted that Mike Mulkern was NOT married at the time of this escapade and had not yet even met Deirdre. The following are the words of Mike Mulkern:

"During the 1979 season which was Bill's first with Montreal, the Expos had made the playoffs, and Bill had just purchased a house on Landsdowne Street in the Westmount section of the city and he wanted me to renovate the home. I had never been there before but when I arrived in Montreal, Bill was at the ballpark (Olympic Stadium), so he told me he would leave the front door unlocked. Bill had given me the address.

"I was with this other guy, Dougie Price, and my brother Bob, and a girl named Patti who was working with us. Since Bill was at the ballpark, we decided to arrive early and begin our renovation, but upon arriving at the address, we found that the door was locked! Typical Bill! I looked up at the second-floor window and I noticed that a window was cracked open. So, I told the girl, Patti, that I would lift her up to the overhang above the front entryway so she could climb through the window and let us in.

"When Patti came down to the front door and let us in, we brought all our luggage and equipment in. The place was practically empty—Bill had just bought the place—so I figured I would get an early start with the project, so I began ripping wallpaper off the walls to check on the condition of the plaster, so I could start hanging sheetrock the following day. Now this is precious! We went to meet Bill later that night and I complained that he forgot to leave the front door unlocked. Bill turned completely white. He had given us the wrong address. We had broken into and entered the wrong fucking place!

"Bill had given us the address of the home he ALMOST bought, but the one he really purchased was farther up the street. So, we all rushed back to the scene of the crime, and we had to break back into the house. What a friggin' mess! There was wallpaper all over the floor and our suitcases were inside the door. Rather than breaking and entering, we could have been arrested for breaking and leaving. Can you imagine what the folks that lived there thought when they returned home? What the fuck! Is this some sort of joke? Burglars broke in, tore all the wallpaper off the walls, but didn't steal anything!"

If you think that story is hilarious, Mike Mulkern's initial visit to see the Spaceman in Montreal is about to get even more bizarre.

As Mike Mulkern recalled:

"I initially arrived in Montreal on a Friday. Once we got into the correct home and everything had calmed down, I was exhausted. My then-girlfriend, Lisa, was going to come up from Massachusetts to join us on Saturday. Keep in mind that in those days I had blonde hair. Well, it was late, so I went downstairs and climbed into a futon to get some sleep. Also keep in mind that unknown to me, Bill's drug dealer, Gustavo, who I had never met, had the run of Bill's house. Gustavo had a blonde girlfriend named 'Shirley.' So, it was pitch black in the room and I was asleep. Suddenly, I felt someone climb into bed with me. I immediately thought that my girlfriend Lisa had arrived early from Boston to surprise me, and my first thought was, 'This is going to be nice and perhaps very rewarding.' I was thinking 'Let me see how this plays out.' Suddenly, I felt a hand rubbing across my chest. Gustavo cried out with his Venezuelan accent, 'You ain't no fucking chick!' and he jumped out of bed! Gustavo saw the shock of blonde hair, and thought I was his girlfriend, Shirley. That was the extent of my homosexual experience."

4

CHAPTER TWO

Welcome Intruders

"Be careful in search of adventure. It's ridiculously easy to find."
—*William Least Heat-Moon. Only the Spaceman can unwittingly crash a secret meeting of Elon Musk's "Space-X!"*

"The time you enjoy wasting is not wasted time." —*Bertrand Russell*

With the specter of Covid-19 hanging over the entire Earth late in the year of 2020, Diana Lee, the beautiful wife of the earthling known as Bill "Spaceman" Lee, did not think it was a good time for travel. However, Bill and Diana had visited Iowa where Bill had fulfilled a prior commitment and delivered some of Louis LeDoux's (Axis Bat Company) bats to a group of kids, during which one of the moms thanked Bill for providing her son with some sound hitting instruction, and by "hitting" his bats with his pitches.

"She thought I was Jesus Christ. She was close, but I explained that I'm always good at hitting bats."

The Spaceman continued:

"So, Diana thinks we're heading home and she's asleep in the car and we're driving through the area that 'the Spirit Lake Massacre' took place in 1857, an attack by a Wahpekute band of Santee Sioux on Iowa settlements. We went through Wisconsin on our way home, and nobody had a fucking mask on, and everyone was sick. It's where Eugene McCarthy was from and it's where everyone inserts rectal thermometers. I went through a resort town in an area called 'the Wisconsin Dells.' I ran into a guy who gave up two home runs to Mike Boddicker in the Iowa State Championship. I was at four different 'Field of Dreams.' There was even a field named after Dana Kiecker, an obscure pitcher with the Red Sox who won a total of 10 games in his entire career. It was a beautiful field. Hell, I won 119 games, but I don't have a field named after me."

Now it gets worse. As the Spaceman and Diana were driving through Iowa, they stopped briefly at a ballpark that, as Bill stated, was, "In the middle of fucking nowhere." Jim Fanning, for those who read *The Spaceman Chronicles,* was one of the primary villains responsible for Bill Lee being blacklisted from baseball. The great journalist Pat Jordan, the author of the classic, *A False Spring*, also clearly documented Jim Fanning's abject cruelty towards him at the tail end of his once promising career. As the Spaceman explained:

"We're on our way to Northwest Iowa State University to conduct a clinic for kids, so, we're out in middle of fucking nowhere, which in this case was Hartley, Iowa, when we come across a little ball field. Never passing an opportunity to pay homage to a ball field no matter how small, I got out of the car for a closer look. I see a sign hanging on the fence. The fucking thing read 'Jim Fanning Field!' The sonofabitch was born in Chicago and died in London, Ontario, but there is a goddamned field named after him in the boonies of Iowa! My son Andy coached the Northwest Florida State Raiders, so there was a connection. Even in death, I cannot escape the SOB Fanning!

"Diana was still asleep and had no idea that I was still not driving home. When she awoke, we were in Indiana. When we were approaching Vermont from our long trip to Iowa, there's a sign that read 'If you intend to stay in Vermont, you have to self-quarantine for 14 days,' and that means crossing Lake Champlain, so I say 'Fuck you, Phil!' (Phil Scott is the governor of Vermont) I've got to get to Cape Cod, so I went to Cape Cod and spent a great night with Rico (Petrocelli) and the gang. While there, I gave a nice speech for 'the Military Veterans of America' about Otis Air Force Base and my days on the Cape and in the military. There was a golf tournament going on and four guys came over and talked about their kids and bats. One guy is from Andover and he told me he's part owner of a metal fabrication company up in the Lyndonville/St. Johnsbury area (Vermont) and that they have a meeting on Tuesday with Space X."

NOTE: For those not aware, "Space X" is an aerospace manufacturer whose founder is none other than their highly controversial CEO, CTO, and chief designer Elon Musk, who is also renowned for his work with Tesla. Musk, a native of Pretoria, Transvaal, South Africa joined Tesla as their chairman and product architect and became their CEO in 2008. Musk promotes "friendly artificial intelligence" and is a billionaire and one of the richest men on Planet Earth.

Now it gets "tricky." Elon Musk has apparently held "secretive meetings" where he has instructed "Mars colony meeting attendees" to keep them secret! He has apparently hosted a "Space X Mars Colony Convention." It is rumored that Musk has had a few clandestine meetings with the Pentagon!

After the overtly friendly part owner of the "metal fabrication company" informed Bill Lee of the scheduled meeting with Space X on Tuesday, he cordially invited Bill to the event! He informed the Spaceman that the meeting was originally slated to take place in China but had been relocated to Vermont. As Bill stated:

"What the heck, I figured. I was going to drop some lumber off in the area. I headed to see my woodworker, a German named Doug, so I figured I would drop in and say hello to the Space X folks. I drove up this Class 4 road and Diana and I headed to the address which was the Burk Inn. It's a beautiful inn, the bar and the restaurant were closed and there was no one there. There were only two people at the hotel. The guy told me there was a meeting there, but that it wasn't the group I was talking about. It's dark and it's getting late, so we went home.

"The next morning, we got up to go see this fabrication plant over in St. Johnsbury. We arrived at this industrial center where we saw a whole bunch of Hummers and other military vehicles. I went inside and a guy in the reception area looked at me and then walked away. He came back moments later and asked, 'Can I help you?' I identified myself and told him that I had a meeting with Space X. The guy looked at me quizzically and replied, 'They cancelled, I can't help you.' Just then a guy named Lionel approached, recognized me, and said, 'Hey, I know who you are, you're Bill Lee! Are you still pitching?'"

The Spaceman continued:

"Lionel asked, 'How the hell did you know there was a meeting of Space X?' I explained I had been invited. He looked at me and confessed, 'Those guys are in another building across the river between Lyndonville and St. Johnsbury.'"

"I crossed the river and there were six hundred people working and they were all pressing metal for 'Concept Two Rowing' and 'Peloton Bikes.' Man, the high-end manufacturing and welding! I spoke with a young woman down below named 'Royer'; I had played basketball and softball with her dad, Mike. She recognized me. She says, 'I know who you are, but how did you know there was a meeting?' Everyone was paranoid; I had somehow crashed a highly secretive and classified meeting! They probably thought it was a coup. Several people asked us to identify who sent us, but Diana got the guy's name wrong, but soon they texted each other and confirmed we were really invited. Then we found out that the meeting had been cancelled and that the primary architects did not show up. But after their paranoia was quelled, they took us on a tour of the entire plant, and we got to see everything!"

Bill continued:

"The young woman named Royer was apparently some sort of secretary for the Space X group, and her dad, Mike, had a brother we called 'Chubby' who played for our team up there in the Northeast Kingdom. Chubby was a good ballplayer, but kind of nuts, too. He worked on the farm in Irasburg, Vermont. Chubby used to fish on the Willoughby River, and he tried to catch some 'landlocked salmon' that were running back to the lake where the rivers run north. We are part of 'Upper Canada Village.' Well, one day, Chubby was playing center field for us and there was a long drive hit to the left-center field gap which is cavernous. Early in the spring we saw two kill-deers out there (killdeer are robin-sized birds that frequent lakes, ponds, and rivers) and they had built a nest. In that nest, we found three eggs, so we made sure to protect that nest at all costs. The wildlife people really wanted to protect that nest. Chubby tracked the long drive to the outfield, but he stumbled on a rock, the ball hit off his glove and rolled right into the nest and crushed all three eggs. Hey, for a 'deer-jacker' it comes with the job."

What is a "deer-jacker," one might ask? Well, the following tale may very well explain that Chubby Royer, and perhaps other Royers, are not exactly beloved by conservationists worldwide. As the Spaceman explained:

"During the hunting season, Chubby was up in North Troy at the Canadian border, and was embarrassed when he was caught firing a rifle at a mechanical deer. It was 11:00 p.m. when sirens sounded off and flood-lights turned night into day. Since he was practically right on the Canadian border, Chubby Royer was suddenly surrounded by state police vehicles, the Vermont Wildlife Commission, and Canadian government officials. The mechanical deer was placed there to catch poachers. Well, they caught more than one!

The sheriff of North Troy, Vermont asked Chubby Royer what he was doing and what his young son was doing in the car with him at eleven o'clock at night. Chubby Royer truthfully responded, "Sheriff, you caught me fair and square. His grandfather was a poacher, his father is a poacher, and he's going to be a poacher, too."

The Royers, despite their work for Elon Musk, are not likely to receive any nominations for "Environmentalist of the Year."

Just another day in the life of the earthling known as "Spaceman" Lee. Seriously, who else but Bill Lee could possibly crash a secret meeting of Space X?

CHAPTER THREE

Get Off My Lawn!

"We have to stop asking, 'How stupid can you be?' Too many people are taking it as a challenge." —*Anonymous*

The earthling known as "Spaceman" Lee, as affable as any member of our species, upon leaving on a "road trip," often checks in with the Major League Baseball Players Association to learn in advance if any of his former teammates or opponents are living in any of the destinations on or near his itinerary, no matter if they were friendly or not. It is merely a neighborly gesture and one that most of the Spaceman's fellow athletes appreciate regardless of their prior relationship. Notice I said, "most." Former Chicago White Sox outfielder Jim Landis does not fall under the category of "most." In fact, when Bill was kind enough to visit Mr. Landis, although the Spaceman was not anticipating a welcoming reserved for a long-lost friend, he received the following decidedly unfriendly greeting:

"What are you doing here, you goddamned California pinko commie bastard?!"

The Spaceman's initial response was, "Listen, you old fart, I didn't come here for gratitude, but I certainly didn't come here for attitude!"

Jim Landis, the septuagenarian former White Sox outfielder was not about to offer an apology for his discourteous remark, however, as he spewed:

"Oh, so now you're a pretty boy California commie poet, eh?"

Since the Spaceman knew he'd be traveling through Napa Valley in his former home state of California, he figured he'd "reach out" to one of his former foes, the erstwhile legendary Chicago White Sox centerfielder, Jim Landis. Landis, "old school" as you may have surmised by now, was living at an outstanding assisted health care facility called "Piner's Nursing and Guest Home" in Napa. In fact, it was nearby another facility, "The Pine Ridge Nursing Facility" in San Rafael that Bill's mom and dad had spent their final years at, and where Bill's wife, Diana, had procured her initial job as a nurse.

The less than appreciative Jim Landis had been one hell of a ballplayer. A native of Fresno, California, Landis played eight seasons as a great defensive centerfielder, won five consecutive Gold Gloves, and is generally considered one of the best fielding outfielders in major league history. Landis was an integral member of the legendary "Go-Go-Sox," a fabled AL championship team renowned for its speed. Landis's teammates included Hall of Famers Luis Aparicio, Nellie Fox, and Minnie Minoso who *should* be in the Hall of Fame, and the White Sox went on to play the World Champion Los Angeles Dodgers in the fall classic, and Landis batted .292 in that series.

Jim Landis was also, as you may have also ascertained, an arch conservative, much like Bill's dad, William F. Lee, Jr. Jim Landis served in the US Army in 1954-55 during the Korean conflict. It is also interesting to note that Landis had played in Alaska before beginning his professional career, the same as the Spaceman had done years later. However, Landis was twelve years Bill Lee's senior, and in more ways than imaginable.

"You old curmudgeon," Bill Lee continued, "I'm nice enough to come visit you, and this is the way you greet me? I'm probably the first person to visit you in five years! Why don't you have another e-cigarette, you old fool?"

The irascible Jim Landis was not about to offer Bill a seat to reminisce about the old days, however.

"You know," said Landis, "the door swings both ways, and I wouldn't be surprised if you did, too. You can leave anytime you'd like!"

Bill Lee was not about to pass up on the opportunity to bust Landis's balls:

"Your old roommate Gary Peters was my roommate with the Red Sox, too!"

Unimpressed, Jim Landis retorted:

"Yeah, and he couldn't stand your ass, either!"

The Spaceman got in the final zinger, however, as he countered with:

"Listen, Landis: If you didn't wake up on Christmas morning with a hard-on, you'd have nothing to play with!"

It should be noted that Jim Landis passed on October 7, 2017 at the age of eighty-three, and yes, the Spaceman mourned his death.

"Hey, at least Landis's wife liked me," said the Spaceman.

It may also interest baseball fans, that Jim Landis's son, Craig Landis, is one of the most powerful sports agents in professional sports history. Craig is the agent for arguably the greatest current player in major league baseball, Mike Trout, and Craig is the man who brokered Trout's record-breaking twelve-year $426 million contract!

CHAPTER FOUR

Beware the Precocious Child

Walter O'Malley's "Revenge"

"Five out of every six people say that playing Russian roulette is entirely safe." —*Anonymous*

Walter O'Malley, forever a villain in the hearts and minds of Brooklyn Dodgers fans, had seen enough. He was entirely fed up having his storied major league team get their asses handed to them by their upstart, albeit championship Los Angeles neighbors, the University of Southern California Trojans. Hell, USC was a collegiate team, not a major league ball club.

For 16 seasons, the Dodgers had regularly scheduled a spring training exhibition game or two versus the perennial Pac 10 powerhouse USC "Men of Troy." In those sixteen years, USC had a record of 8-7-1 versus the residents of Chavez Ravine. This was akin to the Washington Generals defeating the Harlem Globetrotters. O'Malley, being ridiculed in the press, was not going to allow this humiliation to continue. Therefore, he ordered his manager, Hall of Famer Walter Alston, to field his "A Team" and teach the nouveau riche collegians a lesson they would never forget.

The game was played at Bovard Field on the campus of the University of Southern California on February 21, 1968. With Walter O'Malley's instructions, manager Walter Alston sent his professional regular team out to exact revenge against the collegians of USC. There would be no more ridicule in the press. The benefit game began at 1:00 p.m. PST and tickets were sold for $2.00 to the public and $1.00 for the students.

The Dodgers varsity that day included starting pitcher Claude Osteen, who would start opening day for Los Angeles. Osteen twice won 20 games for the Dodgers and would pitch eighteen years in the major leagues with an ERA of 3.30 accumulating 196 victories. Osteen threw 140 complete games during his illustrious major league career. The Dodger lineup sent out to destroy Rod Dedeaux's youngsters that afternoon included Wes Parker, Jim Lefebvre, Paul Popovich, Bob Bailey, Ron Fairly (a former Trojan!), Willie

Davis, Al "The Bull" Ferrara, and Jim Campanis. The uppity USC Trojans would be provided a long overdue lecture in humility.

Rod Dedeaux took one look at his opponent's lineup and sent his young eccentric lefthander, the earthling known as Bill Lee out to face them. Bill, not yet "The Spaceman" in those days, would be the sacrificial lamb.

The Trojans also had a first baseman named Bill Seinsoth in those days, prominently mentioned in the recently released biography of Bill Lee, titled *The Spaceman Chronicles.* Seinsoth, a great slugger, would blast a three-run home run that fateful afternoon.

As for Bill Lee, who has gone through his entire life in various types of trouble, he would induce Wes Parker, Bob Bailey, and Al Ferrara to ground into double plays on that glorious day. The final score on February 21, 1968 was 5-1 USC and as Casey Stengel often stated, "You can look it up," Collegian Bill Lee had defeated the Los Angeles Dodgers and Claude Osteen, whose pitching mates included Don Drysdale, Bill Singer, Don Sutton, and Phil Regan, and who would often throw to their catcher, Tom Haller.

Ah, but Walter O'Malley would indeed exact his revenge. You see, soon he would cease scheduling the rank amateur USC Trojans on his spring training schedule.

It should also be noted that among those Los Angeles Dodgers Bill Lee faced that afternoon, were the following:

Jim Lefebvre—one of the officious blowhards who as a member of the San Francisco Giants front office, continued to "honor" the blacklist imposed by MLB by preventing Bill Lee from being added to the Giants roster despite the fact that the Spaceman had an outstanding spring training in 1982.

Jim Campanis—the son of Al Campanis, the Dodger front office executive, who had uttered moronic opinions regarding the intelligence capabilities of African Americans on national television, and the same Al Campanis who, as documented in *The Spaceman Chronicles,* offered a thumbs-down as the Spaceman was mowing down outstanding hitters in a "comeback" attempt.

Bob Bailey—the washed-up veteran that Don Zimmer chose as a replacement for clutch-hitting Bernie Carbo during the 1978 season, as Bailey failed to knock in a single run as a pinch-hitter, which, of course, was Bernie's forte.

In the process, Zimmer blew a fourteen-game lead to the Yankees, the largest "choke" in MLB history, one that Zimmer in his "autobiography" with Bill Madden (Zim) stated he was so "proud of."

Tom Haller—the Dodgers catcher who did not appear in the lineup versus the Spaceman that afternoon at Bovard Field, but who, along with the aforementioned Jim Lefebvre as another Giants blowhard "executive," prevented Lee from being added to the roster.

On occasion, there is "logic" in our universe.

CHAPTER FIVE

Violence Erupts at a Lame Costume Party Hosted by the Nitwit President of the United States

A Confederacy of Dunces

"When a stupid government is elected in a democratic country, the best thing about this is that you learn the number of stupid people in that country!" —*Mehmet Murat ildan*

"Stupid people make stupid people famous."
—*Abhijit Naskar,* Mission Reality

"There are many men of principle in both parties in America, but there is no party of principle." —*Tocqueville*

"An honest politician will not be tolerated by a democracy unless he is very stupid, because only a very stupid man can honestly share the prejudices of more than half the nation." —*Bertrand Russell*

"From barbarism to civilization required a century, from civilization to barbarism needs but a day." —*Will Durant*

On January 6, 2021, a group of mental defectives that were egged on by a complete imbecile, who at the time was president of the United States, marched on Capitol Hill in Washington, D.C. in an alleged attempt at insurrection, although the lot of the group was not capable of defining the word, nor were any mentally competent enough to even spell it. As the old saying goes, you can't make this shit up.

The president, a man named Donald R. Trump, who resembled a cross between a human turnip and a farm animal wearing a godawful toupee (the Spaceman suggests you read George Orwell's *Animal Farm*), encouraged his "followers," as it were, to "take back the country" he had lost in a democratic election. Not only did he manage to incite his faithful cortege; he somehow managed fomenting a full-blown attempt at a hostile government takeover. Once the president's group of agitated loyalists had arrived en masse at Capitol Hill, none of them seemed to have even the slightest idea of how to carry out their noble assignment. They seemed more intent on snapping "selfies" and taking a few souvenirs from the interior of the buildings they had commandeered.

This illustrious group of dimwits, many of them wearing rather bizarre costumes and carrying Confederate flags and numerous other misspelled signs and placards, proudly overpowered the few law enforcement officials assigned to guard the symbol of free America. The gaggle forced its way into the quarters normally occupied by members of our legislature, several of whom were present and scurried away from the imminent danger posed by the dolts, some of whom apparently sought to harm them, or perhaps inform them that their "leader," Donald Trump, had requested their intervention. Incredibly, Donald Trump, indeed, literally invited them to his "re-election party."

Note: the Spaceman reminds us that Nixon's troupe at Watergate were known as "the Plumbers," and that most of the legislative escapees from the mob found themselves hiding in the basement and were merely following protocol, which apparently included, "hots on the left, colds on the right, and be grateful shit does not run uphill. Oh, and we should've remembered to bring our own toilet paper."

Several of the insurgents appeared to be the sordid results of crossbreeding and incest, but their enthusiasm was palpable. By God, they were going to take back Trump's country, furniture be damned! Sadly, some of the more seriously inbred brain-damaged rebels had armed themselves with implements of destruction and a few fatalities resulted during the stampede.

From his home in Vermont, the earthling known as Bill Lee looked upon the scene unfolding at Capitol Hill, and was neither surprised by the event, nor was he even remotely astonished by the overwhelming stupidity it required to pull off such an act of brainlessness. Said the southpaw:

"The insurrection attempt would've lasted much longer, but the crowd knew that it had to return the outfits they had rented from the costume company by noon of the following day, or their mommies and daddies would have to pay additional charges for late fees."

Note: The Spaceman conjured up an old joke he suddenly recalled, which went as follows:

"This guy rented a tuxedo for his father, and he kept receiving bills for it, but he didn't pay them. You see, he had buried his father in the tuxedo."

Bill Lee continued:

"News broadcasts made it sound as if this was some sort of an original idea. When Donald Trump is your leader, you aren't capable of thought. They were like animals taught to do tricks, but animals are much more intelligent. Throughout history, in fact, humans learned how to function by watching animals."

The Spaceman took a deep breath and continued:

"How do you think humans learned how to eat? Primitive man watched a seagull drop a clam shell on the rocks below to have it crack open. Then the gulls swoop down and eat the slimy insides. Who told the humans that the gross looking insides of a clam were a delicacy? That's why man invented fire. Man took the first oyster and boiled water once they invented fire. They added some herbs and spices and the next thing, you have bouillabaisse!"

After the cooking advice from the Spaceman it got even better:

"This attempted overthrow was not unique. The great John Kennedy Toole originated this type of insurrection in his hilarious novel, *A Confederacy of Dunces*. The protagonist in *A Confederacy of Dunces* is Ignatius J. Reilly, an obese, slovenly and lazy, albeit hilarious observer of the human condition. Ignatius somehow secures a job at a New Orleans clothing manufacturer called 'Levy Pants' and what happened had an eerie similarity to what occurred in Washington, D.C. on January 6, with pretty much the same results."

The following is a synopsis of the events surrounding what Ignatius, a sentient version of Donald R. Trump, instigated on that fateful day:

Ignatius J. Reilly, the aforementioned protagonist, after attaining employment at "Levy Pants," begins to assert himself. In fact, it was Ignatius's mother who decided to have her son seek gainful employment. Although Ignatius believed the job to be beneath his dignity, he figured he may as well make the best of his job, which is a filing position.

The owner of the company, Mr. Levy, briefly stops by the Levy Pants office to see if he has any personal mail. Soon after being introduced to his new employee, Ignatius J. Reilly, he is made aware that one of the distributors, Abelman's Dry Goods, had complained that the last shipment of trousers had pants only two feet long in the leg. Mr. Gonzalez, another employee, assures Mr. Levy that he had written Mr. Abelman and will resolve the matter quickly. However, Ignatius overhears the conversation and having no inclination whatsoever to cater to the complaints of what he considered ungrateful clients, took it upon himself to revise the letter to Mr. Abelman. Ignatius is convinced that "If Levy Pants were to succeed, the first step would be imposing "a heavy hand upon its detractors." The amended letter is addressed to "Mr. I. Ableman, Mongoloid, Esq." and claimed that Levy Pants intentionally had sent the defective pants to test Abelman's Dry Goods. Certainly, insisted Ignatius, a loyal and dependable outlet of Levy Pants products would be able to make the two feet long pants into a fashion trend and therefore, sell them to the public. Ignatius's letter to Abelman informs him in no uncertain terms to never have the temerity to ever again insult Levy Pants again, and if he dared to, "he shall feel the sting of the lash across his pitiful shoulders."

As Bill Lee stated:

"As crazy as the attack on Capitol Hill appeared to be, it was also hilarious in its inherent hopelessness and futility. This was the mastermind of Donald R. Trump and it was nothing more than orders barked out by a subhuman with the brains of an orangutan and was 'carried out' by an inept group of abject failures. The entire fiasco was doomed to failure because the people who arrived on the steps after being summoned by their 'leader,' would intrinsically disassemble quickly due to boredom and disinterest, much like the group of employees assembled at Levy Pants by Ignatius J. Reilly. Hell, look at the outfits they wore. Ignatius wore a pathetic green hunting cap and viewed himself as a modern-day Don Quixote. None of the people storming Capitol Hill had a clue as to why they were even there. This wasn't an 'insurrection attempt,' it was a fucking costume party.

"As the insurgents left, I think I heard them singing to the tune of 'Stormy Weather,' 'I got no buttons on my fly, stormy weather.' These are the people who had elected Donald Trump in 2016, the final nail in the coffin of the dumbing down of America, the political version of *Fun with Dick and Jane*. Just listen to the orange turnip speak. 'They're good people. They're bad people. Fake news!' Trump's vocabulary consists of thirty words. He appealed to morons."

The Spaceman continued:

"These people went to sleep one night in their parents' homes and as they slept QAnon snuck in and sucked out their brains. The outfits they wore on January 6 looked like they had all been bought at an ebay closeout for juvenile birthday parties. The entire group had apparently raided a Bass Factory Outlet and made off with their entire wardrobe.

"One look at the clothing worn by these imbeciles is enough to ascertain that these people had a collective IQ of eleven. They breached security while adorned in horns, animal pelts, flag capes, Trump jackets, superhero outfits, flag jackets, and some were even so ignorant that they arrived in clothing with the addresses and telephone numbers listing their places of employment!

"In *A Confederacy of Dunces*, Ignatius J. Reilly's attempt at 'insurrection,' met a similar fate. Rather than achieve a victory for social justice, Ignatius wound up being terminated.

However, Ignatius would soon achieve additional 'success' upon being hired by 'Mr. Clyde,' the proprietor of Paradise Vendors, a hotdog vending outfit. Ah, but the plans of brilliant entrepreneurs are often short-lived."

The Spaceman drew further analogies between the occurrences on January 6 and Ignatius J. Reilly's attempted insurrection of Levy Pants in *A Confederacy of Dunces*.

"Ignatius J. Reilly's mother managed to have her wayward son procure a job as a hotdog vendor with Paradise Vendors, but quickly Ignatius falls into disfavor with his boss and proprietor, Mr. Clyde. Ignatius winds up eating a larger amount of the product than he sells, so it is decided to move him to New Orleans's famed French Quarter. Ignatius is instructed to dress in a pirate's costume to attract more business, once more serving as a great analogy to the events surrounding January 6 in Washington, D.C."

Ignatius J. Reilly, of course, the character created by John Kennedy Toole, the genius who wrote *A Confederacy of Dunces*, was magnificent, and as the Spaceman concluded, "John Kennedy Toole was the greatest satirist in the history of mankind."

Oh, if only the ass clowns who arrived at the behest of Donald R. Trump on January 6, were also a satirical creation. Sadly, they were not, are not, and will never be.

As for Ignatius J. Reilly, the earthling known as Bill "Spaceman" Lee reminds us of the words of Jonathan Swift:

"When a true genius appears in the world, you may know him by this sign: that the dunces are all in confederacy against him."

CHAPTER SIX

Improbable Liaisons

"Sometimes people don't want to hear the truth because they don't want their illusions destroyed." —*Friedrich Nietzsche*

"If only God would give me a clear sign! Like making a large deposit in my name in a Swiss bank." —*Woody Allen*

"The problem with politicians is that they attack the symptoms and not the disease." —*Bill "Spaceman" Lee*

Only the earthling known as Bill "Spaceman" Lee could possibly draw an analogy between Albert Einstein and Gene Wilder's character, "Leo Bloom" in Mel Brooks's epic motion picture, *The Producers*.

In Mel Brooks's masterpiece, Leo Bloom is an accountant sent over to audit Max Bialystock's books. The legendary Zero Mostel perfectly portrays Bialystock, a formerly successful theatrical producer who had recently fallen on hard times.

Leo Bloom is a conscientious but rather introverted accountant. As he is in the process of doing Max Bialystock's books, the timid Bloom is told by the gregarious Bialystock, to "move around a few decimal points" to lessen the blow of his questionable theatrical business. As the reluctant and honest Bloom looks for loopholes, he makes what he perceived as an innocuous observation, and states that "a failed production can actually make more money than a successful one. Let's assume for the moment, that you are a dishonest man."

Zero Mostel (Max Bialystock) replies, "Assume away."

Max quickly adds, "So, in order for this scheme to work, we'd have to find a surefire flop!"

The shy and honest accountant, Bloom responds, "What scheme? I meant no scheme. I merely posed a little academic accounting theory. It was just a thought."

Max, of course, seeing dollar signs, loudly exclaims, "Worlds are turned on such thoughts. You bloody little genius!"

Leo Bloom, of course, is somehow talked into the proposal by the hilarious, but forceful and overbearing Max Bialystock, which is where the

Spaceman's analogy to Albert Einstein enters the mind of the iconic south-paw. As the Spaceman exclaimed:

"Albert Einstein was Leo Bloom! His invention of the atomic bomb was much like Leo Bloom's role in *The Producers*. You see his mere equation, 'E = mc2' created the bomb! Like Leo Bloom and so many others through-out history, inventions are often created while looking for something entirely else! Einstein invented the atomic bomb despite his being a peaceful human being. It was merely an equation he was working on, but he wound up kill-ing more people than Cecil B. DeMille!"

Folks, if you believe Bill Lee to be batshit crazy, you are likely correct; however, "science" has indeed proved him to be accurate in his assessment of inventions. The author, either "Scott Russell," or most likely Kilgore Trout, and Bill Lee, suggest you read James Burke's epic tome, *Connections*, in which you will learn that nearly every great invention was discovered while looking for something entirely else!

The Spaceman is a true believer in something he refers to as "cross dis-cipline." As he has stated, "The key prerequisite for success is to think across discipline. Through the import comes the expert. Applying knowledge to new situations and considering different viewpoints, evaluating all options and evidence will create a critical thinking disposition. For instance, bicy-cle guys discovered aviation. Your brain somehow 'clicks over.' Another guy attempting to invent a substance wound up tossing it down the drain, and in the process wound up inventing plastic."

Had enough? Wait, because there's more. The Spaceman was reading a book written by Norbert Wiener, who happened to be around in the nine-teenth and twentieth centuries. At the age of seven, Wiener was already reading books on biology and physics. Wiener was also a renowned math-ematician. It should be noted that since he reached the age of reason, Bill "Spaceman" Lee has been a true believer that everything in our lives is con-nected. Consider the following: The Spaceman drew an analogy between Albert Einstein and the character "Leo Bloom" in a Mel Brooks movie. The protagonist in *The Producers* was played by Zero Mostel and his name was, of course, Max Bialystock. The mathematician, Norbert Wiener, who had a great influence on Bill Lee, had a father named Leo! Not Leo Bloom, but "Leo" Wiener, who was born in……….Byelostok, Russia!

By now you are most likely beginning to feel some empathy for the late Don Zimmer.

CHAPTER SEVEN

In Which Will Durant Meets Bertrand Russell as Nietzsche Finally Receives a Shot of Penicillin

Sort Of

"Men are born ignorant, not stupid. They are made stupid by education." —*Bertrand Russell*

The earthling known as Bill "Spaceman" Lee is a devout follower of philosophers such as Friedrich Nietzsche and Jared Diamond. The Spaceman, who believes strongly that agriculture was the biggest mistake in the history of mankind, enjoys the works of Professor Diamond, despite the fact that Diamond taught at UCLA and not the Spaceman's alma mater, USC, which he refers to as the "University of Spoiled Children."

Professor Diamond was born in Boston in 1937 and was professor of geography as well as a physiologist but expanded into evolutionary biology and biogeography. The Spaceman raves about his book, *Upheaval: Turning Points for Nations in Crisis.*

Bill Lee consistently quotes Nietzsche and has proudly exclaimed, "Nietzsche only sold forty books and he had to self-publish!" Nietzsche, who is renowned for his claim that "God is dead," originally published *The Joyful Wisdom* in 1882, and according to the Spaceman, "He only sold forty books and had to self-publish!" Nietzsche, a hero to erudite free thinkers everywhere, published a second edition in 1887 after the completion of *Thus Spoke Zarathustra* and *Beyond Good and Evil.*

As the Spaceman explained, "You've got to live in the present, but that brings in nihilism." Listen, you folks do the research; I am mentally exhausted. However, the Spaceman did offer, "Professor Jared Diamond of UCLA basically disproved everything in the Old and New Testament in a great course he taught at UCLA, including all of the contradictions including 'Thou Shalt Not Kill,' not unless, of course, the guy fucking deserved it." *

> * This, I believe was a reference to an actual character in the Jack Reacher novels named Clay Allison, who was quoted as saying, "I never killed a man who didn't need killing." Don't laugh. This series of books written by Lee Child, whose real name is James Dover Grant, are *New York Times* bestsellers.

The Spaceman then offered his take on what God might say after receiving a less than glowing review of His Bible:

"Critics are everywhere. My book has sold more copies, and in more languages than every one of theirs put together!"

Once more, it was time for Bill Lee to wax philosophical:

"The arrogance of most modern day 'Christians' is astounding. They all believe, or claim to, that God will come back during their lifetime. Their 'lifetime' spans maybe eighty, ninety years tops. He hasn't returned in over two thousand years, but He'll be back by this October, for sure. That's why these evangelists charge so much for their shit. Because they can. Remember, the thinking brain is not driving the fucking car. Mark Madsen covered the subject perfectly in *Everything is F*cked*. He said this book is about hope, but not Bob."

There have been countless philosophers who have sought the truth. One of these noble men was Will Durant, who not only sought out the great Bertrand Russell for advice, but in the process also forwarded copies of his missive to Russell and various other luminaries in the hope of learning more about the human condition. Therefore, his letter to Bertrand Russell (who, Bill Lee observed, "looked exactly like Harpo Marx") written in 1931, was also "copied," as it is in the modern vernacular, to President Herbert Hoover, the Hon. Ramsey McDonald, Winston Churchill, Guglielmo Marconi, Igor Stravinsky, Marie Curie, Thomas Edison, George Bernard Shaw, Mahatma Gandhi, Eugene O'Neill, Joseph Stalin, Richard Strauss, H.G. Wells, Sigmund Freud, Albert Einstein, and even Benito Mussolini!

It certainly appears as if Will Durant, himself a noted observer of mankind, desired answers to eternal questions, and therefore, his three-page letter to Bertrand Russell, read in part:

Dear Earl Russell,

Will you interrupt your life for a moment and play the game of philosophy with me? Write briefly if you must, and at your leisure if you can possibly respond. However, every word from you will be precious to me.

Sincerely,
Will Durant

It speaks volumes that Bertrand Russell did not respond to Will Durant, but that the genius, Dr. Albert Einstein, replied to Bertrand Russell!

As one might expect, this occurrence conjured up thoughts in the far reaches of Bill Lee's brain, and Bill responded with:

"Can you imagine the pressure of receiving a letter seeking advice from you as to the condition of the human species, while seeing that the sender has forwarded the copies to political leaders, scientists, composers, sociologists, inventors, physicians and other geniuses, and that he expects YOUR response?!"

I then asked how he would have reacted. The Spaceman's reply was priceless:

"There was a complete imbecile, as most political appointees are, back in the 1960s. His name was Earl 'Rusty' Butz, and he had the brain of a flea. Of course, since he was entirely useless, President Nixon appointed him Secretary of Agriculture. This guy couldn't spell cat if you spotted him the 'C,' the 'A,' and the 'T.' He would've thought it was a trick question. After Nixon, he worked under Gerald Ford.

"In 1974, at a World Food Conference in Rome, Butz made fun of Pope Paul VI's opposition to population control by using a mock Italian accent. Butz said, 'He no playa the game, he no maka the rules.' Then in 1976 after the Republican Convention, Butz was on a commercial flight from California. He was seated with Pat Boone, a right-wing conservative, and White House Counsel, John Dean (Watergate). Pat Boone asked Butz why the party of Lincoln couldn't attract more blacks, and Butz's answer was colossally ignorant and racist. It's how I would've written back to Will Durant's letter. I would've paraphrased Butz just to blow Will Durant's mind. Butz told Pat Boone, 'I'll tell you what the coloreds want. It's three things: First, a tight pussy; second, loose shoes; and third, a warm place to shit.'"

The Spaceman said that incredibly, in the year 2021, not only are appointees such as "Rusty" Butz still around; one was an orange-haired lowlife prick who recently lost his presidency.

As a footnote, I should add that the great, and that he was, Friedrich Nietzsche, succumbed at the age of fifty-six in 1900 to syphilis. Shit happens.

CHAPTER EIGHT

In Which the Spaceman Mentors Ted Williams in Hitting

"Do you know what keeps me grounded? The same thing that keeps the beer in my glass – gravity." —*Bill "Spaceman" Lee*

"I never questioned the integrity of an umpire. Their eyesight, yes." —*Leo Durocher*

"By the time you know what to do, you're too old to do it." —*Ted Williams*

Ted Williams, aka "Teddy Ballgame," aka "The Splendid Splinter," is generally regarded as the greatest hitter in major league history. The last man to bat .400 some eighty years ago, a war hero as a US Marine pilot, a man who legendary astronaut John Glenn referred to as the best pilot he had ever flown with, Williams was also renowned as the ultimate authority on the art of hitting and was also famous for not being exactly shy when regarding his own genius in the art form. Therefore, when the earthling known as Bill "Spaceman" Lee sat down on a bench next to Teddy Ballgame in Winter Haven, Florida during the 1970s, where Williams was in the process of providing helpful tips to Red Sox hitting hopefuls during spring training, and Lee began offering, without being asked, of course, his theories regarding left-eye, right-eye dominance as it pertained to hitting, very few expected the conversation to be taken seriously by the legendary #9.

Shortly after seating himself next to the man that nearly every baseball player in the world would absolutely give nearly anything to discuss hitting with, the Spaceman somewhat implausibly began holding court. Bill informed the man who batted .406 in 1941:

"You know, you're the luckiest sonofabitch in the world, because you're right-eye dominant."

As most people who listen to the Spaceman expound his theories, Ted Williams appeared incredulous, but Lee continued:

"Ted, you are right-eye dominant and since you bat left handed, your right eye is on the pitcher and your big fucking horn of a nose isn't blocking your vision."

The conversation between the great Ted Williams and the erstwhile southpaw pitcher went on for several minutes. Those that observed it were convinced that when it concluded, Ted would merely walk away, shake his head, and perhaps exclaim, "The man is nuts!" There is a photo of the two men having this conversation, and one can plainly see that Ted Williams is laughing uproariously but witnesses also saw Ted nodding his head affirmatively during the Spaceman's science lesson.

The conclusion of the now historic meeting between the greatest hitter who ever lived and the earthling known as "Spaceman" Lee spoke volumes about the similarities and differences between the two icons. Williams, who was truthfully impressed by Lee's left-eye/right-eye dominance theory, believed it was time to offer a theory of his own. Therefore, he asked the Spaceman the following question:

"Do you know what makes a curve ball break?"

Shockingly, the Spaceman did not respond by asking perhaps the most opinionated baseball player of all time for the answer to the question. Instead, Bill Lee reacted by exclaiming:

"Yes, I do. This movement was explained by a Belgian physicist named Daniel Bernoulli in what is now commonly known as 'Bernoulli's Principle.' Bernoulli discovered it in 1738 and published it in his book, *Hydrodynamica*. This theory also can be applied to the fluidity of a baseball bat and the arc of a swing," said the Spaceman.

Bill Lee noticed a somewhat confused look on Williams's face; however, he continued:

"Bernoulli's Principle proves the increase in the speed of a fluid occurs simultaneously with a decrease in static pressure or a decrease in the fluid's potential energy."

Bill Lee most likely did not notice the vacuous expression on Ted Williams's face, but Teddy Ballgame shook his head affirmatively and that is when his personal caddy, Al Forester, arrived to rescue the marine fighter pilot, a hero of both World War II and the Korean War. Ted Williams hopped aboard Forester's golf cart, and as the Spaceman observed:

"As Forester drove Ted away on the golf cart, Williams was excitedly pointing at a fucking palm tree and covering one of his eyes! He was testing my dominant-eye theory."

It is telling that as Al Forester drove Ted Williams to safety, and keep in mind that Williams often expounded regarding his belief that hurlers lacked intelligence, Ted suddenly and unexpectedly remarked, "All pitchers aren't as dumb as I thought they were."

It should also be noted that in May of 1750, the brilliant physicist and mathematician Bernoulli, who was born in the Netherlands, was elected a "Fellow of the Royal Society." However, over two centuries later, the earthling known as Bill "Spaceman" Lee would be "elected" into "The Royal Order of Buffalo Heads."

Soon after recounting his meeting with the greatest hitter who ever lived, the Spaceman was informing the author that "all snipers are left-handed." Bill backed this theory by alluding to Lee Child's Jack Reacher novels. Somewhat insanely, it all made sense, although, as I told Bill, "If you think I'm about to research the history of left-handed snipers, you're even crazier than I thought!" I began to Google, "Was Lee Harvey Oswald left-handed?" but immediately regained whatever was left of my questionable sanity and never hit the "enter" button on my computer screen. After all, just earlier in the morning, the Spaceman, after watching a number of Marx Brothers films, had quoted Chico Marx, who had exclaimed, "There is no Sanity Clause."

CHAPTER NINE

Orderly Chaos

Storming the Casull (*sic*)

"Do not let a flattering woman coax and wheedle you and deceive you. She is after your barn." —*Hesiod*

"Don't knock on my door unless you know my Rottweiler's name." —*Warren Zevon*

In the foreword to this astounding book, we waxed ecstatic (all right, we were merely content), and made mention of how the State of Vermont prodded the earthling known as Bill "Spaceman" Lee into naming the three-tenths of a mile driveway leading up to his home for the purposes of guiding prospective emergency vehicles up the road in the event of such an emergency, and the fact that the Spaceman, when pressured, offered his choice as the "Ted Kaczynski Memorial Thruway." Bill's response to what occurred should not surprise anyone who has ever met the southpaw:

"First of all, the 'thruway' is a dead end. Government officials have nothing better to do than justify their salaries, so they look for things to discuss while drinking their coffee at their town meetings or whatever it is that they do. Seriously, who the fuck needs to place a road sign on the three-tenths mile of a dead-end road that leads to my home? I guarantee that sign wouldn't last a month with all the snowplows, logging trucks, and MBI Plant vehicles driving to the dump. I'd have three strong chances of having that sign knocked down daily by one of those trucks."

The Spaceman then expounded on the reasons he came to reside in the Northeast Kingdom of Vermont:

"I originally came up on this ridge because I knew it was the dividing point between Canada and the US, and that all the water here would not be polluted. I picked this exact spot because it contained the wellspring that sprung out of the ground that was exactly like the one in John Steinbeck's *To a God Unknown*, one of his first novels. The confluence of the rivers was the dividing line between Upper Canada Village and the United States. When they made it the Forty-Fifth Parallel,* the Americans, in all their brilliance, cheated the Canadians out of three hundred yards."

> * The Spaceman, in his holy wrath, is actually accurate upon researching history, since it seems that in 1771 to 1773, it was decided that the 45th Parallel which separates Quebec from New York State and Vermont was the halfway point between the equator and the North Pole.

ONLY the earthling known as Bill "Spaceman" Lee could possibly offer the following:

"The true halfway point is 16.0 km (9.9 miles) north of the 45th Parallel; this was amended after the War of 1812. This is because the Earth is an oblate spheroid, that is, it bulges at the equator and is flattened at the Pole."

Note: The author was tempted to ask the southpaw how this affected Santa Claus, if at all, but wisely passed on the opportunity. Bill Lee continued:

"The 45th Parallel runs across the continental United States and we screwed Canada out of some valuable territory. This is why in Grey Cup Canadian Football, there are 55-yard lines and the fields are wider. This enabled Doug Flutie to scramble for additional yardage. In Canadian football you can also get away with illegal procedures and the players are permitted to run around like someone stepped on an ant hive. That's why I love pond-hockey, because you can chase the fucker into the next county."

After the author, that would be yours truly, took a deep breath, I sat back and asked the Spaceman if Canada ever attempted to have the United States government correct their egregious land theft, and he responded:

"No, but the Canadiens (as in the Montreal Canadiens) got even on May 10, 1979 in game seven of the NHL playoffs. The Boston Bruins enjoyed a 3-1 lead going into the third period and were still up by a goal with only 2:34 left in the game, when the Bruins were called for too many men on the ice. Guy LaFleur scored on the power play and the Canadiens won in overtime for their fourth consecutive Stanley Cup Championship. All because we fucked up the 45th Parallel!"

As sociable as the Spaceman is, he also loves the seclusion and privacy of his home atop the rural road. One of the Spaceman's neighbors is a gentleman named Scott Reed, a character in his own right. As the Spaceman explained:

"If it were not for Scott Reed, I would've never moved up here. I would have never walked on this property. Scott Reed was the only white guy that my buddy and teammate, George 'Boomer' Scott liked at our fantasy camp."

The Spaceman continued:

"The road was originally called 'Rural Route One,' but then Scott Reed's marriage changed all that. Scott Reed's 'serial' wife came up here from a farm in Hardwick, Vermont with evil intentions. This woman from Hardwick married Scott, divorced him within a year, and attempted to steal his farm. She went through husbands like shit through a goose. She ran the farm and turned the basement of the house into an online gambling parlor. She was running numbers and everything out of her basement in Craftsbury. She actually was the one that named the road as 'Common View Drive!' She and her father came running up here to attempt to steal the property."

Drastic times require drastic measures and as the earthling known as Bill Lee explained:

"I may be a liberal, but I'm a liberal with a gun. I'm your worst nightmare. I took out my Casull handgun with a scope and shouted to this vile woman and her father, 'If I catch you on this driveway again, I will kill you both!' I never saw them again. Punishment deferred is punishment wasted."

The Spaceman then quoted the great American bard, Chris Rock, who stated:

"Guns don't kill people, people kill people. If these bullets didn't cost $1,500, I'd cap your ass!"

Upon researching Casull handguns, they are apparently manufactured by the "Freedom Firearms Corporation," and are considered as the most feared handgun in the world.

Please consider that the Spaceman is not a violent person, and in fact, treats all members of our questionable species with compassion, but this apparently ignoble woman and her father were in the process of attempting to pilfer Bill's good friend, Scott Reed's home. This, then, was perhaps the Spaceman's Dr. Hunter S. Thompson moment. We will explain that analogy shortly.

On another occasion some visitors suddenly appeared near the summit of the Spaceman's driveway unexpectedly. The situation, of course, was not similar. As Bill stated:

"A couple walked up here with their children. At the time I was flying a Cuban flag atop my home, but that didn't seem to deter them.* They arrived at my door. They apologized and explained that they were looking for Arnold Brown's Farm (not to be confused with 'Yasgur's Farm' made famous at Woodstock in 1969). Arnold Brown is a good friend of mine, and his farm can be reached by a trail through a forest behind my property that extends out on Coborn Hill Road which comes out at Arnold Brown's Blueberry Patch. I told them they had found the shortcut and that they were very welcome. I told them to park in my driveway and ride their bicycles and travel about half a mile through the woods to reach their destination."

* The Cuban flag atop the Spaceman's roof was explained as follows:

"The first two ballplayers who visited me up here were Tony Oliva and Julio Becquer, two Cubans who had played with Washington and Minnesota. Becquer was part of the only all-Cuban triple play in history, and that appeared in the most hilarious sports book ever written, *A Season in Hell*, by the great Mike Shropshire, who is one of the guys we dedicated this book to. Whitey Herzog, a great manager, was then playing for the Kansas City Royals, and in the top of the third inning on July 23, 1960, he lined the ball back to Pedro Ramos, who fired it to Julio Becquer, who in turn, threw it to José Valdivielso, completing the lone all-Cuban triple play in baseball history. Not only that, but the third baseman for Kansas City that day was my first manager in Boston, and my first manager in Montreal, the great Dick Williams! Oh, and Williams went 3-4 in that game."

And to think that the Spaceman visited Cuba for nineteen consecutive years, once more proving his theory that everything is connected.

During this period, Scott Reed's home had been abandoned, during the "war" with his then soon-to-be-former wife.

Hardly the greeting that Scott Reed's former wife and father received from the Spaceman. Bill Lee then went on to introduce Arnold Brown, the owner of the blueberry patch as follows:

"Arnold Brown was an immigration officer who had been blind for the past twenty years of his life. Arnold was the one who swore David 'Big Papi' Ortiz in as an American citizen. He loved listening to audio tapes. I once drove both Scott Reed and Arnold Brown to the Junction and after the trip I told Arnold, 'I don't think I can ever wear glasses again.' He asked me why, and I replied, 'Because you just talked my fucking ears off!'"

Oh, I had mentioned earlier how the incident in which the Spaceman had scared Scott Reed's ex-wife and father-in-law off the property with his Casull handgun was reminiscent of a typical Dr. Hunter S. Thompson incident. Well, many years ago, the great singer and composer, John Denver, purchased a home in Aspen, Colorado approximately a quarter mile away from that of Dr. Thompson, a brilliant but unpredictable and zany counter-culture award-winning journalist.

Many of the homes in Aspen were both quite expensive and equally remote. Upon moving into his new abode, John Denver, who was by then a renowned and successful performer, began to hear gunshots. He soon learned that Thompson, living up the road, was firing a shotgun indiscriminately towards Denver's new digs. Arriving at the sentient conclusion that this type of neighborly greeting was not amenable to friendship, and quite frankly, was life-threatening, young John Denver sprang into action. One early evening, Denver arrived at Hunter S. Thompson's front door, armed only with a couple of cases of Coors Beer in his arms. Denver cautiously rang the doorbell. The door opened slowly, and John Denver was immediately staring into the barrel of Dr. Hunter Thompson's rifle, which was aimed at his head. John Denver smiled and said:

"Hi, my name is John Denver and I just moved in down the road. Therefore, I thought I'd be neighborly and offer this gift."

Dr. Thompson slowly lowered his rifle. With a quick and deft move, he grabbed the two cases of beer out of John Denver's hands, tossed the brews inside, and slammed the door in John Denver's face. John Denver laughed as he explained:

"As soon as he slammed the door closed, I heard him bolt the door, and from inside I heard him say, 'He's not that bad of a kid after all.' The firing of shotgun blasts towards my home ceased immediately thereafter."

CHAPTER TEN

Close Encounters of the Weird Kind

"You will never understand the damage you did to someone until the same thing is done to you. That's why I am here." —*Karma*

Julia Phillips, the earthling known as Bill "Spaceman" Lee reminds us, ended up being an outcast from Hollywood because she had the audacity to expose what really goes on behind the scenes. All Julia Phillips accomplished was to become the first woman to ever win an Academy Award for the best motion picture, *The Sting*. Julia, along with her husband and others, wrote three prominent films of the 1970s, including *Taxi Driver* and *Close Encounters of the Third Kind*.

During postproduction of the groundbreaking *Close Encounters*, Julia, who was apparently a cocaine abuser, came under heavy fire from one of the stars of the film, Francois Traffaut, who publicly accused her of being incompetent, a charge she rejected, and countered that she had, in fact, nursed Truffaut through his self-created nightmare of implied hearing loss, sickness, and chaos during the production. He said, she said.

Julia Phillips, to her credit, admitted that she was a notorious cocaine addict and detailed her indulgence in the drug in her memoirs. With Traffaut's "assistance," Julia was fired from the postproduction of the amazingly successful motion picture.

In 1991, Julia penned *You'll Never Eat Lunch in This Town Again*, a powerful exposé about her experience in Hollywood. The book topped the *New York Times* bestseller list, but its revelations about high-profile film personalities, Hollywood's drug culture, and the "casting couch" practices of numerous male Hollywood moguls who preyed upon aspiring young women attempting to make it in Hollywood, drew ire from the all-too-powerful hierarchy of the film industry. Upon considering the recent disclosures of such predatory practices in recent years, Julia Phillips was apparently way ahead of her time; however, she paid dearly for exposing the brutal truths.

Julia Phillips, a brilliant and courageous woman, died in 2002, at the tender age of fifty-seven.

As Bill Lee stated regarding Julia's *You'll Never Eat Lunch in This Town Again*, he half-jokingly offered, "When our books are completed, I may never be allowed to eat another meal in Boston!"

Keep reading, though. As the Spaceman also exclaimed, "When all things are said and done, I'm going to be the guy that wrote the modest proposal. If one must live in an absurd society, the best way to attack it is through satire."

CHAPTER ELEVEN

For Whom the Bell Tolls

"A stiff cock has no conscience." —*Dick Radatz*

"When the blood flows from the big head to the little head, bad things happen." —*Dick Radatz*

As we mentioned in "Letter from the Author," if it were not for the great, late Jim Bouton, the entire genre of "tell-all" sports books would not have been possible. Not only did Bouton forever open the doors for all to follow, but he did so at great cost to himself. By exposing the truth and, in effect, revealing the athletes as fellow human beings with their frailties and shortcomings, he essentially ended his playing career and firmly established himself as a pariah to those that desired to maintain the myth that major league players were somehow elite men incapable of wrongdoing.

Those of us old enough to realize that our heroes were not to be confused with the geniuses of the twentieth century were already aware it was folly to even consider that they were all exemplary citizens incapable of committing acts of indecency, or perhaps even having untoward thoughts. Well, maybe Bobby Richardson, but you get the picture.

Speaking of Richardson, who was one of those holier-than-thou type players, he had the countenance of some sort of religious deity, and in fact became a minister after his playing days concluded. The author had a dear friend, an Irishman, who, for lack of a better description, had what we often suggested, was an insatiable thirst for the healing grape. During those rare occasions that Patrick and I were not in the process of visiting New York City watering holes, he would telephone me, while drinking, of course, and offer his most recent eyewitness account of current newsworthy events. On one of these occasions, Patrick, as he was wont to do, awoke from his most recent stupor, flipped on his television set, and watched as Pope Benedict XVI was being chauffeured around the playing field at Yankee Stadium. The date was October 4, 1965 and I picked up my telephone and heard Patrick ask:

"What the fuck is going on at Yankee Stadium? Is this 'Bobby Richardson Day'?"

Well, Jim Bouton, for those of us that recognized flawed humanity for what it really was, became a spokesman for a generation of fans who desired enlightenment and not the genuflection by the acolytes of absurd divinities. Hell, Mickey Mantle was suddenly exposed as less than a superhero, which, at least to most discerning people, made him MORE of an exemplary, albeit flawed, member of our species. Who knew? In truth, we were all aware, but refused to allow our distorted illusions to be shattered by reality. Mickey apologized to Jim Bouton many years later, and it speaks volumes regarding Bouton's character that he accepted the apology.

One of, if not the most endearing character in Jim Bouton's classic *Ball Four* is Gary Bell, an outstanding right-handed pitcher, who was not only a teammate of Bouton's, but also of Bill Lee on Fantasy Camp teams once both their major league careers had ended. Gary Bell, a native of San Antonio, Texas, was perhaps even a zanier and more colorful character than the earthling known as Bill "Spaceman" Lee. Upon Lee uniting at Fantasy Camps with "Ding Dong" Bell, as he was nicknamed due to his eccentricities; both Bell and the huge former Red Sox closer, Dick "The Monster" Radatz, did not immediately take too kindly to the Spaceman. Both Bell and Radatz, who were, it should be noted, never known to pass up an opportunity to imbibe a refreshing alcoholic beverage, considered Bill Lee to be a "stoner." However, Bill was with Gary Bell the very first time that Radatz smoked dope, and Bell divulged that before the evening was over, the three of them were throwing footballs around in their hotel room.

Although Bell and Radatz were correct in their assessment of their new left-handed teammate, the three men soon became fast friends.

Gary Bell was an outstanding major league pitcher. Between the years 1958 and 1969, Bell compiled a mark of 121-117 with an excellent 3.68 ERA. Alternating between starting roles and the bullpen, Bell hurled 71 complete games and earned 50 saves. The free-spirited Texan became Jim Bouton's teammate in 1969 with the expansion Seattle Pilots, a season that would spell the final year of Bell's career and arrived during the latter stages of Bouton's. In Bouton's hilarious tales regarding both his teammates and opponents, Gary Bell would come away as delightfully eccentric, and a man with a great zest for life and an unparalleled sense of humor.

Despite their rocky start as prospective friends at Fantasy Camp, both Gary Bell and Dick Radatz quickly began to appreciate the Spaceman for what he was, a fellow fun-loving goofball. Not only did the three men "invent" new methods of getting into all types of trouble, but they recounted tales of the past, all of which were equally hilarious and mischievous. Gary Bell told of the time that Radatz was out in the bullpen in Chicago and was "in the process of being blown by "Chicago Shirley," when the phone rang, and it was manager Johnny Pesky calling to alert the bullpen catcher, Bob Tillman to "get Radatz up." Bob Tillman peered over to where Shirley was crouched beneath an overhang on her hands and knees performing oral sex on the huge relief pitcher, and responded, "He's already 'up.'"

Gary Bell roomed with the hulking six feet six, 250-pound Radatz and awoke one morning and heard Radatz snoring loudly. He peered over to where Radatz lay, to see that Radatz had a sizeable hole in his underwear, out of which his penis was protruding, and Gary Bell described the scene as follows:

"It looked like a baby's arm with an apple attached to it."

The Spaceman really loved Gary Bell, who he described as "Slick as owl shit on a sycamore tree. I mean, no wonder Jim Bouton loved this guy."

As for Dick Radatz, and the Spaceman was dead serious; he believes the following epitaph appears on the tombstone of the legendary relief pitcher:

"Can't a Man Unwind?"

It should be noted that Dick "The Monster" Radatz was bigger than life, both literally and figuratively. The six-foot-six Radatz, a former lineman at Michigan State, was listed at 240 lbs., however, that was obviously an understated measurement as anyone who ever met the man would attest. Radatz was an imposing man on and off the field and unfortunately a man whose career and life were shortened by his addiction to alcohol. Radatz was a fun-loving mischievous sort whose escapades remain almost mythical. What Radatz was, however, was the man who forever changed the perception of the Red Sox as losers and pushovers.

During Radatz's first three seasons in the major leagues, 1962 through 1964, Dick Radatz was the most overpowering relief pitcher in baseball history. During those three years, Radatz won a total of 40 games! That is not a typo. Not saved 40 games but WON 40 in relief. His ERAs for those years were 2.24, 1.97, and 2.29, and he didn't merely pitch the ninth inning, he was frequently called upon in the seventh and often made back-to-back lengthy appearances. During those three seasons, Radatz struck out a total of 487 men in 414 innings! And then liquor took over.

Legendary Red Sox broadcaster, Ned Martin, seeing Radatz warming up in the bullpen, would occasionally remark, "They are assembling 'The Monster.'"

As unpredictably, hilariously bizarre and eye-opening as Bouton's groundbreaking *Ball Four* was, can one even begin to imagine what was NOT divulged in those side-splitting chapters? Well, recently the Spaceman gave Gary Bell a telephone call to check up on his old buddy. Bell, now eighty-four and still enjoying life to the fullest, resides these days in lovely Wickenburg, Arizona, a great old western town with an enormous amount of wonderful American and Mexican history. Much like the great Arizona town of Oatman, approximately an hour and a half's drive from Wickenburg, where donkeys freely roam the streets, there are also several donkeys that can be seen outside of the legendary "Palomino Club" on Frontier Street, a drinking emporium Gary Bell is quite familiar with.

During the Spaceman's lengthy conversation with his old pal, Gary Bell, the subject of Bell's former wife, Nan, came up, or as Bill referred to her, "Nasty Nan," but the moniker was intended fondly. Those that read Bouton's masterpiece, *Ball Four*, may recall that Bouton wrote, "Nan told the story of the time she called Gary on the road to check on a flight she was supposed to catch. She called him at 4:30 a.m., his time, and his roommate, Woodie Held, answered the phone, and said without batting an eyelash, that Gary was out playing golf."

How hilariously outrageous is that? Obviously, most wives would be furious at that response, but as the Spaceman observed, "'Nasty Nan' just laughed and accepted the reply as gospel."

The Spaceman continued:

"You see, what Jim Bouton did not write, but I'm sure he was aware of, was that Nan Bell was a hooker." Yes, Gary Bell met his future wife at the time she was a prostitute.

CHAPTER TWELVE

Eunuchs, Hookers, Lifeguards, Managers & Other Unfortunate Pairings

"It's poor planning to schedule a Nymphomaniacs Convention at the same hotel as an annual Eunuch Rally." —*Bill "Spaceman" Lee*

"All managers are losers. They are the most expendable pieces of furniture on the face of Earth." —*Ted Williams*

Ted Williams, who normally had disdain for most managers, truthfully, never desired to be a manager. As a manager, however, his strength was in his ability to discuss hitting with both his players and members of the press. Being a native of San Diego, Ted wanted no part of managing in Texas, where the heat and humidity was nothing like the comfortable dryness he normally enjoyed on the West Coast.

The author recalls seeing Ted Williams during spring training in Winter Haven, Florida in 1977. Ted was in the process of instructing Red Sox batters in the finer points of hitting, and the "Splendid Splinter," given that sobriquet because of his prior tall slender build, was wearing a jacket in what was stifling heat and humidity. At 10:00 a.m., the temperature was already approaching ninety degrees, the humidity was oppressive, and the middle-aged Teddy Ballgame was no longer the slim version of the youngster that had batted .400 some thirty-six years earlier.

During that morning workout, I was seated at Chain O' Lakes Park, when the Spaceman approached and took a seat to my left. I immediately asked Lee, "What's with Williams's jacket? I can hardly breathe." Bill Lee immediately responded, "Ted is so vain that he doesn't want anyone to see his gut. That jacket is a rubber 'Hodgman' jacket." Bill then pointed to his rotund friend and teammate, George "Boomer" Scott, and continued: "Boomer is wearing the same exact jacket to lose weight. The problem is that as much as he sweats, he eats twice as much."

I laughed as I recalled the time that a wonderful elderly woman named Mrs. Hayes had regaled my wife, Peg, and yours truly about Ted Williams's visits to the elegant "Hayes Guest House" on the Shore Road in beautiful Ogunquit, Maine. Being aware that Ted had been a frequent visitor to the lovely inn, I had inquired if she had any tales to tell. She sure did.

"Ted was a pig," giggled Mrs. Hayes, a gracious lady. "I would bake pies for my guests, and Ted would join me for breakfast and devour the entire pies, and they were huge!"

As for the Spaceman, he told me of the time that Ted took his entire Red Sox Fantasy Team out for lunch, "but he got so hammered (as he frequently did) that he wound up hurling an entire fucking pu pu platter up against the wall. You just didn't discuss politics with Ted Williams, especially when he got older, because the 'branch water'* was affecting his thought process too much."

> * Of course, I had to research "branch water," and I learned that "branch water" is commonly used in the making of bourbon, which was Teddy Ballgame's favorite libation. As the Spaceman explained:
>
> "Branch water is preferable if it has been limestone filtered, in which case it removes the iron from the water." I mean, who knew?
>
> For some reason still unknown to me, the Spaceman then quoted Otto von Bismarck, who stated:
>
> "Laws are like sausages. It is better not to see them being made."

Many of Bill Lee's most interesting colleagues would congregate in the bullpen. In 1972, the Red Sox had some of the more "unusual" members of our species, and if anyone is aware of unconventional individuals it would be the Spaceman. Consider:

"Two of my nuttier teammates were Gary Peters, a great athlete, and Lew Krausse, who was also offbeat. During rallies in the late innings, Peters had this little ritual in which he'd begin to strangle Krausse. He would choke Krausse until he passed out. I just learned that Krausse died a short time ago, and if he succumbed due to strangulation, the first guy I'd question is Gary Peters. Gary Peters told me that when he was with the White Sox, his manager was Eddie Stanky. Peters was the left-handed ace and Joel Horlen was the right-handed star of the team. Stanky would buy them a new suit of clothes if they got twenty-one outs on ground balls. That's a great manager! Not like Don Zimmer. We were mismatched. Hell, anyone with a brain was mismatched if they played for Zimmer."

The Spaceman's thoughts were now running rampant:

"Do you know what the most useless job is in the world? Did you know there are lifeguards at Olympic swimming events?"

The Spaceman, who often lives dangerously, recently described his beautiful bride, Diana as follows:

"She has that gene where her body is producing its own alcohol when she doesn't eat. Her body goes into a mixture of butane and propane, two enzymes in her liver that combine for a volatile solution. If you put her next to an open flame, she'd blow up. Gradual shock. People get pulled over for DUI when they haven't been drinking. I'm pretty sure only the Irish get it. She's Austrian-Irish. That makes her a helluva house cleaner, but only when she's hammered."

I did not ask the Spaceman to elaborate.

CHAPTER THIRTEEN

Golden Jets & Goofy Newfies

"My wife made me a millionaire. But I had three million dollars when I met her." —*Bobby Hull*

The earthling known as Bill "Spaceman" Lee absolutely loves New-foundland and its improbable inhabitants, often referred to as "Goofy Newfies." Newfoundland is part of the Canadian province of Newfound-land and Labrador. The residents of Newfoundland are seldom offended by their designation; one need only to visit their large island off the east coast of the North American mainland to witness the pride they have in being a province of well, "Bill Lees." These denizens of Newfoundland are nearly all deliciously delightful and bask in the glory of their questionable sanity.

There is a marvelous 2001 motion picture, *Rare Birds*, and despite its near virtual anonymity, it is one of the most hilarious films of all time. It stars the great William Hurt, and features terrific roles by Andy Jones and beautiful Molly Parker. The movie is based on a book written by Edward Riche, who having been born in Botwood, Newfoundland, is a native of the world's sixteenth largest island. Riche, in fact, has not moved from his birthplace, as he currently resides in St. John's, Newfoundland. The film is directed by Sturla Gunnarsson, himself also a native of the north. Gunnarrs-son hails from Reykjavik, Iceland.

Bill Lee explains Newfoundland as well as any "outsider" possibly can:

"Goofy Newfies just sit in their garages and watch the world go by. As people drive by, impromptu parties break out. It's natural and spontaneous. When the folks of Newfoundland are forced to leave the island, they break down and cry. There was even a boat that refused to leave the island."*

---

* The Spaceman was referring to a wonderful book written by the late, great Canadian author, Farley Mowat, who hailed from Belleville, Ontario, birthplace of Bill's wife, Diana, and where leg-endary NHL hockey player, Bobby "The Golden Jet" Hull, played minor league hockey. In fact, Diana's aunt once dated Bobby Hull. In Mowat's *The Boat Who Wouldn't Float*, the protagonist grows

tired of living life ashore, and decides to take a boat to Ontario, but the boat will not leave the island. He builds a boat that leaks like a sieve and has numerous other issues which prevent its leaving Newfoundland. It is a love story in so many ways.

For further proof that "Newfies" are indeed, goofy, a tale told in Farley Mowat's magnificent book indicates that even death can be hilarious on the island. Hold on, please, this is factual:

Dildo, Newfoundland is located on the east side of Newfoundland and is, and I'm not making this up, is the "Dildo arm" of Trinity Bay about thirty-seven miles west of St. John's. Now, take a moment to clean up the coffee you just spit out.

Well, in Mowat's book, which is NON-fiction, there are two boys living with their father in Dildo Bay, on an island off the coast of Dildo. These boys were taught to hunt moose and after killing a moose, they would hang the moose in a shack until carving him up for the venison. The boys arrived home one evening and found that their father had died. Upon alerting the local authorities, a neighbor came out to the property and asked, "Where is your father?" The boys pointed to the shack, where they had hung their father, as they would have a moose. That's all they knew about what to do with dead "things."

Bill "Spaceman" Lee, himself a lover of Newfoundland, described his visit to one of his favorite places on Planet Earth:

"We're driving through Gros Morne National Park (the second largest park in Atlantic Canada) we're probably headed out to 'Cow Head,' and it's beautiful, but they're paving the friggin' road and there's only one lane open. We're driving in the area where the famous 'High Cliffs' are. This area is listed on the register of the most picturesque geological formations on Earth. The fjords are amazing. We had to stop for a while until they finally reopened the road. My son, Andy, and I are driving, and Diana is in the back. We're driving on a patchwork quilt of pavement. We begin driving at 100 km an hour—the speed limit is 80—but when we reached 90 km, Andy said, 'Do you hear that, Dad? Do you hear the wheels on the pavement? The car is playing 'Oh Canada!' We were stone-cold sober, no weed, no nothing! Diana thought we were nuts, but each time we hit 80 clicks it played 'Oh Canada!' At 100 clicks, it played Led Zeppelin."

The Spaceman expounded further:

"Diana finally agreed that every patch you hit, it was playing 'Oh Canada.' When we got up to Newfoundland, they were supposed to be flying a group of girls from Cuba and we were picking them up at the airport. They were arriving for a hardball tournament, but when we arrived at the airport to pick them up we found out that they were really a ballet troupe, and that none of the girls played hardball. So, here I was assigned to coach a team of ballet dancers playing in a hardball tournament!

"Incredibly, we won one of the games. The game was played in Pasadena. Pasadena, Newfoundland! Even that story is strange, as are most from Newfoundland. The town was named after a couple from Newfoundland that had traveled to Pasadena, California, where Jackie Robinson had been raised, and were so impressed they named their town, 'Pasadena.' I had to teach these ballet dancers in three days how to play hardball. Only one of the girls even knew what the gloves were for. It was déjà vu all over again. It was definitely a Yogi Berra moment."

Bill Lee reminds us just how different Newfoundland is:

"Consider that Newfoundland is located at a time zone unique in North America. It is half an hour later than 'Atlantic Time,' one-and-a-half hours later than Central Canada, and four-and-a-half hours later than the west coast of the country. While everyone else tells time by the hour, the 'Goofy Newfies' tell time by the half hour! They're precious! Even their brains are off by at least a half hour."

The Spaceman was then reminded of still another Canadian adventure:

"Several years ago, there was a guy named Brown, out of PEI (Prince Edward Island) and he was tight with the old Chicago Blackhawks legendary NHL stars. He had Bobby Hull, Stan Mikita, Pat 'Whitey' Stapleton, and a group of Newfoundlanders and Nova Scotians who were also good players. During their hockey games, they would roll a pitching mound out on the ice, and I would demonstrate pitching while standing on the ice.

"Bobby Hull, a great guy, was also nuts. We partied everywhere we went. Once we were in a small city in Labrador, and these women he knew brought us back to a cabin Hull was familiar with. We were all getting shit-faced and raunchy and suddenly these skidoos appeared outside and the women all shrieked, 'Oh, no! Our husbands are back!' Hull and I jumped out of a second-story balcony into a fucking snow bank! That was Bobby!"

The Spaceman repeated a tale about the great Stan Mikita, told by Mikita's longtime teammate and friend, Bobby Hull:

"Mikita could be a nasty guy on the ice, just like the Flyers' Bobby Clarke. He would always hit people on the ankles with his stick; he was an asshole, but a great hockey player. He was always serving time in the penalty box for his infractions, but one time Mikita's five-year-old daughter asked her father, 'Daddy, why do you have to sit all alone in that box for two minutes all the time?' Mikita looked at his daughter and replied, 'Sometimes it's five minutes, dear.' Shortly after that, Mikita changed his ways and was soon awarded 'The Lady Byng Trophy,' the award for being the cleanest player in the NHL, and all because his five year-old daughter had influenced him."

How outrageous was the great Bobby Hull? Well, as the Spaceman stated:

"When Bobby jumped to the Winnipeg Jets in the WHA, with two great Swedish players, Anders Hedberg and Ulf Nilsson, they formed one of the greatest lines in professional hockey history. They were called 'The Hot Line.' How tight were these guys? Well, one day, Hull received a call from his teammate, Hedberg, who pleaded in his Swedish accent, 'Hey, Bob-bee. Please come over right now. I'm here with my wife and I don't think I can have sex with her if you're not in the room.'"

CHAPTER FOURTEEN

Hockey, Eh?

"Where's Moose Jaw? It's about six feet from a moose's ass."
—*Bill "Spaceman" Lee*

If the earthling known as Bill "Spaceman" Lee had played hockey rather than baseball, there is little doubt that he would have been a Philadelphia Flyer. The Flyers, a motley crew of miscreants, drunks, brawlers, and otherwise disreputable reprobates, were one of the legendary professional sports teams of all time. It is likely that the hilarious motion picture, *Slap Shot*, was influenced greatly by the Flyers' collection of unprincipled vagrants. The Spaceman's dear friend and teammate, the great Luis Tiant, once told Bill Lee, "You know, Bill, you shouldn't fight. You always lead with your face." There is a great photograph of the Spaceman which pretty much proves El Tiante's assertion. It shows Lee on the mound pitching against the Mets. Bill had removed his teeth that day; shortly thereafter an opponent had "removed" Lee's actual teeth with a well-placed right hand.

The Philadelphia Flyers were beloved by their fans in the "City of Brotherly Love," but nowhere else. This collection of ne'er-do-wells was quite capable of getting into an altercation at a church bazaar, and it would surprise very few if such an event really occurred.

Bill Lee was representing Quebec in the Canadian National Championship several years ago, and they had lodged his team in dormitories at the University of Newfoundland in beautiful St. John's, as the Spaceman refers to it, "a great drinking town. It's where Marconi sent the radio telegraph across to Europe."

Bill and his former wife, Pam, then took off cross-country in their Volkswagen VW Bus. The Spaceman explained that trip as follows:

"I had been invited to speak at a charity event, a giant fundraiser for children, and of course, I agreed to. They had given me a twenty-gram black ball of hash, the same shit I had smoked when I crashed it all the way out west in Saskatchewan. We were going there, and I was one of several speakers; most of the others were former Philadelphia Flyers players, and they included Bobby Clarke, Dave Schultz, Marcel Dionne, and Clark Gillies. The bash was in Moose Jaw, which is approximately six feet away from a moose's ass.

"The night before the banquet, we had parked the VW bus in a ceme-tery in Swift Current, the same town as my former teammate, Reggie 'Sas-katchewan Fats' Cleveland. That was my first mistake. It was a warm humid night, so we slept with the top pulled up. There was a storm coming out of the northeast. That is rare; most storms come out of the west out in west-ern Canada. I awoke at first light in Swift Current, there are gravestones around, and I wind up pissing on one that was part of a family plot, and it was marked 'Speier.' Until I looked more closely, I had no idea where I was peeing. I yelled out, 'Shit, I just peed on my shortstop's grave!'"*

* Note: Bill Lee's shortstop in Montreal was Chris Speier, and for the record, this was NOT his tombstone, because Speier is still alive. The Spaceman continued:

"You don't piss on your shortstop's grave. It's a bad fucking omen. So, after we were fully awake, we drove to Moose Jaw for that hockey legends thing. The event was terrific. Everyone got hammered, especially the Phil-adelphia Flyers players. The great Bobby Clarke was one of the keynote speakers. Clarke is in the Hall of Fame and was a three-time 'Hart Trophy' winner. Bobby Clarke was from Flin Flon, Manitoba. The old joke was that all you had in Flin Flon were whores and hockey players. Someone once mentioned that to Clarke, and Bobby answered, 'Hey, my wife is from Flin Flon!' The guy replied, 'What position does she play?'"

The Spaceman then spoke about perhaps one of the most unique char-acters in NHL history: Dave "The Hammer" Schultz, renowned for being perhaps the greatest enforcer in the history of the sport:

"Schultz was born in Waldheim, Saskatchewan but lived in Rosetown, Saskatchewan. He was always impeccably dressed and wore the most beau-tiful shoes. He looked like a fucking bank president. At the banquet I was seated right next to Shultz. Schultz had more fights than any man in NHL history. He still holds the record for most penalty minutes served in a single season, 472 fucking minutes! I mean, why even return to the ice? He should have just stayed in the fucking penalty box. I think he even got into several fights during the time he was in the box!"

Among the hockey greats present at the ceremony was Marcel "Little Beaver" Dionne of Drummondville, Quebec, another terrific hockey player, named as one of the 100 greatest players of all time despite his diminutive five-foot, eight-inch height. As the Spaceman described:

"Marcel got absolutely hammered on red wine that night. He looked like the Joker. His lips were all red and he was grinning from ear to ear. Marcel was supposed to be the last speaker at the event, but he was so hammered, he couldn't even talk, so he staggered up to the podium, and clumsily asked the audience if there were any shorter people than him present. When seven people raised their hands, he motioned for them to come up to the stage. He then marched them around the room! He couldn't talk, but he could march. They looked like Snow White and the Seven Dwarfs! I think they sang, 'We are the lollypop kids.' Dionne is a pisser. He's precious."

While Dave Schultz was speaking, "The Enforcer" looked out into the audience and acknowledged the great Clark Gillies seated. Schultz beckoned Gillies to join him and as the Spaceman described:

"Gillies told of the time that Schultz had him in a headlock, so Gillies headbutted him so he could free himself, but the referee gave Gillies a game misconduct! They changed the fucking rules in the middle of the game!"

The Spaceman said that Dave Schultz stole the show, however. As Bill Lee repeated Schultz's speech:

"I was still in school in Saskatchewan, and I was about to be drafted by an NHL team. The headmaster at the school warned me, however, that I was in danger of not getting a diploma because of my poor marks. The headmaster said, 'Do you realize if you don't pass, you won't receive your diploma and that you won't graduate? Dave, right now you are getting three Fs, a D, and only one A. What do you think your problem is?' I looked at the headmaster and answered, 'Maybe I'm concentrating too much on one subject.'"

CHAPTER FIFTEEN

Skating on Thin Ice

Fat Man in the Bathtub

After appearing at the fundraiser in Moose Jaw, Saskatchewan with the hockey legends, it was time for the earthling known as Bill "Spaceman" Lee and his then-wife, Pam, to begin their trek back east. However, there was some bad mojo left behind. First, of course, was the possible karma of "peeing on my shortstop's grave." Secondly, the organizers of the event asked if they could in any way reciprocate and reward Bill for coming all the way out west to aid in their cause. Bill Lee, in fact, responded in the affirmative:

"I knew the weather was about make a turn for the worse, and I didn't really want to drive the VW bus all the way back east, so I asked if they could put the vehicle on a C & N Rail and ship it back to Montreal. I could see that the weather was deteriorating rapidly, and I had a premonition of doom. I was told, 'Sorry, we can't,' I could see it coming. Crash! Boom! Bang!"

As they headed back east, Bill and Pam didn't get very far:

"Our VW bus crashed in fucking Chaplin, Saskatchewan. And I thought I lived in East Bumfuck, Vermont! I knew I shouldn't have pissed on my shortstop's grave. The road was a sheet of ice. I can still visualize the entire scene. It was like it was in slow motion. It was the slowest crash I've ever seen. It seemed to last forever on that fucking sheet of ice. A truck had pulled away from in front of us and a gust of wind hit us. We began sliding at a ninety-degree angle and we're not slowing down. Our VW is now backwards, and I'm looking back from where we'd been in Swift Current. I could feel our car going off the road and down an embankment, backwards. It struck something and flipped over backwards and that gave us momentum. Pam was in the front seat in a sleeping bag. I grabbed her and used the momentum to throw her in the trunk. We went over backwards down the embankment and that was the last thing I remembered. I managed to save Pam's life. When I finally came to, the tape was still playing! It was Lowell George and 'Little Feat' singing 'Fat Man in the Bathtub with the Blues.'"

Some folks on the other side of the road had witnessed the accident. However, the icy conditions were so bad that they couldn't even walk over to help! The Spaceman resumed telling of the potentially disastrous occurrence:

"After the RCMP arrived to turn our vehicle upright, we had already been taken to the hospital. Pam and I suffered the same exact injuries; we were both bleeding from the same spot on our hands. Incredibly, the VW bus was fine! The VW was like a hockey player that gets the shit kicked out of him but just keeps on playing. The RCMP did not cite us. Their report, and it was accurate, blamed the icy roads. Of course, they had searched our vehicle thoroughly once they returned it to its upright position. The fucking thing could run on ice and grass. When I picked up the VW bus, for no apparent reason I looked up to the upper left-hand corner and wedged into the joint was the giant ball of hashish. Despite rolling over and down the embankment, the fucking ball of hash was undisturbed. It looked like a giant moose turd."

CHAPTER SIXTEEN

Another Man Named Williams

How ironic is it that the immortal Ted Williams, arguably the greatest hitter who ever lived, was NOT the Williams who turned the perennial underperformance of the Red Sox around? And even more than turning the Red Sox's entire climate around, this other Williams accomplished that long overdue feat by driving Teddy Ballgame away from the hallowed grounds of Fenway Park?!

Richard Hirschfeld Williams, commonly known as "Dick," was the man most responsible for removing the losing culture in both the Red Sox clubhouse and on the field. For so many seasons the Red Sox wallowed and were forced to grovel at the feet of the mighty New York Yankees. However, then Tom Yawkey, after years of malaise and indifference, gave nearly full autonomy to his new manager who promised, "I know this: We'll win more games than we lose," who then stripped Carl Yastrzemski of his captaincy (a designation Yaz loathed anyhow) and then instructed, and finally insisted, Ted Williams cease confusing the young hitters with his complicated instructions.

Teddy Ballgame left Fenway in a huff, and the shroud of a defeatist attitude left with #9................Harsh, you say?

Dick Williams was, of course, the earthling known as Bill "Spaceman" Lee's initial major league manager. Dick Williams was also Lee's manager in Montreal! Recently, Bill Lee and the author reread some of the finest prose ever written in regard to the Boston Red Sox, and I'm referring to Richard Johnson and Glenn Stout's enormously great book, *RED SOX CENTURY: THE DEFINITIVE HISTORY OF BASEBALL'S MOST STORIED FRAN-CHISE*, edited by Bill Nowlin and Dan Derochers, Mr. Johnson, of course, being the curator of the Boston Sports Museum since 1982.

CHAPTER SEVENTEEN

The Author of This Book Is a Nitwit

The Time I Lost a Split Decision to a Golden Gloves Contender (I Think)

The Brawl at West Farms Road

Saturday Night's All Right for Fighting

(Well, actually it was a late Friday afternoon, but I digress)

Muhammad Ali and Joe Frazier had their "Thrilla in Manila." In Zaire, Ali and George Foreman fought in "The Rumble in the Jungle." In the distant past, I engaged in "deadly" combat in "The Brawl at West Farms Road."

My "opponent" in this comical saga, was my dear friend, a stocky five-foot-eight crazed Irishman named Patrick, and the epic physical dispute I refer to took place around 1966 in the South Bronx, under the train tracks at West Farms Road, Tremont Avenue and Southern Boulevard, right outside of the doors of the famed Chester Theater, which was home to many great motion pictures starring John Wayne, Tyrone Power, Yul Brynner, and many other legendary swashbucklers.

Patrick, at the time, foolishly entertained the suicidal thought of entering the "Golden Gloves" boxing tournament, a much-ballyhooed event held annually at places such as Sunnyside Gardens in Queens and other boxing venues. Pat and I would invariably attend professional bouts at Sunnyside Gardens each Wednesday evening and follow that up with our pilgrimage to Madison Square Garden every Friday night.

The difference between Patrick and yours truly, is that I was painfully aware that I could not fight. When skirmishes broke out, as they frequently did in the various watering holes we frequented, it was my MO to either hide behind my largest friend present, or if all else failed, attempt to diffuse the situation by infusing humor into a potential donnybrook.

Patrick, on the other hand, fancied himself as a brawler. He envisioned himself as "welterweight champion of the world." Ironically, Patrick's often battered face housed more welts than anyone his weight. Fueled with false bravado, a half pint of scotch, and a brain lacking the necessities to prevent getting his ass kicked, Patrick often found himself in positions beneath his adversaries.........literally.

Patrick, a fine lad, had the old proverbial map of Ireland on his face. He had that map, that is, on those rare occasions one could see his countenance beneath the contusions, bruises, and other assorted lacerations he had accumulated from insulting the wrong individual or individuals. For those of us privileged to have known the little Irishman, Patrick was a hilarious and brilliant human being. However, upon entering an Irish pub, Patrick once walked up to the largest man in the establishment, who was heretofore a complete stranger, and proceeded to point a finger at his face while exclaiming, "I don't like your shirt!" This type of "aggressiveness" was often Patrick's downfall, both literally and figuratively.

Upon Patrick informing me of his intentions of entering the "Golden Gloves" boxing competition that fateful year, I responded in no uncertain terms, that he had taken permanent leave of his senses. "Bullshit, Charlie (he called EVERYONE Charlie), I'm entering the sub-novice division. No one in that class has any fighting experience." I then advised my crazed friend to consider, though, that perhaps some of them could actually, you know, "fight!"

Patrick, a proud if foolish Irishman, took affront to my insinuation and barked at me, "What are you saying, I can't fight?" I smiled and replied, "Well, frankly, YES, that is indeed my inference. Hell, I can kick your ass, and I cannot fight to save my ass!"

This disagreement took place, and alcohol may have been involved, outside of the fabled Chester Theater on West Farms Road. The next thing we knew, my dear friend and I decided to prove our points (hey, I've never been accused of being sane, either). A "brawl" ensued and we agreed that if Patrick was defeated by yours truly in the manly art of fisticuffs, that he would abstain from submitting his Gold Gloves application. Therefore, we two nitwits squared off beneath the West Farms Road train stop as folks calmly walked by. In New York, most inhabitants do not take such a "dispute" between two moronic inebriates as anything serious.

Our pathetic effort at manhood resulted in my suffering a swollen eye and a cut lip. Such is the price of friendship. I did have a distinct height and reach advantage over the feisty Irishman, however, and managed to bloody his nose and blacken his eye with some desperate, but accurate, jabs. After approximately five minutes of this abject foolishness, Pat suddenly raised his arms skyward to call a halt to the proceedings and proudly declared himself the winner of this now historic match.

The good news is that Pat never did get around to submitting his entry to the Golden Gloves. I would like to think that the fact that I fought him to a draw had something to do with his wise decision to withdraw.

As I recall, immediately after our altercation, Patrick and I attempted to purchase some liquid refreshment at a neighborhood gin mill, but were denied the privilege by the sage bartender, who peered at us as we entered sweating, somewhat battered, and seemingly incoherent. I, of course, accepted the bartender's edict. A disheveled Patrick, of course, took issue with the decision, and I was forced to drag him out of the establishment.

If only the earthling known as Bill "Spaceman" Lee had been provided with such deterrents during his turbulent career in baseball, it is possible that he would have undergone a bit less dental surgery.

CHAPTER EIGHTEEN

The Lies That Bind

"A lie does not consist in the indirect position of words, but in the desire and intention, by false speaking, to deceive and injure your neighbor." —*Jonathan Swift*

"A liar who will deceive with his tongue will not hesitate to do the same with his pen." —*Maimonides*

The earthling known as Bill "Spaceman" Lee had already exposed many of those that lie and deceive in the first of this trilogy, *The Spaceman Chronicles*. He has resorted to frequently using facts in laying to waste numerous alleged generally accepted illusions. The Spaceman has not only defended himself, but in so doing, has defended reality and integrity, something too often foreign to those merely seeking best-selling books, rather than having to perhaps consider truthfulness. In these pages we are about to debunk the complete bullshit spewed in a few *New York Times* bestsellers, albeit ones rife with enough manure to fertilize all our nation's Midwestern states.

In *The Spaceman Chronicles*, we clearly leaned on hard evidence to entirely disprove the prevarications told by Don Zimmer to author Bill Madden, ones that Madden, perhaps in his haste to move onto another project, repeated as if he really believed them. Hell, maybe he did, but the effort he made in researching the subject matter was faulty, and to be truthful, debatable at best. "Poor," in fact, would be our rating.

We also cast aspersions as to Keith Hernandez's selective memory while he was under oath as he testified at the major league drug trials in Pittsburgh in 1985. As we stated, immunity from prosecution can be a powerful narcotic.

One of Bill Lee's best traits, in the author's opinion, remains his willingness to point fingers at himself. As the Spaceman has often said, "A self-deprecating sense of humor is a necessary factor when attempting to have credibility."

Which brings us to:

Earl Wilson

Those of a certain age might recall the name Earl Wilson. Wilson was a terrific right-handed pitcher, a powerful slugger and a kind, thoughtful, and considerate humanitarian. However, for those who read the *New York Times* best-selling piece of crap, *Hitman,* penned by Howie Carr, one would believe Wilson to be a drunkard, a drug addict, a womanizer with loose morals, and a less than admirable ballplayer willing to dump games for murderous mobsters. Before we get into Carr's work of downright litigious fiction, let me tell you who Robert Earl Wilson really was.

Bill "Spaceman" Lee's major league career was just beginning as Earl Wilson's was ending, and therefore, Bill stated, "I didn't know Earl Wilson, but I knew of him and what he accomplished for so many others that played the game, especially those less fortunate."

Earl Wilson stood six feet, three inches tall and was an imposing figure on the mound and at the plate. If queried, many baseball historians upon being asked to identify the first African American signed by the Boston Red Sox, would respond, Elijah "Pumpsie" Green. However, although Green was the initial black player to take the field for the Red Sox, the very last team to integrate, it was Earl Wilson of Ponchatoula, Louisiana who was the first to sign a contract. Earl Wilson made his major league debut with the Red Sox on July 28, 1959, seven days after "Pumpsie" Green broke the "color line" for Boston. Wilson's ascension to the big leagues was delayed, likely intentionally, by the Red Sox racist front office, despite their being pressured by local Boston legislators to integrate. In fact, it was noted Boston journalist Al Hirshberg who hinted that Wilson, who was originally inked as an outfielder and then moved to catcher, was told to become a pitcher when it was determined that he was "ready for the majors," thereby further delaying his promotion.

Just how racist was the Red Sox organization? Consider the following written by noted Canadian historian and SABR member, Don Hyslop:

"A 1953 scouting report sent to the Red Sox front office, reported, 'Earl Wilson is a well-mannered colored boy, not too black, pleasant to talk to, well educated, has a very good appearance and conducts himself as a gentleman.'"

Gee, "not too black."

It should be noted that the Red Sox did not sign "Pumpsie" Green until 1956. Earl Wilson was also drafted into the marines in 1957. It is also interesting to note that Earl Wilson compiled an impressive 121-109 won-lost record with an ERA of 3.69. The fact that he blasted 35 home runs, 33 as a pitcher and 2 as a pinch-hitter, is even more remarkable. The 121 victories were two more than Bill "Spaceman" Lee would total during his major league career, albeit one which was shortened due to his being blackballed from the game he loved.

Earl Wilson was on his way to stardom with the Red Sox, when the specter of racism once more reared its ugly head. During spring training in 1966, Earl Wilson joined two of his white teammates at the Cloud Nine bar in Lakeland, Florida. As journalist Howard Bryant wrote in his superb volume, *Shut Out: A Story of Race and Baseball in Boston*, the following incident occurred:

"So, what happened on that steamy night Wilson and two white pitchers, Dennis Bennett and Dave Morehead, showed up at the Cloud Nine bar in Lakeland, anyway? The first thing to remember is that spring training in the 1960s did not exist for the sake of commodity. It wasn't yet a business, and those flat and nasty Florida towns did not easily welcome blacks, even if they were ballplayers. Spring training wasn't yet 'family entertainment,' and those old towns were strictly Klan. Bradenton, Sarasota, Port Charlotte were all run by the local KKK. Even the slightly more cosmopolitan St. Petersburg held a rigid social order. That meant no blacks and no Jews."

Howard Bryant, whose equally brilliant biography of Henry Aaron, *The Last Hero: A Life of Henry Aaron*, continued:

"As Wilson remembers it, the scene at the Cloud Nine was brief and hostile. Bennett ordered a beer. The bartender looked at Morehead, who like Bennett was white, took his order but followed by angling toward Wilson and telling Morehead, 'We don't serve niggers here.' Wilson left the bar, teeth clenched. A million images flashed. It was he and Pumpsie Green being rousted one night by cops in the South. It was more than just another humiliation; it was also a reminder that in certain parts of his country he was just another nigger, so beneath human decency that he couldn't even order a cold beer without being harassed."

As Howard Bryant continued:

"Wilson went to Red Sox management, expecting to be backed by the organization. With thirty-five years of perspective, he still isn't exactly sure what he expected the Red Sox to tell him."

As Howard Bryant reported, "Billy Herman, his manager, coldly rebuffed him. Forget the incident, it never happened, he was told. Also, if any of the members of the press ask, Wilson was told in no unclear terms to tell them nothing. It was this point that the Red Sox were most strident. To Wilson, the club's chief concern was the press did not write about the incident."

Earl Wilson, a proud man, responded, "It was the most humiliating experience of my life."

Howard Bryant went on to explain that Earl Wilson had little choice but to speak out about his experience. Once the Boston press got wind of the story, of course, they printed the entire story, but keep in mind that this was 1960s Boston, not exactly a bastion of integrity or fairness, for that matter. As Bryant wrote:

"The choice was clear. He would tell the press the story in its entirety. The Red Sox would now have to respond."

And respond they did. The young strong-armed hurler, first coming into his own as a legitimate major league star, would be soon traded to the Detroit Tigers, for a journeyman outfielder named Don Demeter who Wilson would out-homer, and a pitcher named Julio Navarro who would never even pitch a game for the Red Sox. Earl Wilson would finish the year as one of the aces of a strong Detroit Tigers rotation, finishing the season with a 18-11, 3.07 mark, and would follow that up with a dominant 22 win season in 1967, and then in 1968, he would combine with Denny McLain and Mickey Lolich on the World Series champion Tigers. But it was what Earl Wilson would accomplish off the diamond that was even more impressive.

Bill "Spaceman" Lee, himself an active member of the Major League Baseball Players Association, often reaches out either by telephone or in person to check in on many of his former teammates and foes. However, as Lee informed me, what Earl Wilson accomplished during his post-playing career is worthy of great admiration.

Earl Wilson was particularly acute in his regard for players who played in the era before great financial benefits and free agency became the norm. By 1992, Earl Wilson was named as the vice-president of the "Baseball Assistance Team," commonly known as "BAT." This organization remains dedicated to assisting former players who have become indigent or otherwise fallen on hard times. However, in 2000 Earl Wilson was promoted to president and CEO of BAT, thereby making him the first African American to be appointed to the lofty and meaningful position. Wilson served in that capacity through 2004 and was still active as the vice president until his death in 2005, at the age of seventy.

To further support those in need, Wilson developed the "Earl Wilson Celebrity Golf Tournament." Wilson's former teammate Willie Horton was once quoted, "Earl taught me it is more important what you do outside the field than what you do on it." On the field, though, Earl Wilson finished with nine seasons of double-digit victories and 69 complete games. But when considering his service to his fellow athletes, there is a special place in heaven for him.

During his tenure, Earl Wilson, the son of a school custodian and a mom and housekeeper in segregated Louisiana, was obviously a gifted and generous human being. However, in 2011, Earl Wilson, as we mentioned at the beginning of this chapter, was portrayed as a drunkard, a drug addict, a womanizer with loose morals, and a less than admirable ballplayer willing to dump games for murderous mobsters, in *Hitman, the Untold Story of Johnny Martorano*, by Howie Carr, who should have written the book on toilet paper.

Firstly, it should be noted that like most baseball players not named Bobby Richardson, Wilson enjoyed a drink or two. Some of these drinking tales have been expounded upon by "Spaceman" Lee in these volumes. However, the portrait Howie Carr paints of Earl Wilson is akin to portraying Ted Williams and Stan Musial as weak batsmen. It's unadulterated bullshit.

The "book," *Hitman,* is allegedly a biography of the mobster, Johnny Martorano, who was nothing more and nothing less than a lowlife scumbag murderer for renowned mobster James "Whitey" Bulger's notorious "Winter Hill Gang." Martorano, who has the credibility of a mangy yak in the final throes of tertiary syphilis, was also known as "John James Vincent Martorano," "Vincent Joseph Rancourt," "Nick," "Nick the Cook," "The Executioner," and "The Basin Street Butcher." Just the kind of man you would want your daughter to date. Martorano has admitted to twenty mob related killings. The mere fact that Martorano is a free man these days is enough to tell you the state of our "justice" system.

To preface how Howie Carr and Martorano have besmirched the legacy of an honorable human being such as Earl Wilson, all one needs to know about the state of "journalism" in the year 2021, or in this case 2011, the year that Tom Doherty Associates, LLC, found it fit to publish this trash.

For full disclosure, I had absolutely no intention of reading *Hitman*. The subject matter just did not interest me. However, upon seeing excerpts of Carr's "frightening tale" in the *Boston Herald*, something caught my eye. It was the mention of former Red Sox pitcher, Earl Wilson. Why the hell would a tome about a murderous reprehensible degenerate include Earl Wilson, a respectable and revered athlete?

The following paragraphs contain excerpts from *Hitman*, the alleged "facts," which I have easily laid to waste. My comments follow each defilement of Earl Wilson's character. It should also be noted that Earl Wilson was incapable of defending his character since there is little doubt in my mind that both Martorano and Carr chose Earl Wilson primarily because he is no longer among the living, which is another reason I found the book to be repulsive. In *Hitman*, which would have come in handy, pun intended, during the great "Toilet Paper Shortage of 2020," Carr wrote the following sacrilege:

"By 1962, even the Boston Red Sox had integrated. They had two black players – infielder Pumpsie Green and a promising young pitcher named Earl Wilson, who roomed together in an apartment in the Back Bay. Like most of their Caucasian Red Sox teammates, they liked to drink. Wilson especially enjoyed the nightlife, which for black high rollers in Boston in 1962, was largely centered at Basin Street South."

Note: I'll let this one go, but the line, "Wilson especially enjoyed the nightlife," seems as if he is setting him up as perhaps an inebriate.

"One Saturday night—June 25, 1962—Earl Wilson rolled into Basin Street, looking for a party."

Note: This one I will not let go. You see, June 25, 1962 was a Monday, not a Saturday.

"Separated from his wife, Johnny (Martorano) was swilling his drink of choice, champagne. He had nothing better to do, so he invited Wilson over to his table. After closing, Martorano rounded up some of the chorus-line dancers, as well as plenty of champagne, hard liquor, and marijuana. Everyone then headed over to Wilson's apartment in the Back Bay, where the party continued all night, into Sunday morning."

Note: The likelihood of a notorious hit man for the Winter Hill Gang joining a black athlete in Boston's Back Bay in 1962 for a party at his apartment is unlikely enough, since Boston was the most racially polarized town I had ever seen upon my arrival in 1973, but I'm even willing to at least partially tolerate its absurdity.

"Around eleven the next morning, with most of the women and assorted hangers-on asleep or passed out around the apartment, a bleary-eyed Earl Wilson walked unsteadily up to the couch where Johnny (Martorano) was dozing off.

"'Johnny,' he said, 'can you give me a ride to the ballpark?'

"'What?' Johnny said.

"'I gotta get to the park,' Wilson said. 'I'm pitching the first game of the doubleheader.'

"'You're kidding, right?'

"'No, man, I gotta go.'

Note: As I read the excerpt in the *Boston Herald*, I became more suspicious. To begin with, as I stated, June 25 was a Monday, and therefore, there was no way there was a daytime doubleheader at Fenway Park the following day.

"Johnny (Martorano) and Wilson made their way unsteadily downstairs, into Johnny's car. During the short drive to Kenmore Square, Wilson nodded off a couple of times, but awoke long enough to give Johnny directions to the green door in Fenway's centerfield wall that served as the player's entrance. With the street still deserted, Johnny stopped the car. Earl Wilson opened the door, tried to get out, and tumbled face first into the gutter. Johnny helped him to his feet, leaned him up against the green door, and rang the bell. Then he ran back to his car. He didn't want to answer any questions about the condition of the Sox's starting pitcher for the first game. He stepped on the gas, keeping his eye on the rearview mirror as the door opened and Earl Wilson fell inside."

Note: If you are not entirely incredulous by now, check for a pulse. But wait, you'll be knee high in bullshit shortly.

"Johnny drove back to his own apartment, slowly sobering up during the ride, and realizing his opportunity. This was exactly the kind of 'inside information' he'd always heard so much about in the stands of Braves Field and Fenway Park with his father. Now if he could only take advantage of it.

Back at his own apartment, he began calling every bookie he knew, getting as much money down on the Los Angeles Angels as he could. The Angels' starter was Bo Belinsky, another party animal who'd already thrown a no-hitter earlier in the year.

"'I was in for everything,' Martorano said. 'When you're twenty-one, twenty-two, but you can't get that much money up, but I put down everything I could against Wilson. I figured it was guaranteed.'

"But Wilson threw a no-hitter. He was the first black pitcher ever to throw a no-hitter, and he also hit a home run—only the third pitcher ever to do that while tossing a no-hitter. Wilson outpitched Belinsky, 2-0."

Note: Holy crap! I immediately hit the ceiling! I was now aware that what I was reading were ALL fairytales. Earl Wilson, driven to Fenway Park by one of Whitey Bulger's murdering thugs, had pitched a no-hitter in the first game of a doubleheader on a Sunday, while hung over! This despite the fact there was no doubleheader on June 26 (which was a Tuesday!) at Fenway Park, plus on Sunday, the Red Sox were still in Baltimore! On top of everything else, Earl Wilson's no-hitter came on a TUESDAY NIGHT! I know. My high school graduation ceremony had been held earlier in the day at Roosevelt High School in the Bronx (I had graduated from Morris High, but our auditorium was too small to accommodate us), and I "celebrated" by going home and listening to Earl Wilson pitch that no-hitter on WTIC in Hartford, Connecticut on my trusty transistor radio!

If Earl Wilson had been drunk in Baltimore on that Saturday night, God bless him, but Johnny Martorano wasn't with him, and I'm now ninety-nine percent certain that Martorano never even met Earl Wilson! However, he and Howie Carr apparently did as much research as Bill Madden in his nearly equally ludicrous book, *Zim: A Baseball Life*, or should that have read "A Baseball Lie"? Unfortunately, Earl Wilson's honorable name had been forever tarnished by the nitwit, Howie Carr, and a murderer named Johnny Martorano. But wait, Martorano and Carr were not through with their blasphemous bullshit.

"That night I'm sitting in the club, wondering what to do to come up with all the money I owe every bookie in town. I had already told everybody in the club they're not getting paid this week. And in walks Earl Wilson. He says to me, 'This is the best day of my life, and it started right here, last night. Johnny, I owe it all to you!' Then he ordered champagne for the house.

"Johnny said nothing to him that night, but a year or so later, on another late evening at the club, Martorano finally confessed to Wilson what he'd done, betting against him the day he pitched his no-hitter.

"'Why didn't you tell me, Johnny?' Wilson said, smiling broadly. 'I'd have thrown the game for you.'"

Note: It wasn't apparently enough to denigrate Earl Wilson, a noble man, by the prior absurd allegations, ALL of which were entirely false, but to then claim that he actually offered to throw a major league game is beyond unconscionable.

"Spaceman" Lee and I hope that speaking the truth will at least serve to partially eradicate whatever damage has been done in a horrific book of lies and will perhaps restore the reputation of the late Earl Wilson, a man who has earned and deserves admiration.

The Spaceman also suggests that donations be made in Earl Wilson's name to: https://www.mlb.com/baseball-assistance-team

CHAPTER NINETEEN

The Asshole Departs for More "Hospitable" Folk

In March of 2021, Curt Schilling announced his plans to relocate from Massachusetts to Tennessee. The former successful right-handed pitcher was fed up with the denizens of the Bay State.

The earthling known as Bill "Spaceman" Lee thereby bid Mr. Schilling a fond adieu.

CURT SCHILLING IS MOVING TO TENNESSEE & THE SPACE-MAN IS WILLING TO HELP HIM PACK

Curt Schilling is moving to Tennessee and exclaimed, "We're just trying to find a place to live out our lives where people are nice, and Tennessee is it."

It is my guess that Schilling feels that Massachusetts, where Schilling has lived since 2007, just isn't very nice. Schilling, never at a loss for disparaging words, stated:

"Outside of our circle of friends, it really hasn't been a really pleasant experience in Boston."

So long, Curt. Perhaps we were a bit upset when, upon seeing the January 6 attempt at insurrection on Capitol Hill, you started spewing, "There is so much awesome going on here!" on social media.

Or maybe it was when you wrote, "You cowards sat on your hands, did nothing while liberal trash looted rioted and burned for Air Jordan's and big screens. Sit back, shut up, and watch folks start a confrontation for shit that matters like rights, democracy and the end of government corruption."

Or perhaps we were merely bothered by your impressive collection of Nazi memorabilia. Or maybe it was the millions of dollars Schilling literally stole from the state of Rhode Island to fund a video game company that had no actual video games to sell, thereby bankrupting the entire state.

Well, Herr Schilling, Bill "Spaceman" Lee is ready and willing to make your moving experience more pleasurable. Being a thoughtful, compassionate and amiable fellow, the Spaceman offered #38 a few suggestions. They are as follows:

"You'll do fine with the Clampetts and the McCoys in that little hollow down there, but if you do go, I'd advise you to bypass Rhode Island, as there might be a bench warrant awaiting you in Pawtucket or Warwick. When you do arrive, I suggest going on a canoe ride down the Cahulawassee River. When you see the blind kid playing his banjo, you'll know you're home. Oh, and Curt, watch out for the 'relative humidity' down there. That's the amount of sweat that falls off your balls when you're banging your first cousin."

The Spaceman concluded with:

"I've arranged to manufacture a few 'Ned Beatty masks' for you to wear. It should be fun. They'll ride you like a rented mule. Sorry you didn't like us. They'll just love your white ass down there!"

A BRIEF INTERMISSION

Go Get a Cold Drink and Some Popcorn

Death on a Rooftop, a Childhood Long Gone, and a Phone Call from a Hollywood Icon

A Floodgate of Memories Open

In 1963, I was one year removed from graduating from Morris High School in the South Bronx. Although I was attending Bronx Community College, I was nearly entirely devoid of direction or purpose. I suppose that isn't necessarily a far distance from where I reside today. I do write, on occasion.

Back in the day, my friends and I would attend boxing matches at Madison Square Garden each Friday night and at Sunnyside Gardens in Queens every Wednesday evening. We loved boxing.

Even while in high school, despite the fact I could not fight my way out of a paper bag, we would frequent the Mount Carmel CYO in the Bronx. I was akin to a mosquito with an erection floating up the river while lying on its back and exclaiming, "Raise the drawbridge." We were young imbeciles, as opposed to the aging morons we are today.

While hanging out at the Mount Carmel CYO, I began to admire a young boxer named Billy Bello. He trained under the watchful eye of trainer Charlie Caserta. Billy was a classic stand-up boxer, a Golden Gloves welterweight champion who was being primed for a professional career. Billy had a beautifully devastating left hook and he was reminiscent of my hero, Joey Giardello, the former middleweight champion.

On July 6, 1963, Billy Bello, then twenty, fought in his first main event at Madison Square Garden. My friends and I eagerly traveled via the IRT subway to cheer him on. I wanted to be Billy Bello, a good-looking youngster admired in his entire neighborhood in the Fordham Road section of the Bronx. On the night in question, Billy was matched against a great veteran boxer named Gaspar "Indio" Ortega. Ortega was awarded a close and disputed split decision, but there was no doubt in the minds of the boxing experts that Billy Bello was on his way to greatness.

On July 20, 1963, exactly two weeks after Billy Bello's initial main event, he was found dead on a tenement rooftop on Fordham Road in the Bronx. There were fresh needle marks on Billy's left arm. He died of a heroin overdose. He was twenty years old..........................Memories fade.

Many years later, I was privileged to write the biography of my childhood hero, Carmine Tilelli, aka Joey Giardello. The book is titled *Joey*. One day upon answering my phone, a woman's voice informed me, "Scott, I've got Mr. Chazz Palminteri on the phone. Hold on, please."............. *Yeah, sure,* I thought, *and I'm Bugs Bunny.* Within seconds, the unmistakable voice of Chazz Palminteri stated, "Scott, I just wanted you to know how much I enjoyed your book, *Joey.*"

I was floored as if I was hit with a Joey Giardello left hook. Chazz Palminteri, Hollywood icon, author, and star of *A Bronx Tale*, liked my book! The conversation I had with Mr. Palminteri, who immediately insisted I called him "Chazz," lasted the better portion of an hour. What I learned during that conversation and the conversation itself, remain indelible.

Mr. Palminteri, I mean "Chazz," informed me that his dad's idol was Joey Giardello and that his father had also trained under the legendary Mount Carmel CYO trainer Charlie Caserta, and that *Joey* brought back many pleasant memories.

During that unlikely conversation with Chazz Palminteri, we realized that we knew a lot of the same people in the neighborhood, people such as Charlie Caserta! I admitted, rather sheepishly, that Charlie had tossed my sorry ass out of the Mount Carmel CYO on occasion, and I laughed uproariously as Chazz responded, "Scott, that puts you in good company. Charlie threw a lot of us out!"

Amongst the guys in our neighborhood we both knew was Tony Tozzo, a former Gold Gloves Champion who was also a member of the toughest street gang in the Bronx, "The Fordham Baldies." Trust me, no one screwed with the Fordham Baldies, whose members included a young man named Dion DiMucci....................Yes, that Dion, the lead singer of "Dion and the Belmonts!" Dion, of course, went on to settle down and today is a complete gentleman with an extraordinarily great family.

Towards the end of my conversation with Chazz Palminteri, I brought up the name of Billy Bello, the actual reason I began hanging out at the Mount Carmel CYO. I wanted to be Billy Bello.

Chazz Palminteri was astounded. He hesitated before replying, "Scott, do you recall the line in *A Bronx Tale*, the one in which my father (portrayed by Robert De Niro) told me, "'Son, there's nothing worse than wasted talent'?"

"Of course," I answered.

Mr. Chazz Palminteri then told me, "Scott, my father was referring to Billy Bello!"

Before ending our conversation, one which I will cherish for the remainder of my lifetime, Chazz Palminteri gave me perhaps the greatest compliment I've ever received. There isn't a more meaningful compliment in the Bronx than the one Chazz Palminteri gave me that afternoon. Said Chazz:

"Scott, I know this: You're for real!"

CHAPTER TWENTY

The Trouble with Harry

The Trouble with Billy

A Tale of Two Assholes

East of Eden

"Some people have a chip on their shoulder. Billy Martin has a whole lumber yard." —*Jim Murray, the legendary writer of the* Los Angeles Times

"You are not in control of your destiny. Your destiny is in control of you." —*Bill "Spaceman" Lee*

Note: Upon writing the first of our trilogy, The Spaceman Chronicles, *the subject of the biography, Bill Lee, and the author, regardless if he is "Scott Russell" or Kilgore Trout, suggested that to more fully understand the life of the Spaceman, that you read Kurt Vonnegut's* Cat's Cradle, Slaughterhouse Five, *and* Breakfast of Champions. *As you are now reading (at least we are hoping you are reading this volume and not using it as a projectile)* The Final Odyssey of the Sweet Ride, *we suggest you now view the great motion picture directed by Alfred Hitchcock, titled,* The Trouble with Harry.

It would stand to reason that the eccentric earthling known as Bill "Spaceman" Lee would eventually wind up among the denizens of the "Northeast Kingdom" in northern Vermont.

Bill Lee resides atop a hill in scenic Craftsbury, Vermont. The location of Bill and Diana's home is in the EXACT spot where one of the most hilarious motion pictures in cinematic history was filmed. The film, directed by the incomparable Alfred Hitchcock, was called *The Trouble with Harry*. Even the advertisements and previews of the classic were sidesplitting funny, as they showed townsfolk dragging a dead body all over Craftsbury and burying him, digging him up, and then reburying him. The promos boldly announced, "The trouble with Harry is that he's dead."

The premise of *The Trouble with Harry* is that "Harry Worp," the deceased subject of the movie, was a complete asshole, and that his passing was not particularly mourned by the residents of Craftsbury. However—and here is where the hilarity ensues—you see, nearly everyone in town believes that he or she was the one responsible for Harry's death, one that appeared for all intents and purposes to have been a murder.

Harry Worp's lifeless body is found atop a hill near the woods, and he has apparently been killed by either a gunshot wound to the head or a blow from a blunt instrument. "Captain Wiles," portrayed by Edmund Gwenn, is convinced that he shot Harry with his rifle while rabbit hunting; but "Miss Gravely," portrayed by Mildred Natwick, is certain that she killed Harry by striking him with the steel heel of her hiking boot; and "Jennifer Rogers," portrayed by Shirley MacLaine in her motion picture debut, is certain that she killed Harry, who incidentally is her husband, by clobbering him over the head with a milk bottle. They are all hilariously wrong, of course, as Harry, as it turns out, was felled by a heart attack. Another protagonist, "Sam Marlowe," portrayed by the great John Forsythe, is a local artist who is perfectly willing to assist his "suspect" friends by any means possible. Even more absurd and equally hilarious, is that all "involved," attempt to keep their "secret" from the town's dimwitted, humorless, and hapless deputy sheriff, Calvin Wiggs, who "earns" his living by the quantity of arrests he makes!

Every one of the townspeople of Craftsbury, Vermont in this epic black comedy is a delightful dingbat. Bill Lee will inform you that this is art imitating life. Or is it life imitating art?

"Spaceman" Lee and Craftsbury, Vermont appears to be a marriage made in heaven, or perhaps somewhere else with an absurd sense of humor. In a typical morning in Craftsbury, Bill Lee can often be found at the town's cemetery doing stretching exercises at the gravesite of his neighbor, Mahlon "George" Allen. The grave marker is a black piece of granite. I'll let the Spaceman explain:

"In the morning I go up to George's gravesite to do my Achilles stretching on his grave. His wife, Claudette, is buried there, and on George's tombstone there is a birthdate, but no expiration date. This enables me to talk to him. While I'm stretching, we talk, and I have a beer. I always tell George, 'You're not quite dead yet, you know.'"

Obviously, this requires an explanation, therefore:

"You see, George, whose real name was Mahlon Allen, is buried at the plot along with his wife, Claudette, who was a beautiful woman. However, the granite stone only lists his birthdate of December 8, 1960. There is not yet a deceased date, so I talk to him as I do my Achilles stretching exercises and have a beer 'with' him."

I did not ask if "George" ever responds during these "conversations." After all, this is Bill Lee I'm speaking with.

Mahlon, or "George" Allen, as he was known, died on August 7, 2014 in Craftsbury, of course. I did not inquire as to why there exists no expiration date on his grave marker in fear of receiving an answer from the Spaceman; however, I did receive the following additional data:

"While Mahlon was hauling trees several years ago, a limb hit him across the face and left him with a scar that ran perpendicular at a forty-five-degree angle from his nose. It was grotesque, and yet beautiful. You couldn't avert your eyes from it."

Oh, and get this: Mahlon "George" Allen is a direct descendent of Ethan Allen, who is one of the founders of the State of Vermont! It gets even better, but there is little that would surprise anyone who is aware of the past and present inhabitants of the town of Craftsbury, made famous by a lot more than Alfred Hitchcock's *The Trouble with Harry*.

Incredibly, the townsfolk of Craftsbury, Vermont, population slightly over 1,100, are as delightfully eccentric as the actors in *The Trouble with Harry*. As the Spaceman says, "They are all dingbats," and therefore, as Bill Lee admits, he fits right in.

Bill Lee refers to his adopted hometown of Craftsbury as "the jewel of the Kingdom. It's like a giant jewel in your bellybutton."

The rolling green hills of northern Vermont with its picket fences and family-run farms provide for an idyllic setting, but one that has attracted off-the-wall characters for generations, Bill Lee included.

Bill Lee knows batshit crazy when he sees it. After all, he peers into the mirror on occasion. The Spaceman continued:

"When you live up here in 'the Kingdom,' even the sheriff (the Orleans County sheriff) will not come to Craftsbury. I went to the sheriff's office in Newport, Vermont to report that my saw was missing and the dispatch girl in the sheriff's office told me, 'Sorry, we don't go to Craftsbury! If you happen to find someone lying dead at the top of a hill, you work it out among yourselves!'"

In *The Trouble with Harry*, as we stated, Captain Wiles, portrayed by Edmund Gwenn, is convinced he killed Harry Worp with a single shot to the head while rabbit hunting. However—and you cannot make this up!—Bill's neighbor, Scott Reed's father, David Reed, really did accidentally shoot his best friend and neighbor atop the same hill that Harry Worp had been found! This bizarre incident occurred several years ago, and the Spaceman expounded regarding the bizarre incident:

"Fortunately, the guy did not bleed out as it was so brutally cold that nature provided its own tourniquet."

The Spaceman went on to explain that the shooting victim's daughter can often be seen walking down the Black River Road. As for the "shooter," David Reed, he was a marine in the 28th Marine Regiment whose famed artillery division captured Mount Suribachi on February 23, 1945! Yes, Iwo Jima! David Reed had enlisted at the age of sixteen! "David Reed was seventeen when he got to the island where the Japanese would come out of their tunnels at night to terrorize everyone."

In chapter nine, we had mentioned that the Spaceman had driven the ex-wife of Scott Reed and her father off the property by "threatening" them with a shotgun. They were there to steal Reed's home and his farm. So that completes the dichotomy—Captain Wiles, believing he had killed Harry Worp with his shotgun, David Reed really shooting his best friend with his rifle atop the very same hill, and the Spaceman aiming his Casull at two would-be thieves, thereby proving his worthiness as a resident of the idyllic and oft-times zany town of Craftsbury, Vermont.

After the "lawman" known as Bill "Spaceman" Lee drove Scott Reed's ex-wife and her father away by brandishing his weapon at the top of the same hill that the fictional Harry Worp's body had been found, and the same spot where David Reed had accidentally shot his friend, Scott Reed's former wife charged the Spaceman with assault because he had aimed his weapon at her and her father. Bill, of course, was merely defending Scott Reed's property, which was rightfully his. The Spaceman further explained:

"All of this happened because Craftsbury is 'East of Eden.' It's all

Steinbeckian because in *To a God Unknown*, the oldest son of a disgruntled farmer who is upset because they hadn't enough food to feed everyone, leaves Vermont and travels to California to find his fortune and acquires a piece of property in the Salinas Valley amid the foothills above it. Then other Vermonters arrived and they "girdled"* the tree that caused the drought."

> * And you folks thought this was not educational. "Girdling," as it is known, is also known as "ring-barking." It is the complete removal of the bark from around the circumference of either a branch or trunk of a woody plant. A branch completely girdled will fail, and when the main trunk of a tree is girdled, the entire tree will die. For the record, the Spaceman always wanted to be a forest ranger. This is not the same type of "girdling" your heavy-set Aunt Matilda used to appear thinner, however.

The Spaceman also recalled that his family traveled from California to Vermont (The Hunts) in covered wagons. As Bill stated:

"So, six generations later I went 'back' to Vermont unknowingly and end up East of Eden. It's a natural progression, sort of like the swallows returning to Capistrano."

The Spaceman pretty much explains the 1,100 or so inhabitants of Craftsbury as follows:

"Normal people come up here to seek the foliage and the isolation and can be left alone. That is why we have so many former CIA agents who settled here (there are at least three). There are very few men capable of keeping their wives up here in Craftsbury. There's a high rate of pregnancy, though, but there is only a three-day breeding period."

Note: I did not ask for an explanation, but the Spaceman continued:

"Pregnancy generally occurs in the spring when the temperature warms up to sixty-five degrees after a cold winter. It happens every spring."

As for the location of the house the Spaceman built in Craftsbury, he explained:

"I built this house on this ridge and turned it towards the morning sun so that all the cold weather and my past were facing my ass. I came here to get away from my past, but it's back there."

As for Mahlon "George" Allen, the gent the Spaceman often converses with at his grave atop the hill in Craftsbury, he was indeed a direct descendent of Ethan Allen, who was born in Litchfield, Connecticut in 1737, but settled in the area that is now Burlington, Vermont, which is where he passed on February 12, 1789. Ethan, for those of you that paid attention in history class, was a farmer, land speculator, philosopher, writer, lay theologian, and American Revolution war patriot and general. However, Ethan Allen is best known for being one of the founders of Vermont and for his role in the capture of Fort Ticonderoga in May of 1775 during the Revolutionary War.

Ethan Allen and his brothers, Ira and Frances, purchased tracts of land that became Burlington, Vermont. Ethan married twice and fathered eight children. Allen also played a leading role in the formation of the "Green Mountain Boys." Allen died after suffering an apoplectic fit in 1789 and is buried in the Green Mountain Cemetery in Burlington.

However, another amazing fact goes far in further proving, as the Spaceman fervently believes, that everything is connected. Ethan Allen had two grandsons: Henry Hitchcock, the attorney general of Alabama; and Ethan Allen Hitchcock, a Union Army general in the Civil War. It was, of course, Alfred Hitchcock who directed *The Trouble with Harry* which made Craftsbury famous!

The Spaceman also points out that the capture of Fort Ticonderoga took place in 1775, and that two hundred years later, Bill Lee led his troops into battle with the Cincinnati Reds in an epic World Series! It should also be pointed out that General John Burgoyne's eight thousand-man army occupied the high ground above the fort under the command of General Arthur St. Clair during the French and Indian War. I was not about to ask the Spaceman if Tom Burgoyne, aka "The Phillie Phanatic," is a direct descendent of General John Burgoyne, again, in fear of receiving a positive response.

As for other wonderfully improbable characters in the area, the Spaceman's dentist is Dr. Kenneth Burchesky, DDS, of Lyndonville, Vermont, a "good ballplayer," as Lee describes him, "a helluva good dentist, and to my knowledge, the only Rastafarian dentist in the Northeast Kingdom." However, the Spaceman, himself a Rastafarian, added, "I wouldn't let him touch my cow! Plus, he's the worst switch-hitter in the history of the world."

Craftsbury, Vermont is also home to the annual "Fiddlers Festival," which, not surprisingly, brings in additional nonconformist-type characters. The hills are alive with the sound of fiddles. During one such festival in

1976, it rained like hell for several days, but this is Craftsbury we're talking about, and mere elements of nature will not serve to deter the denizens of such an eclectic yearly gathering. With the ground muddy, each competitor mounted a tractor trailer to perform one at a time. Most of the crowd was barefoot and drinking beer. The performers were dressed in a combination of bib overalls, straw hats, and dinner jackets.

Get this: In the wonderful motion picture, *The Trouble with Harry*, there is a scene where Captain Wiles is enjoying blueberry muffins at Miss Gravely's home, and those muffins were baked by the REAL Audrey Reed, David Reed's wife! The real shooter's wife, feeding the actor shooter! Again, you cannot make this shit up.

Bill "Spaceman" Lee is about to also draw an analogy between the "victim" in *The Trouble with Harry*, Harry Worp, and another complete asshole, former Yankee second baseman and longtime major league manager, Billy Martin! Hang on tight.

In the motion picture *The Trouble with Harry*, we are made fully aware that the deceased Harry Worp was a complete asshole. However, it is never fully spelled out as to why, but because of the genius of Alfred Hitchcock and his wonderful cast of actors and actresses, there exists little doubt that the character Harry Worp was a useless elongated turd of a human being. Then there was former ballplayer and manager Billy Martin, whose exploits on and off the field provided conclusive evidence of his being perhaps the poster child for aspiring assholes. Billy Martin, in fact, who both played for and managed the Yankees, may very well have been the target of an incident involving the Spaceman and his dear friend and teammate Ferguson Jenkins.

One day after the Red Sox had completed their game at Yankee Stadium, the Spaceman and Fergie Jenkins enlisted the help of their third baseman Rico Petrocelli's brother, Dave, in escaping Yankee Stadium's fans as they left the ballpark. David Petrocelli, a sweetheart of a man who also served as an usher in a section of Madison Square Garden where the author of this tome would watch his hometown New York Knicks, was glad to assist. With Dave Petrocelli leading the way, the Spaceman and Hall of Famer Jenkins exited beneath the stands into an alleyway where they came upon a young inebriated naked woman lying supine on the pavement. As the Spaceman and Fergie peered at the scene bemusedly, Dave Petrocelli removed a Yankees cap that was lying a few feet from the downed woman and placed it atop the woman's abdomen. Fergie Jenkins, God bless him, then remarked, "That's the first time I've seen anything other than an asshole beneath a Yankees cap."

It is well-documented that Billy Martin was a contemptible prick of the highest degree. There are few who would argue that point, including several of his friends and associates. It was pitcher Mickey McDermott, who was perhaps one of Martin's closest pals, who once was quoted that, "Billy never felt an evening was well spent unless it included at least one fight." Billy's closest friend and confidante on the Yankees was the great Mickey Mantle, who was quoted in Jane Leavy's superb biography of the Mick, *The Last Boy*, as saying Martin was the only guy he knew who "could hear someone giving him the finger." Jane Leavy went on to write, "He (Martin) negotiated life with a chip on his shoulder, and those in the know gave him a wide berth."

In the great, late Jim Bouton's groundbreaking *Ball Four*, Bouton wrote, "A year after the book came out, I was a sportscaster from New York covering spring training in Florida. Before a game, I spotted Joe Schultz (Bouton's former pitching coach), then a Detroit Tiger coach, hitting fungoes to some infielders. I hadn't spoken to Joe in almost two years. Naturally, I had to go over and say hello. I half-expected him to tell me I was throwing too much out in the bullpen (read *Ball Four*!). Instead, he said he didn't want to talk to me, that he hadn't read my book, but he'd heard about it; when I tried to tell Joe that he came off as a good guy, Billy Martin, the Tiger manager at the time, who's a bad guy, came running across the field hollering for me to get out (This was before Martin wrote HIS tell-all book). Because I've grown accustomed to the shape of my nose, I got the hell out. The sad part is I never had a chance to invite Joe to go out and pound the Budweiser."

To really understand the "depth" of Martin's character, one need only to read Jane Leavy's quote in the aforementioned *The Last Boy*. In it, Jane described the sediment that existed in the ground of the mining town where Mickey Mantle was raised in Commerce, Oklahoma, where the townsfolk worked the mines among "the ashen heap of mineral detritus disgorged from the abandoned Turkey Fat Mine." The mineral waste was known as "chat." Mickey Mantle's first wife was named Merlyn and as Ms. Leavy wrote, "Cruel Billy Martin called Merlyn 'Chat Pile Annie.'" And Mickey was his closest friend and teammate!

The most hilarious sports book ever written was penned by the great Mike Shropshire, who covered the Texas Rangers during the 1973-75 seasons, at which time the ball club was managed by the great Whitey Herzog and then the inebriate known as Billy Martin. The book is titled *Seasons in Hell*, and Shropshire's firsthand tales of Martin's drunkenness and cruelty are powerful, and yes, too often hilarious. Martin fought with opposing players, his own players, sportswriters, bar patrons, strangers, bartenders, fans, and on occasion, the authorities.

As Shropshire explained, sometimes Martin's evening began calmly, but something mysterious came over him, and that something nearly invariably occurred at approximately 12:45 a.m. As Shropshire wrote:

"Billy adored his fans. At least, he did until exactly forty-five minutes past midnight. Then Billy would undergo a swift transformation of personality in which he suddenly became the reigning poultry weight champion of the world and apt to practice uppercuts and jabs into the faces of some of these same adoring fans."

Mike Shropshire further explained:

"Billy was in everyday sipping proximity to his adored companion Mickey Mantle, now enjoying retirement in Dallas. Billy was avidly proclaiming to the world that Texas was his kind of place. He wore Levis, cowboy boots and occasionally even a cowboy hat."

As Shropshire hilariously penned, "Usually at least three and a half hours of persistent consumption were required for Billy to achieve his post-midnight, I'm fixin' to kick somebody's ass mode."

Burt Hawkins, a colleague of Mike Shropshire's, was a baseball lifer. He covered the Washington Senators for the *Washington Star* from 1937-1960 and was nominated for a Pulitzer Prize in 1957 for his seven-part series on the Senators. Hawkins moved to Texas in 1979 and continued to cover the ball club, who were renamed the Texas Rangers. During his lengthy fifty-nine-year career, Hawkins was a sportswriter, the public relations director, and an official scorer. In fact, the press box in Arlington is named after him. However, none of this impressed the drunk Billy Martin on a charter flight from Arlington to Kansas City late one evening.

As Shropshire explained in *Seasons in Hell*, Martin, already deeply into the effects of the healing grape, normally required little if any reason for striking another human being in the face with his fists upon reaching the required amount of intoxication. Therefore, as the 727 headed towards its destination in Missouri, Billy became enraged upon learning that Burt Hawkins's wife, Janet, had expressed an interest in forming some sort of Rangers auxiliary, a players' wives club. Of course, this was apparently sufficient provocation for Billy Martin to punch out Burt Hawkins. Which he did.

After cooler heads prevailed, most of the writers decided to remain contrite, and it was agreed that the incident would not make the press. Of course, there have always been scoundrels such as Dick Young, who never saw a controversy not beneath whatever dignity he possessed, and soon, Billy Martin, who wanted to return to the Yankees anyhow, was once more exposed as the belligerent drunkard he was.

After Billy Martin's Tigers had been swept by the Texas Rangers 3-0 at Arlington Stadium, Mike Shropshire wrote, "After the third and final game, I ventured over to the Detroit clubhouse to see if Billy might have some sort of explanation. There was nothing to fear in attempting that, really. My paper, after all, had a comprehensive health-insurance plan," he half-joked.

During his volatile and *often* volatile career as both a player and manager, Billy Martin got into physical altercations with opposing catcher Clint Courtney, twice; opposing catcher Matt Batts; the great Tommy Lasorda in an epic fight; pitcher Jim Brewer, who he battered on the mound (Brewer, Bill Lee's former coach was severely injured in the fracas); Howard Fox, a Minnesota Twin executive; Dave Boswell, Martin's own pitcher; Jack Sears, a fan outside of Tiger Stadium in Detroit; a cab driver in Chicago whose crime was telling Martin that he preferred soccer to baseball; Burt Hawkins, a Texas Rangers writer and club executive; Ray Hagar of the *Reno Evening Gazette*; Ed Whitson, his own pitcher while with the Yankees; several bouncers at a topless bar; and of course, Joseph Cooper, a marshmallow salesman. Of course, there are countless other altercations that never made the news.

In author Scott Russell's book (hey, that's me!), *Joey*, the biography of former middleweight champion Joey Giardello, he wrote the following:

Joey Giardello was a huge Brooklyn Dodgers fan since the days of his youth. As all Brooklyn Dodgers fans did, Joey had no love for the rival New York Yankees. Joey, of course, was invited to numerous banquets which of course, included meeting many members of the professional teams that had toiled for the Yankees, Dodgers, and Giants. At one of these reunions, the New York Yankees' manager was also a guest.

Billy Martin was renowned as one of the most volatile, trigger-tempered, vulgar and combative players and managers of his era. He was especially contentious when drunk, which was often. Billy Martin was also infamous for not fighting fairly, usually looking for an unfair advantage. In 1952, when the combustible Jimmy Piersall (Fear Strikes Out) of the Red Sox was experiencing mental issues which literally evolved into a total nervous breakdown, Martin jumped him from behind in a runway leading to the Red Sox dugout at Fenway Park and gave Piersall a fearsome beating. As manager of the Minnesota Twins, Martin got into an argument with one of his own pitchers, Dave Boswell. The incident took place at a bar (where else?) and Martin cold-cocked his hurler as he sat on a barstool holding two shot glasses, his and Martin's. Martin had just placed his glass in Boswell's hand before slugging him to ensure that Boswell was defenseless.

Billy Martin, as a player for the Cincinnati Reds, once assaulted pitcher Jim Brewer on the mound while Brewer was in the process of handing Martin's bat back to him. The incident occurred in 1960. Martin had thrown the bat at Brewer for a perceived brushback pitch. Martin punched Brewer, breaking Brewer's eye socket. Brewer sued Martin and won a settlement.

Well, at the reunion in question, Joey Giardello, a man of course, whose fists were lethal weapons, was introduced to Martin, who of course, was once more half in the bag. For Martin, it was a normal state of intoxication. Joey had been an invited guest of the legendary Yankees' teams of the 1950s. Joey politely attempted to make conversation with the tempestuous Martin as follows:"

Joey: Billy, I didn't like you very much when you were beating my Dodger teams in the World Series. You really used to kill the Dodgers.

Joey of course, had meant it as a compliment, since Martin had great numbers versus Joey's beloved "Bums." However, Martin, drunk as usual, did not take it as a compliment.

Billy: I'll kick your ass!

Joey did not take him seriously. However, Joey said, "I was watching for a sucker punch, just in case. You never know, he might have tried it. It wouldn't have been the first time."

Joey Giardello was very aware of Billy Martin's reputation as a cheap-shot artist. As several of Martin's friends got between them, Joey reminded the inebriated Yankee, "I ain't no marshmallow salesman!"

Upon being asked what would have occurred had Martin got out of line, Joey Giardello, who had knocked Sugar Ray Robinson on his behind while in the process of defeating him, responded truthfully and factually, "I would have hurt him bad."

The Spaceman recently told me that the key upon approaching Billy Martin was to "Never approach him with your arms folded or your hands in your pockets."

I was asked if I could compile a list of people Billy Martin has not fought with. Before I could even respond, Lee offered:

"It's a short list, but it includes the Dalai Lama, Leo Tolstoy, and Mahatma Gandhi, although I heard Billy took a swing at Gandhi, but missed and fell into the Ganges River and had to be rescued. Billy was rescued by a Yogi—although it wasn't Berra—a mystic, and a fakir, although they later regretted not allowing him to drown. They attempted to enlighten him with the three levels of consciousness, but that infuriated Billy and he soon got into a nasty brawl with Kahlil Gibran."

Oh, there was the analogy between the characters in *The Trouble with Harry*, all of whom thought they had killed the asshole Harry Worp, and Billy Martin. You see, just as many folks believed they were responsible for the firing of Billy Martin in Texas, but it turns out that the one responsible was Billy Martin himself.

Just as the residents of Craftsbury, Vermont all believed that they were the one responsible for the death of Harry Worp, many of Billy Martin's foes and "friends" apparently believed that they were the ones that were accountable. For instance, the writers covering the team who reported and in addition frequently covered up Martin's late-night brawling escapades believed their accounts of these encounters resulted in Martin's eventual dismissal. The Spaceman himself believed for quite some time that he was really the one that finally pushed Billy Martin to the brink. As Bill Lee recalled:

"We played Texas in a series just before Martin was canned. I began taunting him from our dugout and shouting at him for being the prick he was. Billy began hanging off the roof of the dugout like a chimpanzee. He was swinging back and forth. I thought I was at the fucking zoo!"

Ah, but as much as Bill Lee would have loved to be the one responsible for Billy Martin's fate, Billy, just as Harry Worp in *The Trouble with Harry*, was killed by "friendly fire." He was his own worst enemy, and the one thing he could not sucker punch was the bottle that killed him.

CHAPTER TWENTY-ONE

Genetics, Gene Pools, Witches, Warlocks, Tom Brunansky's Bat & the Dalai Lama

"Our prime purpose in this life is to help others, and if you can't help them, at least don't hurt them." —*Dalai Lama*

"Stop chirping like a bird, you putz!" —*Bill "Spaceman" Lee*

"If you can't justify it through chemistry and physics, you've got to go to Wiccans." —*Bill "Spaceman" Lee*

Suffice to say that if a group of Jehovah's Witnesses descended upon the people in the Northeast Kingdom, Bibles in hand, they would be frustrated in convincing the inhabitants of Craftsbury to perhaps read a Bible passage with them. It's not as if the residents of Craftsbury would be rude, but the bible-thumping, Watchtower-reading Yahweh evangelists would very likely be convinced to go ice fishing or snowmobiling with a group of nonconformists beyond their wildest imaginations. The more the merrier. As the Spaceman remarked, "The thimble of genes in this valley is only four."

In the world of the earthling known as Bill "Spaceman" Lee, there are few surprises. Several years ago, the great Pulitzer Prize winning photojournalist and equally terrific writer of the *Boston Globe*, Stan Grossfeld, who has authored several outstanding books, traveled with Bill and Diana Lee throughout the Maritime provinces and the Northeast Kingdom. In the *Boston Globe* dated July 25, 2015, Grossfeld quoted the Spaceman as saying:

"They recently asked me on the radio, 'What would you be doing if you weren't playing baseball?'" Lee answered as he made his way to the ballpark in Moncton, New Brunswick, "Probably twenty years to life somewhere."

Stan Grossfeld, who has covered many an eccentric character throughout his travels, inquired as to how the Spaceman felt about his being blackballed by major league baseball all these years. In typical fashion, Lee replied, "It may have hurt me economically, but if you're a Zen Buddhist Rastafarian like me, it's in my best interest to not make money."

Note: The author of this book, "Scott Russell," or more likely Kilgore Trout, highly recommends Stan Grossfeld's collaboration with Dan Shaughnessy, *Fenway: A Biography in Words and Pictures*, which includes a foreword by Ted Williams.

While visiting Bill and Diana, Stan Grossfeld's journey took him to the scenic town of Barnet. To offer further evidence that the Northeast Kingdom is never to be confused with anything other than a parallel universe, the towns around Barnet, Vermont are named East Barnet, McIndoe Falls, Mosquitoville, Passumpsic, and of course, West Barnet, which is I suspect (although I did not ask the Spaceman) west of East Barnet. Well, while on Stan Grossfeld's pilgrimage to join forces with Bill and Diana, none other than the Dalai Lama was visiting the area. No, really.

Just south of West Barnet is the town of East Corinth where they filmed the classic *Beetlejuice* starring Michael Keaton. It is where the late great environmentalist Guy Waterman lived and where his widow still resides on their farm.

While in Vermont, the Dalai Lama addressed the students at Middlebury College.

Note: It should be noted that author Scott Russell's novel, *Prophet's End,* is highly centered around Middlebury!

One day, according to the Spaceman, the Dalai Lama was enjoying a peaceful walk through a forest, when the serenity was further enhanced by the sound of a chirping bird. The Dalai Lama paused to take in the tranquil sound. The Dalai Lama then spoke, "Listen. Stop and hear the wonderful sound of nature!" Stan Grossfeld, who was walking behind the Dalai Lama, responded, "I'm sorry your Holiness. That was me whistling."

Again, according to the Spaceman, the Dalai Lama turned and replied softly, "It's not nice to fool the Dalai Lama."

For you ethereal fanatics, the Spaceman would like you to know that this Dalai Lama is the fourteenth in history, and that his spiritual name is Jetsun Jamphel Ngawang Lobsang Yeshe Tenzin Gyatso, but his birth name was Lhamo Dhondup, and that he was born in the Wood-Pig Year, Fifth Month, Fifth Day of the Tibetan calendar, or on July 6, 1935, which would make him eighty-six years old (if this book gets published before his next birthday!) His birthplace is in Taktser.

The Dalai Lama was awarded a Nobel Peace Prize and is the first Nobel laureate cited for his environmental concern.

Lest you think that the Spaceman is a devout Zen Buddhist, consider his vast and differing views:

"I learned genetics by reading Mark Twain's *Pudd'nhead Wilson*, and by watching my grandfather's dog jumping out of his truck. He would see a fucking rabbit and run off, and we wouldn't see him again until nightfall, but his other dog would just remain in the truck and refuse to jump out. He would say, 'Fuck this shit, I'm staying here!'"

In what seems to most sane folks as a contradiction, at least to those that do not know Bill Lee, he explained:

"I'm a warlock because I've got Tom Brunansky's bat in my basement, and I have no idea how it got there. It's the bat that broke during batting practice before the game at Fenway Park on September 29, 1990. I was at the game, but I left after Brunansky was 0-1. Somehow the bat was given to me by Shawn Poirier, a warlock, and Laurie Cabot, a Wiccan priestess from Salem. In an attempt to break the 'Curse of the Bambino' (the Red Sox had not won a World Series since trading Babe Ruth to the Yankees after 1918) Shawn Poirier and Laurie Cabot, the warlock and the witch, held a rally outside of Fenway Park and began waving around a baseball bat and exhorting the crowd, who began chanting, 'Beat Toronto! Beat Toronto! Beat Toronto!' We petitioned the gods to beat Toronto. It was me, Shawn Poirier, and Laurie Cabot waving the fucking bat, but the Red Sox fans never see the big picture. They should've been shouting, 'Win the World Series!'"

Now, it got even stranger, as the Spaceman expounded:

"Laurie Cabot, the high Wiccan priestess, and the warlock, Shawn Poirier, had handed me the bat. I had no idea it was Tom Brunansky's broken bat! As I drove home, I listened to the game on the radio as Brunansky blasted three home runs! When I arrived home, I looked at the bat. It was then I realized they had given me Brunansky's broken bat! Yes, the Red Sox went on to win the division, but they were swept by the Oakland A's 4-0 in the AL Championship Series. All because the Red Sox fans shouted the wrong fucking chant!"

Note: Less than two years ago, I was with the Spaceman at a celebrity golf tournament in Boothbay Harbor, Maine. Upon seeing a pair of cleats in the trunk of his car, I asked as to their significance. Bill responded:

"Oh, those are Cole Hamels's cleats, the ones he wore while being named MVP of the 2008 World Series. I outbid a thirteen-year-old kid for them at a

Matt Stairs fundraiser. I told the kid to quit bidding because I needed them. I told him, 'Tiger, those are mine!' They fit perfectly. They had the pitching toe on the left side."

Oh, and the Phillies haven't won since. Warlock? It's your call.

I also learned that the Spaceman had a friend in a lovely Wiccan priestess named Margot Adler, who wrote *Drawing Down the Moon*. Bill Lee stated, "Margot gave me an amulet, one of those things they give you to rub for good luck."

I haven't as yet added that volume to my reading list.

CHAPTER TWENTY-TWO

Pissing Into the Wind

"Buddha and St. Augustine were hell-raisers when they were kids. I was planning to do everything perfectly today, but when I woke up, I walked right into a fucking wall! I'll never make it as a Buddhist."
—*Bill "Spaceman" Lee*

"There are few moments of clarity more profound than those that follow the emptying of an overcharged bladder. The world slows down, the focus sharpens, the brain comes back in line. Huge nebulous difficulties prove on close calm examination to be merely cloud giants."
—*Tom Holt*

"It's probably better to have him inside the tent pissing out, than outside the tent pissing in." —*Lyndon Johnson on FBI Director J. Edgar Hoover*, NY Times, *Oct. 31, 1971*

Note: The author finds Lyndon Johnson's comment to "Keep your friends close and your enemies closer," to be one of the greatest idioms or euphemisms ever spoken.

Paul Adams Hunt was the son of Rockwell Dennis Hunt, who was an eminent California historian as well as a professor at the University of Southern California. Rockwell was also a prolific author and was named "Mr. California" by Governor Goodwin Knight in 1954. Rockwell was Bill "Spaceman" Lee's great-grandfather and Paul Adams Hunt was Bill's grandfather.

"Grandpa Paul Adams Hunt," said the Spaceman, "was the head controller of irrigation on the Stanislaus River. The Stanislaus is a major tributary to the San Joaquin and the Sacramento, which is one of the few interior deltas in the world (there are only three!). As kids we could go to any reservoir and fish. One day we were at the Tulloch Reservoir and a boat arrives. The guy driving the boat is an idiot and he's got a water skier aboard. The moron doesn't understand the convex, and he hits the fucking dam! My grandfather sarcastically gave him a standing ovation, but he didn't offer to help.

"Later on, we return to where we're parked, and we see the idiot's truck and trailer, but the boat's not on it. The window on the truck is open and my brother Paul—he was nine years old—says, 'Grandpa, I gotta pee.' My grandfather told Paul, 'See if you can pee through that open window.' Paul let out a stream and it looked like the fucking arch in St. Louis! He peed into that truck for a good three minutes. These days Paul can't piss unless his wife lets him!"

The Spaceman continued:

"Hey, it stands to reason that Grandpa Hunt should instruct my brother Paul to piss into the parked truck. After all, he was in charge of irrigation! My grandfather was the first guy in California to offer outreach programs for poor children in Los Angeles. He was way ahead of his time. He was my hero. I always wanted to be a forest ranger."

This remembrance somehow morphed into a remembrance about Bill's former drinking buddy, the great southpaw, "Tug McGraw." As the Spaceman recalled:

"We would go to Rembrandt's Bar in North Philly, just outside of the old prison. It was a three-quarter square bar and all the seats were facing a marble wall. It was an old German bar, and it was a urinal, too. You wouldn't even have to get up to go to the bathroom. You'd just pee against a wall and it would roll down into a gutter. We were in downtown Philly that day somewhere near the Walt Whitman Bridge."

Lest you believe that Bill Lee was entirely proud of his elders, he offered:

"I've been an apologist for my family for too long. My grandfather Paul Adams Hunt and his brother, Lloyd Hunt, prevented the building of the Boulder Dam by blocking the flow. Agriculture is often the enemy of the people."

CHAPTER TWENTY-THREE

The Spaceman's List of "Authors" Who Have Never Actually Read a Book

Mick and Paddy are reading headstones at a nearby cemetery.
Mick says," Crikey! There's a bloke here who was 152!"
Paddy says, "What's his name?"
Mick replies, "Miles, from London."

To pay homage to his fellow authors, the earthling known as Bill "Spaceman" Lee wishes to acknowledge his fellow athletes, the ones that have also "written" books. Therefore, in the spirit of journalistic brotherhood, *the* Bill Lee has graciously compiled a list honoring those loquacious ambassadors of Shakespeare that have so enriched our lives with their prose and profound thought.

The Spaceman has even taken the time to rate these remarkable men of the fourth estate.

#1 KEITH HERNANDEZ—Yes, the legendary former St. Louis Cardinal and New York Mets first baseman and current broadcaster may have never read a book, or owned one, for that matter, but he most certainly has "written" one. However, in all fairness, it is rumored that Keith has had eleven books read out loud to him by eleven different teammates but could not recall the titles of the books or the players that read them to him.

#2 DON ZIMMER—Zim indeed "wrote" a book with Bill Madden, despite not being capable of spelling "cat" even if he were provided the letters "c," "a," and "t."

#3 CURT SCHILLING—Although he apparently owns a few copies of *Mein Kampf.*

#4 BILLY MARTIN—Even Billy has "written" a tell-all volume, although it's more likely that he's used it as a projectile.

#5 ANGEL HERNANDEZ—Although it's unclear if Hernandez has ever read a book, there are some that claim he has read a few in Braille.

#6 HAYWOOD SULLIVAN—In all fairness to "Hayseed," he may have read several comic books.

#7 BERNIE CARBO—It's possible, though, that Bernie has read the Scriptures, but more than likely just memorized a verse or two.

#8 LENNY DYKSTRA—I've heard from some reliable sources that Lenny is in the process of penning "How to Lisp in Fourteen Different Languages," and also a book about business ethics.

#9 JOE PEPITONE—I understand that Joe's classic, *Joe, You Coulda Made Us Proud*, will be available in hair salons across our continent within a few months.

#10 JESUS—Yes, Jesus has written ONE book, but then ceased. Hey, quit while you're ahead. Keep in mind that Jesus's book has sold more copies than any other book in history but has never made it onto the *New York Times* bestseller list, which speaks volumes (pun intended) about the validity of such a canon.

NOTE: Recently, the author learned that Bill "Spaceman" Lee and his dear friend Gordy Grayburn, aka "Dr. Zoom," were thrown out of a Christian bookstore upon Lee asking the proprietor if they offered any "nonfiction books."

CHAPTER TWENTY-FOUR

Elegies for Immortals

Crossing the Bar

"Sunset and evening star,
And one clear call for me!
And may there be no moaning of the bar,
When I put out to sea,
But such a tide as moving seems asleep,
Too full for sound and foam,
When that which drew from out the boundless deep
Turns again home.
Twilight and evening bell,
And after that the dark!
And may there be no sadness of farewell,
When I embark;
For tho' from out our bourne of Time and Place
The flood may bear me far,
I hope to see my Pilot face to face."
—*Alfred Lord Tennyson*

"The only rule I got, is if you slide, get up." —*Bill "Spaceman" Lee*

"I'd rather have a bottle in front of me than a frontal lobotomy."
—*Tom Waits*

Hillel Wright, author, "crossed the bar," as it was written in the *Japan Times* in 2017. It was a reference to the above poem by the great Alfred Lord Tennyson in 1889, and most likely written as a metaphor comparing death with crossing the "sandbar" between the river of life with its outgoing flood and the ocean that lies beyond death, the "boundless deep," to which we return.

Hillel Wright was one of the most indescribably eclectic writers of our time. Hillel's train of thought was deliciously different from the great major- ity of his fellow journalists. I believe that even Dr. Hunter S. Thompson would have been hesitant to drop acid with Hillel, in fear of seeing the eventual result of such an "experiment." Hillel Wright was born in Colorado in 1943, the son of a father who was stationed at Lowery Field in the US Army Air Corps. Hillel was then raised in Hartford and Old Saybrook, Connecticut, where he became a Boston Red Sox fan. Hillel Wright moved to Hawaii in 1969 and began a career as a commercial fisherman. He moved to Denman Island, British Columbia, and married Maureen Fath in 1972.

Wright was a poet, fisherman, a writer, a tree planter, a clam digger, and a radio host who ran for election as a member of the Rhinoceros Party, the very same one that the earthling known as Bill "Spaceman" Lee ran for, as a candidate for president of the United States. It would stand to reason then, that Hillel and Bill Lee would become good friends, and that they did. In fact, Hillel's absurdly delightful book, *Rotary Sushi* is dedicated to the Spaceman! *Rotary Sushi* is described on the cover of the book as "many kinds of stories." And that they are.

In that magnificent volume, the titles of the chapters are ones that even Dr. Hunter S. Thompson would have been proud of writing. Try these on for a few:

Allah's Radio
War Against Treeplanters Escalates
The Ghosts of Sammy Sammy
The Neo-Suburbanist Manifesto
Home Sweet Picnic Table
The Black Cat of Yamato Machi
Showdown at Luigi's
Cadillac Too-Hard-to-Handle Love-God Russell
Bird Lives!
Morgan, Morgan
Hark! The Herald Janitors Sing
That Kinda Guy
Kaiten Sushi
And the Spaceman's very favorite titled – A Borges Trilogy

Hillel Wright, who embraced all religions and non-religions, earned a BA from Temple University in Philadelphia and an MA at Southern Illinois

University, which was where the Spaceman's favorite writer and philosopher, Buckminster Fuller, taught!

Hillel moved to Japan and married Shiori "The Muse" Tsuchiya. Eventually the couple would spend half the year in Naha, Okinawa, and the other half in Canada. After moving south from Kawasaki after the Tohoku "Triple Disaster" in March of 2011. This, of course, was the horrific earthquake that led to the disastrous tsunami as thousands of lives were lost.

Note: On April 10, 2011, the author's beautiful and gifted friend, Taimane, the daughter of a Samoan princess, performed at a concert in Kokua, Japan to benefit the victims of the tsunami. The video is available on YouTube.

The Spaceman's aforementioned favorite chapter titled, "A Borges Trilogy," is priceless. As Bill Lee often states, "I, too, am Jorge Luis Borges." Upon reading Hillel Wright's *Rotary Sushi*, you will understand.

Upon writing about Hillel Wright, I asked the Spaceman if perhaps we were delving too far into unchartered territories, and if maybe we were getting a bit too esoteric and/or eclectic. Bill responded, "Very few understand us as it is, and it really doesn't matter. To fully understand us would require an IQ of at least 140 or less than 6. Anything in between would be undecipherable."

It should be noted that one of Bill Lee's teammates out in Hornby Island, BC was indeed, Hillel Wright—and oh, what I would give to have recorded conversations between those two gentlemen. Bill Lee's team played at Joe King Field ("You've got to be joking," said the Spaceman). Joe King Field is located near "The Forbidden Plateau," which is a small, hilly plateau in the Comox Glacier Island ranges of Vancouver. The Comox Glacier is northwest of the Comox Lake, roughly between Mount Albert Edward to the southwest and Mount Washington to the northeast.

The Spaceman often described Hillel Wright's writing as "Zevonist." When I mentioned that even Dr. Hunter S. Thompson might have been hesitant of dropping some acid with Hillel, Bill replied, "I don't know. There's a lot of psilocybin and mescaline on Vancouver Island."

The Spaceman described the inhabitants of Hornby Island, BC, as follows:

"The folks up there are all poets who live there because it's so desolate. It's just banana slugs and rain all the time. Most Americans settled up there because of the Vietnam War."

I suppose that Hillel Wright, who as we stated, "crossed the bar" in 2017, was so correct when he was quoted as saying, "We're just living quietly in the future."

While discussing the great, late Hillel Wright with the Spaceman, Bill recommended I read another great travelogue written by Will Ferguson, titled *Beauty Tips from Moose Jaw*. Keep in mind that the author was born in a fur-trapping settlement, and his book describes how Scottish Lowlanders and Highlanders initiated fur trading in the region, but that the Highlanders, as Lee stated, "dominated the trade because they were better drinkers."

Seriously, you ask the Spaceman—my head is spinning!—but Bill concluded with, "That's why Lagavulin is my favorite scotch."

Incidentally, the book is hilarious, poignant, and yes, educational, especially after sipping sixteen-year-old scotch.

BRIEF INTERMISSION # 2

A Brief Brush with Nobility

"Sometimes we meet someone and feel like we have known them all our lives." —*Avijeet Das*

"And in a few rare instances, we have." —*"Scott Russell"*

"Y ou're Scott Russell, aren't you?"

The query was directed at me by a familiar looking gentleman as Peg and I took one of our countless walks in our neighborhood of "the Cliffs." The man certainly looked friendly, and I was quite certain I had seen him before. After all, Peg and I have lived here for well over three decades.

"As long as you're not serving me a warrant, I will admit to being him," I responded. The man laughed and then introduced himself:

"Hi, I'm Jack," he offered, "I understand you're a fellow author." It turned out that Jack is the father of my neighbor, Dawn, and her husband, Todd, who were quite familiar with my writings. Upon meeting Jack, we were both surprised that we were born within months of each other. Within moments, we realized that we had much more in common. Soon we were invited into Jack's comfortable home. The walls of Jack's home were adorned with mind-boggling photographs of eminently recognizable people, and Jack was in each photograph! The walls of Jack's den contained impressive caricatures of Hollywood stars, and famous politicians and legendary athletes. It did not take me too long to realize that Jack was not your run-of-the-mill neighbor. This was obviously an extraordinary and gifted artist. Yes, the caricatures were his artwork!

Within days, we exchanged books we had both written. Incredibly, Jack is perhaps the preeminent authority on the Old West, and he is often called upon by those in the motion picture industry to provide pertinent information. But, oh, the tales!

In 1967, Jack, as I was, was a young man of twenty-two, but not yet a writer, but what a caricature artist! One day, Jack had been commissioned to draw caricatures of some friends. He was at a restaurant when suddenly a young woman peered over his shoulder, and said with a rather severe New

York accent, "Hey, you're pretty good. Can you paint one for me?" The young woman was a Brooklynite, and a terrific young singer and actress. She was a graduate of Erasmus High School in Brooklyn, and she had made quite a name for herself onstage and in motion pictures. Her name—and she's still around—is Barbara Streisand, although she is now known as "Barbra" or "Babs." Soon, Barbara, who was married to actor Elliott Gould in those days, would arrange many more opportunities for Jack to paint other celebrities. Peg and I stared incredulously at the photographs of Ms. Streisand, Gene Kelly, Audrey Hepburn, and other immortals lining Jack's wall. There were even photographs of Jack with Bobby Kennedy, Ted Kennedy, and Ethel Kennedy, but the best was yet to come.

Jack regaled us with a hilarious story that took place in 1967. He was seated in a plush restaurant and drawing a few caricatures, when the proprietor of the restaurant approached him to inform him that an exclusive party was about to take place at the venue, and Jack was politely asked to vacate. As Jack gathered his easel, pen and ink and charcoal, the door swung open, and Jacqueline Kennedy entered with an entourage. Jack had not yet noticed her, but he was startled when Jacqueline called out: "Jack, where are you going? Aren't you going to stay and have dinner with us?"

Now, it even gets better. Upon seeing Jacqueline Kennedy warmly greet Jack on another occasion, the often-mouthy Barbara Streisand, shocked at seeing Jacqueline's overt friendliness to her artist friend, exclaimed in her severe Brooklyn accent after Mrs. Kennedy had walked away, "You know huh?! (sic)"

My old friend and collaborator (hell, at least I have one name to drop!) Bill "Spaceman" Lee is a huge student of the Old West. Bill is really looking forward to meeting Jack, something we've arranged in the near future.

"You're Scott Russell, aren't you?"

When Jack meets the Spaceman, I promise to have my recorder on. Ken Burns, you ain't seen nuthin' yet!

Oh, the gentleman's name is Jack Demattos, and check out the magnificent books he has written. They are well worth reading.

CHAPTER TWENTY-FIVE

Make Way for Ducklings

"If animals spoke, humanity would cry." —*Manuj Rajput*

"Animals never worry about Heaven or Hell. Neither do I. Maybe that's why we get along." —*Charles Bukowski*

"I don't believe in the concept of hell, but if I did, I would think of it as filled with people who were cruel to animals." —*Gary Larson*

In Robert McCloskey's wondrous 1941 children's picture book, *Make Way for Ducklings*, the hero of the story is a policeman with a whistle. In *Make Way for Ducklings*, mallards are rescued on an island in the lagoon in the Boston Public Garden. In 1987, artist Nancy Schon created a magnificent thirty-five-foot-long bronze sculpture of "Mrs. Mallard" followed by her eight ducklings. As it stands in the Boston Public Gardens in Boston's Back Bay, it is one of the most treasured attractions for those visiting the city, and of course, for its inhabitants, especially the children who anxiously leaf through the book.

Fast forward to not too long ago, and the earthling known as Bill "Spaceman" Lee was a guest of the Boston Red Sox, his former employer, and he was delivering a speech to a group of fans in the corridor of Fenway Park, when he was interrupted. As the Spaceman described the escapade:

"I was in the process of giving a speech to a group of fans just inside of the fence that faces the Prudential Building when I heard a commotion outside. Folks were shouting and kids were getting all excited out there, and the kids seemed to be upset. I looked out and I saw a female goose attempting to walk across the street, and she had her brood of baby fledglings following slowly behind her. I stopped in the middle of the speech and told everyone that I had to go out and save the geese.

"When I ran out there, the geese had made it to the Sunoco Station on Brookline Avenue. It was ninety degrees out there and the baby geese all looked exhausted. The son of a retired cop, a great guy, began to help by directing traffic away from the geese. The first thing I said was, 'We've got to get a new leader.' Mom wasn't doing too well. The fledglings all had their tongues hanging out; they were spent. I got a giant tub at the Sunoco Station and filled it with water from a hose. We had to get the geese hydrated.

"After all the geese had downed water, the son of the cop helped me herd them across the street to the Fens (the area across Brookline Avenue, where there are lakes and gardens). We pulled open a chain-link fence and herded them to safety, where they waddled into the water. Then I walked back to Fenway Park and received a standing ovation. The son of an Irish cop helped tremendously, and then he told me, 'Thank you so much for what you did. You've always been a gentleman.' When I pitched in relief, I accumulated a bunch of saves, too."

CHAPTER TWENTY-SIX

Many Rivers to Cross

"When I die, I want to die like my grandfather who died peacefully in his sleep. Not screaming like all the passengers in his car."
—*Will Rogers*

"My goals are to hit .300, score 100 runs, and stay injury-prone."
—*Mickey Rivers*

The earthling known as Bill "Spaceman" Lee was always fond of his opponent, the fleet-footed outfielder named Mickey Rivers. "Mick the Quick" was one of the fastest players in the major leagues and one of the true characters of the game. Mickey was never renowned for his ability to communicate in the "King's English," but his choice of colloquialisms made up for his alleged failure to impress those that would ridicule the absence of Shakespeare-type alliteration.

On occasion, there is logic in our universe, and it would stand to reason that John Milton "Mickey" Rivers would eventually don the Yankee pin-stripes and butcher the English language much like the Yankees beloved Hall of Fame manager, the verbose genius Casey Stengel, had done many years before him.

Mickey Rivers's quotes were legendary in their unintentional brilliance. Consider that Mickey was once asked about his relationship with volatile owner George Steinbrenner and his volcanic manager, Billy Martin, and Rivers replied, "Me and George and Billy are two of a kind." Mickey Rivers once asked, "What was the name of that dog in *Rin Tin Tin*?"

Mickey Rivers was, and is, delightful, and one of the more accidentally hilarious human beings to ever don a major league uniform. The great, late journalist George Kimball of the *Boston Phoenix* would often write of the adventures of Mickey Rivers, who as George reported, was fond of wagering on the ponies. Unfortunately, Mickey was not skillful at picking winners, and in fact, his choices nearly invariably finished far back in the pack, that is, if they even managed to make it to the finish line.

Mickey Rivers was also famous for finding willing bookmakers in every town his ball club visited, but due to his proclivity for picking losers, Mickey was often a bit tardy in making payments to his "brokers"; those included various members of organized crime, and their "collection agencies" would arrive at ballparks throughout the United States to gather their bosses' winnings, cash that Mickey Rivers had already spent on mundane items such as food and clothing. These entrepreneurs were often referred to as "leg-breakers," and didn't exactly exhibit patience or courtesy to any of their "clients" that were arrears in their payments.

In one of George Kimball's more entertaining articles about Rivers's inclination to avoid such mob-related individuals, he wrote that while Rivers visited Fenway Park in Boston with the Yankees, there were a couple of rather serious looking goons waiting outside of the Yankees clubhouse after a night game. They were not present to attain Mickey Rivers's autograph. Mickey exited the Yankees locker room wearing a Panama hat, dark shades, and had his collar turned up when these Neanderthal-resembling gentlemen addressed him with, "Hey Rivers, get over here. We want to talk to you!"

In inimitable fashion, Mickey Rivers responded, "Me no Mickey Rivers. Me Miguel Riviera," and in typical Mickey Rivers fashion, he ran towards the exit and into the street and quickly disappeared into the night, leaving the two heavyset collectors flat-footed. George Kimball once reported that it was common for Rivers to receive advances for his salary two months in advance.

Many years later, the Spaceman was in the Midwest appearing in a legends game, one that included Yankees and Angels former star, Mickey Rivers. The Spaceman was given a heads-up that the promoter of the event had been bouncing checks, but it was too late as Bill had already received his bogus check. After participating in the game, Bill boarded a plane to fly back east, when a smiling Mickey Rivers entered the cabin of the aircraft and happily declared while waving a check, "I got my money!"

Mickey Rivers was a pisser. When Mickey played for the incorrigible Billy Martin in New York, the Yankees volatile manager was frustrated by Rivers's lack of bunting ability. No one in the major leagues, at that time, was faster than Mickey from home to first, and Billy Martin knew that if Rivers were better at bunting, he would reach base far more often and score many more runs with his legs. Therefore, Martin insisted that Rivers spend at least twenty minutes a day during batting practice improving his bunting ability. Later that night, Mickey Rivers complained to the press, "I don't know why Billy wants me to practice bunting. Why don't he have me practice something I'm good at."

Hall of Famer Reggie Jackson, an erudite and well-educated man, would often attempt to belittle Mickey Rivers, but as "Spaceman" Lee laughed, Mickey got the best of the brash Yankees slugger. As the Spaceman explained:

"One time, Reggie was busting Mickey's balls as his usual condescending self, and he told Rivers, 'Why do I even speak with you? I've got an IQ of 170.' Mickey quickly responded, 'Yeah, 170 out of a thousand!' Another time Jackson was making fun of Mickey, Rivers replied, 'You know what, Reggie? You don't even know who you is. Your first name is Reginald, and that's British. Your middle name is Martinez, and that's Mexican, and your last name is Jackson, and that's black! You don't even know what you is!"

How can you not love Mickey Rivers?!

CHAPTER TWENTY-SEVEN

Philosophy X Infinity

"Doubt is the origin of wisdom." —*Rene Descartes*

"Never put Descartes in front of de horse." —*Bill "Spaceman" Lee*

"Judge a man by his questions rather than his answers."—*Voltaire*

"I don't ask questions. I know all the answers." —*Bill "Spaceman" Lee*

Their mouths agape, the youngsters on the Stoughton Black Knights baseball team stared incredulously at the septuagenarian gentleman in the Red Sox uniform as he seemingly appeared out of nowhere and began excitedly informing them that he embraces the Cartesian Principle, and that he based everything on Cartesian logic.

It was bad enough that they were about to face an overpowering pitcher, one in fact who was listed by most astute baseball experts as the best pitching prospect in the entire northeast, and perhaps even the best high school pitcher in the United States. But now they were being addressed by a verifiable madman who was busy explaining Michael Lewis's *The Undoing Project* to a group of high school scholars not prepared for such a lecture on a suburban ball field.

On May 18, 2021, the earthling known as Bill "Spaceman" Lee drove 250 miles from his home atop a hill in Craftsbury, Vermont to a ball field in North Attleboro, Massachusetts to see a seventeen-year-old youngster named Dennis Colleran, Jr., a senior at North Attleboro High School, pitch. The occasion was a baseball game between North Attleboro and Stoughton High School, and Bill was invited by yours truly, the author of this magnificent book.

"You've got to see this kid pitch, Bill," I told him, although upon my answering the phone at ten o'clock on the morning of the game, I was not expecting to hear the Spaceman inform me some five minutes into the conversation, "Oh, by the way, I'm on my way."

The Stoughton baseball team, already dazed by Bill's earlier comments regarding Cartesian logic, was somewhat taken aback as the Spaceman scolded, "I know where you live, and I've got the keys to your house."

To fully understand, or even to partially comprehend "Spaceman" Lee, one requires at least a primer to follow his innocuous ravings. You see, since Bill is a locksmith, as we detailed in *The Spaceman Chronicles,* and actually resided in Stoughton during his days playing with the Red Sox, Bill indeed has a "key" to their homes, since he was given a key to the town! Again, there is bizarre logic in our universe.

As for the game itself—the Spaceman and I sat directly behind the screen with various scouts from major league organizations—D.J. Colleran acquitted himself quite well. In a seven-inning contest, Colleran pitched a two-hit shutout, struck out twelve men, and displayed poise, power, and a presence which belied his tender age. For the record, the scouts told me he topped out at 99 MPH. Following the game, I introduced Bill to the young-ster, the one who nearly invariably digs my wife Peg and I out of major snowstorms even before we've climbed out of bed at 5:00 a.m. Bill, at six feet, three inches tall, looked up at the towering strong-armed right-handed youngster and exclaimed, "You're bigger in real life!"

Then it was on to a great Mexican meal in Walpole, Massachusetts, where the Spaceman offered, "It was a magical day. When D.J. comes up to Burlington, it will be an event."

Before leaving for dinner, the Spaceman in typical fashion, told me, "I went back to get my folding chair after the game and there was a man sitting there fighting with his third ex-wife. I told him I would dig a hole for him if he would dig a hole for me."

Note: The Spaceman's dependence on relying on Cartesian logic can perhaps be explained as follows: Cartesian logic is a simple way of ques-tioning and is a form of methodological skepticism. It is an effective way to examine questions and answers from every point of view, especially in a coaching setting.

The following morning, back home in Vermont, the Spaceman found himself on a Little League field. Those in charge thought it a good idea to have Bill umpire the game. As Bill reported on the proceedings:

"They gave me shin guards, a chest protector, a mask, a pitch-counter, and a whisk broom to dust off the plate, but all I wanted was the mask. The friggin catcher never caught a pitch. I got hit in the nuts, on each shin and my toes. I asked the kid behind the plate, 'Why do they call you a catcher? You never catch anything.' The Craftsbury kids were playing a team from Morrisville. The Morrisville team has this one fucking bruiser. His mother weighs four hundred pounds and she sits outside the stadium near their pickup truck. It's a good thing the kid was a pull hitter because if he wasn't, he would've killed at least three children out there. The kid hit two inside the park home runs which were really groundballs to short. They're playing coach-pitch and regular-pitch. His coach was pitching to him and standing only thirty-five feet away. If he had hit this kid's bat, I would've seen a coach die in Craftsbury."

The Spaceman concluded with, "They had this little girl out there playing second base. She couldn't have weighed more than forty-five pounds. She was the smartest player out there. She was always in the right place at the right time."

CHAPTER TWENTY-EIGHT

Keep Your Eye on the Ball

"I have an inferiority complex, but it's not a very good one."
—*Steven Wright*

One day in the not-too-distant past, the earthling known as Bill "Space-man" Lee, once more found himself playing baseball against men half his age. The occasion was the Senior League Spring Classic. The locale was Eddie Popowski Field in Fort Myers, Florida at the Red Sox minor league complex, and Bill was in the process of attempting to avoid being clobbered by a one-hop line drive headed directly at his face. As the Spaceman described the incident:

"I was knocked senseless. The ball struck me on the eye socket. I was knocked unconscious for several minutes. I woke up on the mound as the trainer placed an ice pack on the wound. The doctor immediately placed me on concussion protocol. The ball hit so hard in the eye that it one-hopped the visitor's dugout. My buddy, Mike Mulkern, was with me in Fort Myers and the doctor asked him if he was going to be around me all day. Mike told him he was. 'Good,' the doctor said, 'If he starts acting strangely, call me immediately.' Mike looked at the doctor incredulously, and replied, 'How the fuck would I know if Bill is acting strangely?!'"

Four months later, the Spaceman lost three teeth. Bill claimed it was "a delayed reaction." I did not pursue why in fear of receiving a response. Oh, and get this: the Spaceman went out and pitched both ends of a double-header the next day!

At one of those Senior League games, former Yankees third baseman Clete Boyer was checking out Diana, Bill's wife, and as Bill stated, "Clete started hitting on her. He pointed at me and shouted, 'What are you doing with that asshole?'"

CHAPTER TWENTY-NINE

Colorful Travel Agent & A Bizarre Dream

"I don't know where I am going, but I am on my way." —*Voltaire*

"I was standing on the riverbank one day when a man on the opposite bank called out to me, 'I need to get to the other side!' I shouted back, 'You are on the other side!'" —*Steven Wright.*

O n Sunday, May 23, 2021, the earthling known as Bill "Spaceman" Lee pitched his first game of the Vermont Senior League season. With the snows finally melted, the temperatures more resembling Planet Earth, and his seventy-four-year-old bones creaking, Bill Lee took the bump against another team of aging youngsters in denial of gravity. Hours later, Bill Lee, although the worse for wear, had emerged with a complete four-hit nine-inning victory. However, Monday morning awaited with its claws and teeth bared, and just getting out of bed would prove to be a daunting task. However, the Spaceman is not your prototypical athlete, and after an hour or two of considering assisted suicide, it was determined by a committee of one, that the contents of a bottle of Lagavulin scotch might contain the needed supplement to what mere mortals would require, Super Strength Tylenol be damned.

"How can you drink that stuff?" asked Diana, Bill's long-suffering bride. Bill Lee replied, "Are you kidding? Lagavulin is so smooth it's like maple syrup to a Vermonter."

Before we continue with this chapter, I should point out that there resides in the town of Craftsbury a lovely young woman who shall go nameless. For lack of a better description, this attractive young lady can be loosely described as a "travel agent." However, the "journeys" she offers seldom, if ever, can be found on maps or travel brochures. The young woman's specialty is an excursion of the mind, a psilocybin adventure, as it were, and the "travel guides" are of the plant variety. Book your "'shroom trip" as quickly as possible, as space is limited—or perhaps unlimited, take your pick. As the Spaceman elaborated, "There is a fungus among us." But he was not referring to the young lady's "travel agency."

Note: In no way am I suggesting that the earthling known as Bill Lee booked such an expedition a day after pitching a nine-inning game; however, one can easily imagine the desirable effects of a combination of Lagavulin scotch and a 'shroom pilgrimage.

The Spaceman awoke the morning of Tuesday, May 25, feeling much better than he did the prior morning. The soothing aftereffects of Lagavulin scotch, and perhaps another additional medicinal benefit, rendered the veteran left-hander in a much greater state to consider pitching another baseball game the following Sunday. In fact, Bill made plans to pitch that game and declared his intentions to take Luis Tiant to dinner afterwards, that is, "if I survive the game. If not, Luis can hold a memorial service for me."

However, despite his shoulder and other joint and muscle aches having significantly subsided, there was this matter of a rather strange and vivid dream, one that was frighteningly reminiscent of the type of vision often described by Dr. Hunter S. Thompson. I will allow the southpaw to describe his, for lack of a better term, nightmare:

"I'm in my VW, I'm trying to stop, but I have no brakes. I wind up plowing into a pedestrian. It was the worst nightmare about not having brakes. In the dream, there's a Dunkin Donuts, my ex-wife Pam, a Quebecois baseball team, Canadian government officials, and I wind up having to swim across a river. A gold tooth fell out of my mouth, but I don't even have a gold tooth. The entire dream was like a fucking mélange. A horse-faced girl offered to give me a ride to a ballpark I didn't even know existed. She looked familiar and she was the only amiable person present. What the hell was I doing in Quebec to begin with? For some reason, I was wearing long underwear that had two names on it. One name was mine and the other was the name of some guy in the Mets organization."

Have you heard enough? Well, that's too bad, because the Spaceman was not done with the graphic description of his dream:

"I really don't think my dream has anything to do with 'shrooms. It had everything to do with stuff that has been encapsulated in my body like a cicada. A military officer began questioning me about what had happened. I answered, 'How the hell do I know, I just swam across the fucking river!' It's amazing I even got here. It was terrible. The river was in nasty shape. I had to practically crawl across to a giant place, but I found a hole in the mesh. It dropped down to a medieval street with houses that were built along the river. The town resembled an M.C. Escher* print. Escher was the one who invented the Mobius strip, where water runs uphill, and everything is an optical illusion. I walked out and paralleled this road, and then a ballgame broke out. Don Zimmer was there, and I advised him, 'Don't give me the fucking ball today, Zim.' But then it got worse. My ex-wife Pam brought the car to the dealer and said, 'Here, fix it!' But I think I'm going to be all right. Lagavulin cures lots of ailments."

> * For many years, M.C. Escher, a great and inventive artist, was neglected even in his native Netherlands. However, when a retrospective of his works was held, art "experts" began to recognize Escher's genius. As Bill Lee reported, "There is a lithograph of Escher's that appears to function as a perpetual motion machine. It is magnificent. I have a shirt depicting one of his greater creations that show fish that become ducks and ducks that become fish. The transition is spellbinding."

Following the Spaceman's description of his dream, he said, "Scotty, when you come up here, I can hook you up with my 'travel agent.' Recently I gave her four books written by Carlos Castaneda."

I think I'll lie low for a while, though.

CHAPTER THIRTY

Looking for Fergie

Mexico on $20 a Day

"I was gambling in Havana
I took a little risk
Send lawyers, guns and money
Dad, get me out of this
I'm an innocent bystander
Somehow. I got stuck
Between a rock and a hard place
And I'm down on my luck
Now I'm hiding in Honduras
I'm a desperate man
Send lawyers, guns and money
The shit has hit the fan" —*Warren Zevon*

Those of a certain age will recall the Frommer's Travel Guides and for all I know, they are still helpful to modern-day travelers. Back in 1962, William F. Lee, Jr. and his wife, Paula Theresa (Hunt) Lee, the parents of the earthling known as Bill "Spaceman" Lee decided to take a trip along the Mexican coastline, and they relied heavily on a Frommer's Guide, which included practical advice as to how to complete their trip on a mere $20 a day.

Even back in 1962, the guide strongly advised American visitors to avoid the many areas that were strongholds of the Sinaloa Drug Cartel, who for many years not only controlled many provinces, but also "owned" local authorities. The powerful cartel, considered by most to be more powerful than the infamous Medellin cartel of Colombia, still flourishes today. The Sinaloa gang is primarily based in the city of Culiacan, Sinaloa, but its tentacles reach all over Mexico and beyond. The cartel is perhaps the "leader" in drug trafficking, money laundering, and is unparalleled in Mexico as an organized crime syndicate. Even the arrest of their former leader, Joaquin "El Chapo" Guzman, has not significantly hampered their organization.

Which brings us to the great Ferguson Jenkins, Hall of Fame pitcher, Bill Lee's close friend, and the founder of another infamous group, "The Royal Order of Buffalo Heads," a small, however, influential group that drove Red Sox manager, Don Zimmer, batty.

Very recently (May of 2021) Bill Lee became increasingly concerned regarding the safety of his old teammate, Fergie. There is no way to put this less succinctly, but Bill was experiencing some difficulty in reaching Fergie, who was not returning his phone calls or text messages. You see, Bill learned that Fergie had acquired "a new girlfriend," one incidentally much younger than him, and that the young lady was, um, er, a rather important cog in the machinations of the Sinaloa Cartel. Fortunately, the Spaceman was relieved to hear from Fergie, who is well, thank you, and did not join Dr. Hunter S. Thompson's "Samoan attorney," whose real name was Oscar Zeta Acosta, who apparently "disappeared" in the Sonoran Desert, shortly after a rumored "drug deal." Oscar, a counterculture writer of considerable renown, authored *The Autobiography of a Brown Buffalo* in 1972, and followed that up with *The Revolt of the Cockroach People* in 1973.

Note: The Spaceman's parents, indeed, traveled in their brand new 630 VW down the coast of Mexico in 1962, and with the assistance of Frommer's Guide, stayed for $20 a day. It should also be noted that upon the Spaceman learning that Fergie had been honored by having a bronze statue of the great right-hander erected outside of Wrigley Field in Chicago, Bill exclaimed, "Fergie, you're already bronze!"

CHAPTER THIRTY-ONE

Do the Wrong Thing

The Gary Hancock Syndrome

(Sorry, Spike Lee)

"Without losers, where would the winners be?" —*Casey Stengel*

I was there when it happened. The date was July 16, 1978, and the place was Fenway Park in Boston, and suddenly there were 35,587 diehard fans on their feet cheering wildly as if it were "V-J Day," and we had just won the war. The attendance that afternoon was 35,589; however, only two people remained seated and seemed oblivious as to what the commotion was about. I know. You see, I was one of those two fans that remained seated, the other being my ex-wife who shall remain nameless.

The occasion was the second game of a doubleheader between the hometown Boston Red Sox and the visiting Minnesota Twins. The reason for the tumultuous ovation, which apparently escaped the two of us, was the appearance of a Red Sox player who had just been introduced to the crowd, as follows: "Batting sixth for the Red Sox, the designated hitter, number 38, Gary Hancock." The announcer who had made this apparently unexpected declaration was the legendary Sherm Feller, the longtime PA voice of the Red Sox. Gary Hancock, a relatively obscure minor league outfielder, was about to make his major league debut, an event certainly noteworthy, especially to the then twenty-four-year-old ballplayer.

From what my ex and yours truly could surmise, there was only one other person among the crowd that afternoon who appeared astonished by the raucous and lengthy ovation which began as polite applause, but soon became a groundswell of hysteria reserved for the appearance of the Pope or perhaps the Beatles in the 1960s, and that person was the recipient of the greeting, the debuting Gary Hancock. From where I sat behind home plate, Hancock peered around the ball yard as the noise increased from a mild roar to what one would expect for a religious deity or a war hero. The youngster, about to strike out, incidentally, in his first major league at bat, had a vacuous look on his face which seemed to convey, "Who the fuck do they think I am, the second coming of Babe Ruth?!"

The Spaceman surmised that since Hancock's now legendary entrance came during the second game of a doubleheader, that "most of the fans were shit-faced by then." "No, I don't think so," I replied, "they're merely acting out their sophistication."

Even after Minnesota hurler Roger Erickson fanned the newcomer, the fans reacted with additional, albeit lesser applause as if they were saying, "Don't worry, kid, we'll see you in Cooperstown." Predictably, Hancock went on to have a six-year major league career as a journeyman outfielder, accumulating a .262 batting average with 12 home runs and a total of 64 RBIs.

You may ask who was responsible for such over exuberance from the Fenway Faithful. I am about to point a finger at an old friend of mine, the Hall of Fame journalist, the inimitable Peter Gammons. You see, John Updike notwithstanding, I believe that Peter was at least partially to blame for at least fanning the flames with the foolish notion that "Red Sox Nation," as it grew to be known, was the bastion of sophistication. What better way to display one's own importance than to rise as one to welcome an obscure ballplayer to the major leagues with an absurd and seemingly theatrical and lustrous commencement? It was Peter Gammons, who I admire, incidentally, who referred to yours truly in the *Boston Globe* as, "Scott Russell, a graduate student from Boston," a strange, but rather innocuous comment affixed alongside one of my highly questionable statistical studies which Peter considered worthy of print. I can assure you I have never misrepresented myself as a "graduate student" from anywhere other than Morris High School in the South Bronx, something I'm proud of, incidentally.

Note: The author, either the seemingly fictitious "Scott Russell," or more than likely Kilgore Trout, grew up watching ballgames in New York City, amongst fans that were more "thug-like" than the callous "sophisticates" of Fenway Park, the "Lyric Little Bandbox of a Ballpark," as described by the great author, John Updike, in his magnificent "Hub Fans Bid Kid Adieu," in his *New Yorker Magazine* tribute to both Ted Williams and his fans. I shudder to think that if Updike were around today, he might have penned, "Hub Fans Greet Rookie with Bewildering Hello."

I am certain that many of you are now shuddering in fear and anticipation of learning what the earthling known as Bill "Spaceman" Lee has to offer regarding the debut of Gary Hancock, and not surprisingly, he, of course, does. You see, the Spaceman believes this exact subject was covered in depth by noted author Malcolm Gladwell in his spellbinding tome, *Outliers*. In *Outliers*, Gladwell, the English-born Canadian journalist, asks "What makes high-achievers different?" The Spaceman, of course, is about to explain as follows:

"We pay far too much attention to what successful people are like, and far too little as to where they are from, and that includes their culture and their family, their generation, their idiosyncrasies and the experience of their upbringing. As Malcolm Gladwell attempts to teach us, for instance, that the reason Korean airline pilots are involved in a greater amount of fatal air crashes is because of their culture."

"Please explain," I asked the ubiquitous Spaceman, although I had not as yet read Malcolm Gladwell's *Outliers*.

Bill Lee responded, "Well, you have to understand Korean culture. As both passengers and the pilot's subordinates enter the aircraft, they are obligated to bow to the pilot. This is perfectly all right, but this practice even applies if the pilot had been drinking all night or had spent the entire morning in an opium den and was completely fucked up. Therefore, those entering the plane are placed in a situation where, because of their pride, rather than be disrespectful, they'd just as soon fly into a mountain than display impropriety towards the almighty pilot."

Hey, if you have a problem with this, take it up with Malcolm Gladwell, the Spaceman, or perhaps a Korean pilot, but advisedly before a flight.

Incredibly, but somewhat expectedly, the Spaceman then began making a comparison between his former manager, the hapless Don Zimmer, who routinely flew into many mountains as his small legion of lemmings bowed to him as they attained an inevitable doom. Upon yours truly advising Bill Lee of my "Gary Hancock experience" of July 16, 1978, I was immediately to become aware that once more, as proved definitively by James Burke in his mind-boggling "Connections," that there is logic in our universe. As we documented in *The Spaceman Chronicles* by using irrefutable facts, that Don Zimmer was solely responsible for the historic collapse of the 1978 Red Sox, Gary Hancock's major league debut and its somewhat bizarre ramifications literally were the beginning of what would herald Zimmer's ineptitude being the direct cause of the Yankees overcoming a 14-game deficit.

Following are the comments by the Spaceman, as only he could possibly draw an analogy between Korean airline pilots, Malcolm Gladwell's *Outliers*, and Don Zimmer's leadership, or lack thereof:

"The July 16, 1978 doubleheader Scott Russell (Kilgore Trout?) referred to, the one in which Gary Hancock made his 'screen debut' in front of nearly 36,000 screaming banshees, also was the actual onset of Don Zimmer's monumental collapse. Although Zim would not remove me from the rotation until August 19, the Hancock appearance literally heralded the beginning of the end. In the two-year period of complete incompetence, Zimmer had already removed Bernie from the organization, and Fergie (Jenkins) and Rick Wise from the rotation, but was also in the process of shoving my ass to the bullpen, where I would sit and rot until Bucky Dent's inevitable home run. You'll note that the losing pitcher in game two (the Gary Hancock Theophany) was Jim Wright, who, along with Bobby Sprowl, would replace me in the rotation. I had already won 10 games when Zimmer's abscessed mind told him I was through, and Wright and Sprowl didn't even win 10 games combined during their entire careers."

Upon researching the Spaceman's comments, I learned that Bill had pinpointed the exact date of Boston's largest lead of the season. Following games up to and including those games of July 17, the American League standings read as follows:

BOSTON	61-28	—
MILWAUKEE	52-36	8.5
BALTIMORE	49-42	13.0
YANKEES	47-42	14.0
DETROIT	45-44	16.0
CLEVELAND	42-48	19.5
TORONTO	32-58	29.5

It should stand to reason that another incident occurred on July 17, 1978. New York Yankees manager Billy Martin and his star outfielder Reggie Jackson nearly came to blows in the Yankees dugout. The Yankees were on their way to the World Series, and Don Zimmer was on his way to ignominy and presumably to the dog track. It is written.

CHAPTER THIRTY-TWO

The Rheal Deal

"I've learned that people will forget what you said, people will forget what you did, but people will never forget how you made them feel."
—*Maya Angelou*

"The mediocre teacher tells, the good teacher explains, the superior teacher demonstrates. The great teacher inspires."
—*William Arthur Ward*

"In learning you will teach, and in teaching you will learn."
—*Phil Collins*

The earthling known as Bill "Spaceman" Lee was taken aback upon finding three text messages on his iPhone in May of 2021. The text messages were from his dear friend and pupil, Rheal Cormier, a fellow left-handed pitcher, and one whom Lee had mentored for several years before Rheal became a successful major league hurler. The reason for the Spaceman's surprise was that Rheal had passed away on March 8, 2021 in his native Moncton, New Brunswick, Canada at the tender age of fifty-three.

Upon learning of Rheal's passing, Bill had left a few tender words on Rheal's iPhone in the form of a poem. Yes, the Spaceman, as eccentric as he may be, is also a poet. The delicate and poignant message, Bill Lee reasoned, would drift off into space and never be heard by a living being, at least here on Planet Earth, but then two months passed, and Bill Lee began receiving text messages from who appeared to be his late friend, Rheal Cormier.

For the record, the "messages" the Spaceman was receiving from his dear departed friend, Rheal, consisted of a converted text to his landline phone. It was digitized with an automated woman's voice. Said Lee, "The digitized message sounded like Siri, and I don't take any shit from Siri."

Despite the Spaceman not being a member of the technological society of either the US or Canada, eventually he managed to decode the missives from beyond and in so doing, came to the realization that the sender was none other than Lucienne, the lovely widow of the erstwhile French-Canadian

SCOTT RUSSELL

southpaw. Without going into extreme detail, Lucienne, the mother of Justin and Morgan, two children she had raised with her late husband, Rheal, informed the Spaceman that she had recently checked Rheal's iPhone and had listened to Bill's poem, a loving tribute to his protégé. She responded to Bill with, "I listened to the two messages you left for Rheal, and you made me laugh. You know how much you inspired Rheal! Thank you!"

It should be noted that Rheal Cormier wore #37 throughout his amateur and professional career in honor of his idol, Bill "Spaceman" Lee.

Lucienne had left her phone number where she was staying in Florida, and Bill, of course, called her and they enjoyed a lengthy conversation. During that exchange, Lucienne told Bill that she had heard from some of the guys in Moncton, and that they had submitted Rheal as a prospective name to rename the ballpark in Moncton, which is currently known as Kiwanis Park, the largest baseball field in Canada east of Quebec City. The ballpark is in St. Catharine's and it also accommodates soccer, football, and field hockey. The ballpark is also one where Ralph Chambers managed to get Bill kicked out of the league, but now that they placed Chambers's name on a plaque higher than Rheal's on the tree, Bill complained, "I can no longer piss that high on Chambers's plaque." However, Bill is hesitant about attaching Rheal's name to an artificial turf field. Let us explain:

Both the author and the Spaceman are THOROUGHLY convinced that the artificial turf fields created by Monsanto, Dow Chemical, and other evil conglomerates, were responsible for the untimely deaths of far too many that had the misfortune of playing atop their highly poisonous surfaces. Upon looking closely at the names and the ages and causes of death, especially of those athletes that played on "Astro Turf," as it was called, it is astounding. Take for example Veterans Stadium in Philadelphia (1971-2003), a horrific structure. In 2003, the original "Astro Turf," patented originally as "Chem Grass" in 1965, was replaced by "Nexturf." However, the new turf was not installed properly, and the ugly seams could plainly be seen by all that attended the ballparks. In 1987 Monsanto's Research & Development department implemented a "texturized nylon system." It should be noted that the Phillies and Kansas City Royals played the entire 1980 World Series on Astro Turf. In 1987, the entire World Series between St. Louis and Minnesota was also played on Astro Turf. Some of the legendary players involved are listed below.

116

Sadly, the following are facts:

"Tug" McGraw (played on the ersatz turf from 1975-1984), a great friend of Bill Lee's, died in 2004 at the age of fifty-nine. Cause—Brain cancer.

Darren Daulton (played on the fake turf from 1983-1997) passed in 2017 at the age of fifty-five. Cause—Brain tumors.

John Vukovich (played on the turf from 1976-1981, and then coached on it from 1988-2004) died in 2007 at the age of fifty-nine. Cause—Brain tumor.

Ken Brett (played on artificial turf in 1973 and then again in Kansas City 1980-81) died in 2003 at the age of fifty-five. Cause—Brain cancer.

Dick Howser (managed in Kansas City 1981-85) died in 1998 at the age of forty-five. Cause—Brain cancer.

Dan Quisenberry (played in Kansas City from 1979-88 & St Louis 1988-89) and died at the age of forty-five in 1998. Cause—Astrocytoma (helluva name!), a highly malignant form of brain cancer. Astrocytomas are a type of brain tumor. They originate in a particular kind of glial cells, star-shaped brain cells in the cerebrum called astrocytes. This type of tumor does not usually spread outside the brain and spinal cord. It does not usually affect other organs.

And now, Rheal Cormier dead at the age of fifty-three (played at Veterans Stadium in Philadelphia from 2001-2006). Cause—lung tumor and pancreatic cancer.

We are currently in the process of researching several other all too early deaths of the teammates of these individuals. We strongly believe there is a correlation between the surfaces they played on and their health issues.

As Bill Lee commented upon seeing that Astro Turf was originally patented as "Chem Grass," "That is an indictment right there." The Spaceman also recalled that W.P. Kinsella, the author of *Shoeless Joe*, which was transitioned into the incomparable *Field of Dreams*, had written "Thrill of the

Grass," a short story about the 1981 baseball strike. In the tale, Philadelphia fans snuck into Veterans Stadium with bolt cutters and systematically removed the artificial turf, and when the Phillies returned, they had a natural grass field. As Bill Lee added, "Why do you think Monsanto sold out to Bayer, to protect the 'innocent'?" Bill also reminded us that Ewing Kauffman made millions of dollars from Monsanto, and that his awful surface on the playing field in Kansas City certainly appears to have had a direct correlation to the fatal diseases suffered by his players.

The Spaceman's recollections of his dear younger friend, Rheal Cormier, are wonderful. As Bill stated, "I first saw Rheal pitch in a ballgame in Diep. Up there in New Brunswick, they have midget leagues for kids fourteen through sixteen, junior leagues from seventeen to eighteen and senior ball for kids nineteen and up. It's where hockey players get discovered in Canada, but Rheal was all about baseball. Rheal was just a baby, and he was a phenom. I noticed he was a strong kid, but he wasn't too big. He had a big curve ball, but he'd throw it three times in a row and the third time they would blast it. I told him, 'Did you ever hear of World War I?' Three guys would light up by using one match, but it was the third one who always got shot by a German sniper. They'd zero in on the light."

The Spaceman continued:

"He digested everything I taught him. He was smart, and he was an accomplished hurler early on. He learned his fadeaway change from me."

Rheal Cormier became an outstanding relief pitcher late in his career. In 2003, Rheal had an ERA of 1.70 in 84.2 innings. The following year he appeared in 84 games. The Acadian hurler pitched for the Canadian National Team in the Pan American Games in 1987, and then he pitched for Canada in the 1988 Olympics. Incredibly, in 2003, Cormier won the last game at Veterans Stadium in Philadelphia, but also won the first game at Philadelphia's new ballpark, Citizens Bank Park! In 2012, Cormier was inducted into the Canadian Baseball Hall of Fame, but most of all, as the Spaceman recalls, "Rheal was precious."

Dad (William F. Lee, Jr.) with dumb son.

Bill teaching Andy how to
throw spitter (Note: Tongue).

First MLB player to be fined for wearing hat backwards.

Hi you two!
How about that new name
over there!? Kathrin was
born on 12/18 — she truly
made our Christmas!
How've you been? Not so
sure about that weather out
there. Winter in Malibu is
a little different (surfing at Xmas, etc)
Everyone fine — Bill's busy
working out and helping his uncle
Mike loves school, Andy loves trouble!
See you in Winter Haven! Love — ML.

LOVE IS BORN!

Merry Christmas!

etc)

le

le !

Bill, MaryLou,
Mike, Andy, and Kate Lee
+ the Pretenders
(J. Browne.)

Love is Born – Good News

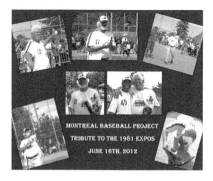

Tribute to 1981 Montreal Expos—June 16, 2012

Road trip food (Arizona).

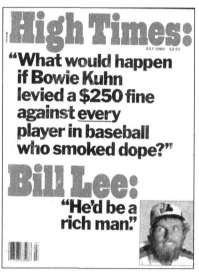

The Spaceman and microphones – A match made in Heaven. Photo by Barbara Tobin

Cover of High Times—July 1980— self explanatory

Not quite Havana. Bill and Diana at the Phoenix Zoo.

SCOTT RUSSELL

THERE'S NO PLACE LIKE HOME

played somewhere warm). It's Thursday, Feb 2.

Lots of baseball excitement here — new baseball coach. Smithy has retired after nearly 30 years. Mike Leonard is a young guy (under 40) a catcher who played in the Red Sox system, made it to AA (Portland SeaDogs) and most recently was the head coach at Bates for six years. Seems great.

Terrific series — I'm rooting for the Tribe as I lived for six years in Cleveland. I wouldn't be heart broken if the Cubs won though.

Take care, Stay warm, Karl

26 Oct 2016

Dear Bill & Diane,

Thanks for speaking with me recently. I enjoyed writing the column and ended up — all about baseball and not politics. You acquitted yourself well in the Channel 5 debate — enlivened the proceedings. This check is not for your Campaign, but because I have stiffed you the last two times you have visited my class — and I'd like you to come back and close my Winter Term class, if you're in VT (and why would you be if there's baseball to be

Note from Karl Lindholm—Dean of students at Middlebury College.

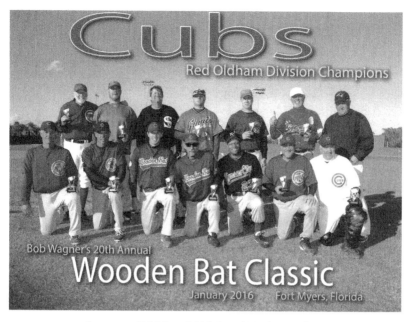

Spaceman at Bob Wagner's 20th Annual Wooden Bat Classic
in Fort Myers, Florida, January 2016 (Cubs)

Bill in Cooperstown   *Legend!*

The bearded national league left-handed Montreal ace—1979

THE SAN ANDREAS FAULT

Whose fault is it? San Andreas of course.

Front yard in Craftsbury.	*100-year reunion at Fenway*

Royal Order of Buffalo Heads—Bernie, Rick, Fergie, Willow, and Bill.

124

Andy (Bill's youngest son), AnnaBelle (A League of Their Own), Mike (Bill's oldest son), and Bill.

Bill and Dad at Fenway—1975 World Series

Bill and Michael

Colts! Bill's dad—upper left with Coach Newbold, Artie McRalls (center, first row—32-0!),
Catcher Vic Miranda (second row, second from left), Coach Newbold's son with his arm around Bill.

Grey Sox—Bill front and center.

William F. Lee (Bill's dad)

*Grandpa William F. Lee, Sr.—
husband of Hazel—with the legendary
Hollywood Stars—1918!*

Bill Lee, USC, pitcher — 1967 or 1968 — Bill was 48 and 9 through his freshman to senior year — Pitched in two College World Series in Omaha, Neb. - 1965 as a sophmore and 1968 as a senior. USC won it all in 1968 — Bill was noted the outstanding pitcher in the series — He won 2 games and relieved in one other game — Paula and I were there—what a great 7 days - I think they came from behind in every ballgame — Believe me, we were physically and emotionally drained.

The fledgling Trojan and Bill's dad's note on back.

Bill at the Axis Bat Co.

Bill Lee and the Weight Band's Brian Mitchell.

Sacred black mountain reflected by Laura Culver, San Rafael

"I'm prone to exaggerate when I'm sober."

-Tomlinson | Ten Thousand Islands

Doc Ford's character Tomlinson is based on Bill.
Signed by Randy Wayne White, the author.

A bear paw print on Bill's truck
at Camp Cripple Creek.

The author with Bishop Anthony Spinoza.

Larry Campbell (Bob Dylan's lead guitarist for eight years), and Bill at Camp Cripple Creek instructing Larry on how to relieve stress in his shoulder.

(L to R) The Weight Band—Larry Campbell, Albert Rogers, and Michael Bram, with the Spaceman.

Larry Campbell, Bob Dylan's lead guitarist for eight years, and Bill.

Bill Lee, the Spaceman infuriating the Fenway faithful.

Albert Rogers, the bass player for the Weight Band, and Peg, Scott's wife, with the author.

Bill, Meg Giffen of the Roy Hobbs League, and Meg's father Tom Giffen.

The Weight Band at Fenway under the rainbow.

CHAPTER THIRTY-THREE

Sneaking Sally Through the Alley

The Four F Club

With the lone possibility of Jim Brosnan, the great late Jim Bouton was the first former athlete to have the temerity to present ballplayers as average members of the male species, and not as religious deities. Bouton, a great writer with an enormously wonderful sense of humor, had the audacity to not only suggest that his teammates and foes were mere imperfect beings, but in so doing jeopardized his own career by exposing his peers as (gulp) normal human beings! I mean, who knew? Mickey liked women as much as we did!

Bouton's epic *Ball Four* was classified as heresy by many in the establishment for displaying major league ballplayers as fallible as our friends and neighbors. And in so doing, Bouton's books made us appreciate our heroes even *more*, as so many of us could finally identify with them. Seriously, who knew that our idols drank, smoked, and often indulged in the very same vices as we mere mortals?

Major league baseball players, for the most part, are not choir boys. The earthling known as Bill "Spaceman" Lee has thousands of hilarious tales that cannot be told, not even in such a volume. Although Bill Lee describes himself as an asshole, as does the author of this tome, regardless of whether such a person is "Scott Russell" (doubtful) or Kilgore Trout (probable), we are not about to disparage, disgrace, or dishonor the names of some of the finest human beings on Planet Earth, are we?

One of the Spaceman's more hilarious revelations—and we realize how politically incorrect this may appear—is the existence of something many major leaguers refer to as "The Four F Club."

Sensitivity alert: The "Four F Club," as it existed, and no doubt still exists, stands for "Find 'em, Feed 'em, Fuck 'em and Forget 'em." Again, if you were offended after the initial thirty-two chapters of this book, why are you still here?

Listen folks: professional baseball players, much like rock musicians, for the most part, are barbarians. However, it should be noted that most forms of debauchery are a two-way street. The term "groupies" is known to any authentic fan of rock 'n roll, and young women, middle-aged women, and yes, even some older women, are generally "available" to rock stars, and baseball players too, are rock stars.

There exists a generic term describing baseball groupies, and that is "Baseball Annies." These women are seldom "the girl next door," and they often derive self-esteem by proxy. These "Baseball Annies" are not only eminently available to traveling ballplayers, but they are just as often just as much "on the prowl" as the players they engage on the road. Many of these women derive pleasure by "scoring"; that is, sleeping with a major league ballplayer. These women completely understand that "romance" is not in the offing and are fully aware that most of these athletes have wives and children back home. As the Spaceman stated, "These groupies have their own 'Four F Club.' That is Find 'em, Finagle 'em, Fuck 'em, and Forget 'em." Marriage is not their goal.

The Spaceman told a hilarious tale, and yes, we are going to name one of the athletes, as he was not married at the time. One of Bill Lee's more delightfully zany teammates with Boston in the late '60s and early '70s was the equally eccentric southpaw reliever Albert "Sparky" Lyle. Sparky had "hooked" up with one of the aforementioned "Baseball Annies," but this young woman was inexperienced in stalking major leaguers to engage in frivolities with the player. After an eventful week-long tryst with Sparky, it was time for Lyle's Red Sox to depart for a lengthy West Coast trip. As the Spaceman described:

"Our bus was leaving for Logan Airport, and this young woman entered the bus to seek out Sparky who was seated at the back of the vehicle. She began wailing and crying, 'Oh, Sparky, please don't go. I'll miss you so much!' At that point, a slightly older and more experienced 'Baseball Annie,' put her arm around the younger woman's shoulders, and consoled her with, 'Quit your crying, girl, the Baltimore Orioles will be here in forty-five minutes.'"

Note: One of the Spaceman's "girlfriends" in those days was a model named Margaret. She was um, er, smoking hot. In fact, she was on the cover of an iconic rock 'n roll album, titled "Sneaking Sally Through the Alley." The album was the debut LP of the great Robert Palmer, and it featured some of the greatest musicians of all time, including Lowell George (a friend of the Spaceman's) of Little Feat, Allen Toussaint, Art Neville, and Steve

Winwood. In a rather bizarre occurrence, Bill received a phone call from the woman's mother not that long ago, and she suggested that the Spaceman and her daughter should "get back together." Bill exclaimed, "Can you imagine that; pimping your own daughter!"

CHAPTER THIRTY-FOUR

The Real McCoy

"I heard that Don Gullett is going straight to the Hall of Fame. I am going to the Eliot Lounge." —Bill "Spaceman" Lee following the seventh game of the 1975 World Series

The earthling known as Bill "Spaceman" Lee never shunned his responsibility to members of the Fourth Estate even on those occasions that he and/or his team lost. The words above were uttered following the Red Sox's heartbreaking seventh game loss to the "Big Red Machine," the legendary Cincinnati Reds team that had just defeated Lee's Red Sox to claim the 1975 World Series championship.

The Spaceman, in fact, outpitched both Cincinnati starters Jack Billingham and Don Gullett, but on both occasions the Red Sox bullpen could not hold on to the lead after the Spaceman was replaced by relief pitchers. Young Gullett had been anointed as a "sure Hall of Famer" by various members of the media, and therefore, the Spaceman's quote; and Lee indeed headed to the Eliot Lounge on Massachusetts Avenue in Boston following game seven, where he drowned his sorrows by downing a dozen or so brews.

The Spaceman remains affable to this day and seldom, if ever, refuses to answer questions directed to him by members of the media, and this includes banal and absurd questions. Keep in mind that the Spaceman is not above providing equally absurd responses to ridiculous queries, but they are often hilarious and thought-provoking. Then there is a growing legion of modern-day athletes who seem to delight in being rude, churlish, nonsensical, and yes, downright ignorant. It seems the money these players "earn" these days gives them the right to belittle, degrade, and humiliate the poor schlubs that write or report for a living.

In May of 2021, a great female tennis player named Naomi Osaka made headlines when she proclaimed that she was done speaking with the media after her matches. It appears that the young woman cited "mental depression and anxiety" as the two major reasons for her decision, and certainly the press and the public, of course, should abide by her decision. However, as is evident in most cases during these turbulent times, there might be more than meets the eye.

Firstly, it is the media that literally humanizes athletes. Rather than be considered an individual blessed with extraordinary physical skills, writers delve into the background and psyches of these headliners and make them out to be more than they really are. I mean, who really cares about who they voted for or what they eat for breakfast? The answer to that is, of course, rhetorical as fans indeed want to know as much as they can about their heroes so that they can identify with them.

Obviously, Naomi Osaka's mental health is far more important than the few banal comments she might utter after a victory or (gulp) a loss, but....... we are obsessed with the mindset of our heroes. Which brings me to: Phil Mushnick of the *New York Post*, the irascible (which is why I LOVE Phil) curmudgeon who reported that it is apparent that Ms. Naomi Osaka's "depre$$ion and anxiety" might be highly $elective. You see, she will, and does speak with the Japanese media, but only if $he is paid for her interview$.

Athletes refusing to speak with the press is not a recent revelation, although it seems the amount of money athletes "earn" these days is often commensurate with their lack of respect for those that write of their exploits. However, even as far as back in the 1970s, the great Hall of Fame journalist, Hal McCoy of the *Dayton Daily News*, would also serve as an official scorer for the Cincinnati Reds games. For those not aware, those Reds teams of the 1970s were known as "The Big Red Machine," and their players are legendary. Pete Rose, Tony Perez, Johnny Bench, Ken Griffey, Sr., and several other notables, are household names to any self-respecting baseball fans. The shortstop on that championship ball club was a slick-fielding shortstop from Venezuela named Davey Concepcion. I'll let the great Hal McCoy tell the story:

Being a baseball official scorer is like taking a long ride on the Trans-Siberian Railroad, nine innings of pain and drudgery...and please, Almighty, no extra innings.

Given a choice of having my testicles removed or scoring a baseball game, I would put in a call to a surgeon. Of course, if you made a call a player didn't like, he would threaten to remove them for you. One fine summer's day was ruined for me by Cincinnati Reds shortstop Dave Concepcion, although the day already was abysmal when it was my day behind the official scorer's microphone.

A ball was hit directly at Concepcion, a wizard with the leather. The ball skipped between his legs and into left field, an easy play for a high school hockey goalkeeper. I clicked on the microphone and authoritatively boomed, "E-6." The inning ended and the press box phone rang. The call was for me.

With no preamble, no greeting, a screeching voice said, "Mac-Koy, how can you call that an error. I deed not even touch thee ball."

Said I, "Davey, the ball went right between your legs. If you had squatted down, as you should have, the ball would have hit you in the cup."

"Okay, Mac-Koy, I no talk to you no more," he said, slamming the dugout phone back on its cradle. So for the next couple of weeks, I didn't try to talk to him. Then, one day as I walked past his dressing cubicle, Concepcion said, "Hey, Mac-Koy, I talk to you now."

I said, "Okay." And I kept walking and didn't talk to him or try to interview him for another two weeks. That'll teach him.

Then we formally made up, but his final words were, "That wasn't an error."

Scott, that's the only real issue I ever had, but my scoring days were limited. I ducked it at every opportunity because it was like being in the Roman Coliseum and it was you giving the thumbs up or thumbs down... and you were never right.

Hal McCoy, a GREAT journalist, knew exactly how to handle a non-talkative athlete. Oh, and Hal would've loved covering the earthling known as Bill "Spaceman" Lee, who was never renowned as a non-talkative athlete. I should also add that Hal McCoy, Hall of Fame journalist, is an advocate of Davey Concepcion's enshrinement into the Hall of Fame, since Davey was an exceptionally great fielder and a championship player.

CHAPTER THIRTY-FIVE

The Doctor Is In

Different Strokes for Different Folks

And I Am the Idiom to Prove It!

"My doctor gave me two weeks to live. I hope they're in August."
—*Ronnie Shaker*

"I was going to have cosmetic surgery until I noticed that the doctor's office was full of portraits by Picasso." —*Rita Rudner*

"Never go to a doctor whose office plants have died." —*Erma Bombeck*

On Tuesday, June 1, 2021, I was seated at my desk when I began to feel a bit lightheaded. Peg would tell you that I'm always "light-headed," since there's "very little in my head," but I digress.

I was looking at some notes I had written (I invariably write all my research notes on lined pads) when the vision in my right eye became rather bizarrely limited. It was blurry, but I had not been drinking, when I noticed a rectangular blue strip which allowed me to see above and beneath it, but not in the middle, sort of like one of the 1960s Cinemascope motion pictures. The vision in my left eye was stable. Oh, and I felt fine.

Being a curious sort, I retrieved my Omron Blood Pressure Monitor, and wasn't exactly shocked at seeing a reading of 176/154/70. As Peg peered over my shoulder, she immediately suggested she call my primary care physician immediately and have me rushed to Massachusetts General Hospital.

"No," I responded.

Listen, I LOVE my primary care physician, but if I even report a hangnail, he immediately insists that I travel to Boston within seconds, and he is apt to rush me in for an MRI, an ultrasound, an EKG, a blood test, remove my appendix, rip out my tonsils, tear out a few glands, and begin my long overdue prefrontal lobotomy.

I insisted to Peg that despite my age and burgeoning insanity that I was completely okay. In fact, I waited five minutes and my eyesight returned to normal, plus I retook my blood pressure, which now read, and I'm not making this up, 96/73/61, and no, the Omron Monitor was indeed, fine. I then told Peg I was immediately going out for a four-mile walk. She put on her sneakers and insisted, "I'm going with you!" Who knew? Apparently, she still likes me.

Rather than call my wonderful physician—and I am NOT being facetious—I called the earthling Dr. William F. Lee, III, aka "The Spaceman" in Vermont, and he agreed with my course of action.

"Of course, you had a stroke. It's common. I've had several myself. I just take a knee and a baby aspirin. All you need to do is dilate your capillaries. It was merely a fucking spike that went through the pupil to the back of your retina where the blood vessel goes. You'll be fine."

I listened to the good southpaw doctor, and I am fine! Oh, and I've walked over twenty-five miles during the following five days and my blood pressure plummeted to 99/68/62, and even better, my primary care physician had not yet removed my testicles.

The Spaceman also prescribed reading Michael Lewis's *The Undoing Project*. I have done so, and I am now awaiting a battle between Kahneman (my new hero) and Tversky as if it were Ali versus Frazier. Besides, if I croak, Dr. Hunter S. Thompson is no longer around to offer his condolences or perhaps a eulogy as he did for Oscar Zeta-Acosta. God, what I would give for someone to eulogize me with "Scott was a high-powered mutant of some kind who was never even considered for mass production. He was too weird to live and too rare to die."

Please tell my primary care to stay away from my left parotid nerve.

Those of you that have read *The Spaceman Chronicles* are aware that Bernie Carbo credited the Spaceman with saving his life. Now it seems that Dr. Bill Lee has also saved mine. Bill once told his closest friend, the inimitable Mike Mulkern, that he saved his life. Mike then asked, "How the hell did you do that?" The Spaceman replied, "I just killed a shit-eating dog." With friends like that...................

BRIEF INTERMISSION #3

The Mother of All Cockroaches

L'il Ol' Palmetto Bugs, My Ass!

Ill-Fated Honeymoons and an Improbable Biology Lesson

> "I'm horrified of lobsters. And shrimp and lobsters are the cockroaches of the ocean." —*Brooke Burke*

In March of 1977, I arrived at the Ramada Inn in Winter Haven, Florida to enjoy my first spring training camp and to watch the Red Sox and the earthling known as Bill "Spaceman" Lee get ready for the '77 campaign. I was on my honeymoon with my first wife, who shall go nameless. Imagine honeymooning with the Spaceman, George Kimball, and being in a "honeymoon suite" next door to Don Zimmer! Yes, he and his wife, Soot, were in the very next room. That itself should have portended doom for my ill-advised marriage.

In both the great Oscar Zeta-Acosta's great volumes, *The Autobiography of a Brown Buffalo* and *The Revolt of the Cockroach People*, Dr. Hunter S. Thompson, in his infinite acumen, offered an introduction to the unique "Dr. Gonzo," the improbable and insane Chicano genius who went missing in the Sonoran Desert in the early 1970s, never to be found. In those introductions, Acosta, who was completely off the rails himself, was described by Hunter S. Thompson as follows:

"I have never liked writing about him, because it makes me think too much, and I can never find the right words to explain the terrible joy that he brought with him wherever he went... You had to be there, I guess, and you had to understand that the man was never comfortable unless he was in the company of people who were crazier than he was."

All right, this is an admission: Dr. Thompson could have also been describing the earthling known as Bill "Spaceman" Lee, and (gulp) yours truly would be one of the crazy people in his company. I believe that this specific chapter very much substantiates that point.

Back to my sorry ass checking into Winter Haven, Florida on March 6, 1977: Upon checking into the Ramada Inn in Winter Haven, the clerk at the registration desk handed me a note which read, "Bill Leed (sic) called, please call him at the Holiday Inn." As my ex and I checked into our ill-omened honeymoon suite, which had all of the amenities of a leper colony in Spinalonga—I had placed the Red Sox tickets the Spaceman had left for us at Chain O' Lakes Park—when I peripherally glimpsed at something moving, or more accurately, crawling beneath the queen bed in our well-lit room. The sight of the crawler immediately grossed me out. Here I was, years and hundreds of miles removed from my upbringing in the South Bronx tenements I was raised in, but there it was, as plain as day. A filthy, sleazy, disgusting cockroach, a huge, unpleasant reminder of my childhood. The cockroach made a brief unscheduled appearance, and then immediately retreated beneath our honeymoon queen bed.

This, I can assure you, was no average cockroach. This was the Ric Flair or perhaps the Charles Barkley of cockroaches, and before he disappeared below the bed, I believe I saw the huge bug smile at me, or perhaps it was a grimace.

Oh, how I despised those appalling creatures. As a small child, I would wait until dark, and then, armed with false bravado and my trusty red plastic water pistol, climb out of bed, suddenly turn on the lights in the kitchen or bathroom, and commence my deadly assault. Arnold Schwarzenegger had nothing on me. Long before Steve "The Crocodile Hunter" Irwin, I was "The Cockroach Hunter." Splat, splat, down they tumbled. I showed no mercy.

So, there I was at the hotel in Winter Haven prepared to make "Space-man" Lee even crazier than he already was, and I was confronted with an ancient, but formidable adversary from my youth: the estimable cockroach. I was ready and prepared to do battle with the hairy beast, albeit this time without my trusted weapon, the all-powerful water pistol. My parents threw that out, but more about that later.

As I reported, this was a fearsome looking cockroach, the size of "Big Daddy" Lipscomb, and likely a descendent of an unfortunate bug that met his demise by way of my plastic, water spraying cockroach killer. This woodlouse no doubt was out to avenge his forefather's untimely death (see A Bronx Tale), and he looked as if he was more than capable of eve-ning the score. Therefore, rather than commit myself to a battle that, even if I emerged victorious, would certainly leave me battered and bloodied, I enlisted the help of a hotel employee. The young lady arrived after my frantic call for help.

"A cockroach, sir? Are you sure? I don't ever recall seeing a cockroach at this hotel," she said with conviction.

Just then, the furry beast emerged from under the bed, making a beeline for the wall. "Look! There it is!" I shouted.

The young lady smiled, peered at me with a quizzical expression and replied demurely in a sweet syrupy southern drawl, "Why, that's not a cockroach, sir. That's just a l'il ol' palmetto bug."

"Ma'am," I insisted, "I'm from the South Bronx in New York and I know a cockroach when I see one, and that's the biggest, scariest, ugliest cockroach I've ever seen. Look, I just saw him flex his biceps! The thing is wearing a leather jacket with a skull and crossbones. He looks like freakin' Lee Marvin!"

The woman responded, "I think you're exaggerating, sir." And she laughed before adding, "Let me know if we can do anything else for you." With that, she turned, captured the beast in a paper cup, and as she left, I made note that she had not killed it.

"She's probably one of them." I exclaimed to my recent bride, "She'll likely come back after we're asleep and release it under the door!"

Later that evening, I dreamed I was locked in mortal combat with a giant lobster, another bug that I never eat.

Oh, I had mentioned earlier that my parents had thrown out my water pistol, and not because it symbolized violence; people did not think that way in the 1950s. However, they had also thrown out my impressive collection of *Sport Magazine* and *Sporting News*. They threw them out because, "Paper makes cockroaches."

Funny, I thought, *I always assumed that cockroaches made cockroaches.* Even at the age of ten, I figured that much, despite never being mistaken for a Rhodes Scholar. Nope, as I learned, as it turned out, paper made cockroaches. Little wonder then that I struggled in biology.

Incidentally, I love spiders. This freaks out my long-suffering bride, Peg. Every time I capture a spider in our house in North Attleboro, Massachusetts, I release it into our backyard to prevent my cats from mutilating it. You see, I always considered spiders to be a sign of affluence, since I would frequently spot them in the "cleaner" abodes in upstate New York. I never saw a cockroach in either Monticello, or South Fallsburg, New York, only spiders, so I reasoned that either the spiders ate all the cockroaches or that only rich people had them. Hey, I never claimed to be sane.

One early spring evening after purchasing our home in southeastern Massachusetts, I put on our floodlights, which illuminate our backyard and deck, and noticed a huge, rather familiar looking insect hanging onto my sliding door. Oh my God, I thought, a cockroach! They've found me! Peg, ever fearful that I'd tear up every floorboard in the house, rip out every tile in the kitchen, tear up the rugs and call the National Guard, attempted to assuage my fears.

"That's just a Japanese beetle," she assured me, "try to relax." I slept fitfully that night.

My insanity, and I am making no excuses, was no doubt inherited from my mother, a woman who was literally certifiable. I say that without malice, but rather just as a fact. My mother, not a dumb woman, but one as crazy as a bedbug, pun intended, was often prone to volatile and too often violent outbursts. It's not that she wasn't funny, although never attempting to be. Hell, she was Ruth Gordon in *Where's Poppa?* The lone significant difference was that "Gordon's" (George Segal) mom was acting and my mother was not.

There was one specific incident that accentuated my mother's insanity. She was so emotionally unstable that she considered the heat and humidity of summer to be tragic. Before the advent of air conditioners—they only seemed to be in movie theaters in the early '50s—whenever a heat wave would grip the South Bronx, my mother would sob uncontrollably. Heat and humidity would render her inconsolable. In retrospect, my allegedly insane mother was more likely a visionary, since her reaction to extreme warmth was perhaps a half-century before Al Gore warned us about "Global Warming." My mother had foretold of the impending disaster!

The incident I refer to as a particularly disturbing example of my mother's irrational fear of heat took place when I was merely five or six years old. On one extremely steamy and uncomfortable evening in the early 1950s my mother began pacing back and forth inside of our fourth-floor tenement apartment, and she proclaimed loudly while sobbing, "Solly (my father), do something!" Her demand came as if my poor father was in possession of some God-given ability to control the heat. Katie, or "Kadie" as it apparently reads on her birth certificate, then shouted, "I can't take it anymore. I need air. I can't breathe! Let's go up to the country."

Note: The "country" my mother was referring to was in reference to the New York State region around South Fallsburg and Monticello, aka the "Jewish Alps," or the "Borscht Belt" as many comedians and entertainers would refer to it. My dad, always attempting but nearly invariably failing to appease my mother's demands, responded, "All right, Katie, we'll pack up the kids (myself and my older brother) and leave first thing in the morning."

"No!" my mother shouted angrily, "I have to go now, or I'll die from the heat!" Death, indeed, lurked. Al Gore would have been so proud.

My father, a semi-functional illiterate, but a nice man, pleaded, "But it's nine at night."

"No!" the crazed woman shrieked like a banshee, "I have to go now, or I'll die!"

So away we went, and transportation circa 1951 was not terribly swift. I had to be awakened, as did my brother. Well, here we were schlepping up to the "country" on a warm, humid summer evening. We finally arrived at a motel in South Fallsburg significantly after midnight. Upon checking into our room, my mother suddenly blurted out, "Solly, I can't stay here!"

"Why not, Katie?" my exhausted father replied.

As God is my judge, my mother, now enraged, the veins bulging in her neck, shouted, "I can't stand the drapes!"

"What?"

"I can't stay here, Solly. I can't stand the drapes!"

"Fine," my besieged father lamented in complete resignation, "we'll leave first thing in the morning."

"No!" my mother shrieked, "I can't sleep here with those drapes!"

Rather than kill my mother, which in my opinion would have been justified, my father picked up the suitcases which hadn't even been unpacked, and we began our slow inexorable trek back to the Bronx, finally arriving in the wee hours of the morning. The sun was coming up, and it was time to face still another day.

Do you see why I consider the Spaceman to be relatively normal? Everything is relative. That is, except my relatives.

CHAPTER THIRTY-SIX

A Cry for Help

Concubines from the Distant Past, Fights with Umpires & Allergies Galore

The earthling known as Bill "Spaceman" Lee was not having a good day. Yours truly, the author, and that would be either "Scott Russell" or Kilgore Trout, returned from a lengthy walk on the afternoon of Sunday, June 13, 2021, and listened to the following voicemail message from Bill Lee. The pauses between comments made them even more hilarious:

"I beat Williston 7-4.............Four unearned runs.........Punched (struck out) out the best hitter in the league twice............Got into a fight............Drove in a run.........Lowered my ERA to 0.337............ That's my name backwards and upside down............And Jane Doe called me fifteen minutes ago from Greenwich Village..............I need help."

All right, obviously some translation is required. I will do my best, since I have apparently been anointed as "Spaceman" Lee's interpreter; not a thankless job, incidentally, but certainly a daunting task.

#1— In his fourth game of the Vermont Senior League season, the Spaceman took the hill against the best hitting team in the league, the Williston, Vermont entry. Nine torturous innings later, Lee escaped with a 7-4 victory, but not without considerable hindrance by his own fielders, who approached each batted ball as if it were a live hand grenade.

#2—Indeed, the Spaceman struck out the best hitter in the league, twice, and got him to pop up another time.

#3—The "fight," Bill alluded to, was between him, the home plate umpire, and nearly with the opposing catcher, who took umbrage with the Spaceman arguing that his runner should not have been called out (Bill was correct according to the rule book), and as the receiver scolded, "You're always looking for an advantage!" but not in those exact words.

#4—Bill did not lower his ERA to 0.337 as he claimed, but to 0.27, which is even better. You see, 1 earned run in 33.2 innings pitched is even better than the Spaceman thought, and when I informed him of that fact, he replied, "Oh, not my name backwards and upside down, but Carlton Fisk's number, making it even worse!" Better is "worse" in the strange universe of Bill Lee. Oh, and the Spaceman was a geography major, not a mathematics major.

#5—"And 'Jane Doe' called me fifteen minutes ago from Greenwich Village."

Obviously, "Jane Doe" is not "Jane Doe," but in fact, someone else. Hey, we've blasphemed enough people in both *The Spaceman Chronicles* and *The Final Odyssey*, and I'm not seeking retribution via way of litigation. Therefore, Ms. Doe will remain anonymous, however...............I have decided to call her "Karen," since those named Karen seem to be the brunt of jokes these days, and who knows? Perhaps she really is a "Karen." We're not telling!

One of the most popular frequent posts on social media these past few years has been a meme referred to as "Woman Yelling at a Cat." The woman's name is nearly invariably "Karen," and the meme features a screencap of *The Real Housewives of Beverly Hills*. The meme juxtaposes an emotionally upset blonde ("Karen") pointing and shouting at a white cat seated behind a dinner plate which contains a salad. "Smudge" is the name of the sarcastic and hilarious cat, and as I stated, the woman is nearly invariably "Karen." The meme has inspired countless incredibly funny "spinoffs," and is a source of great humor with the obvious possible exception of many blonde women.

Even more hysterical is that it is likely, according to various statistical surveys, that fewer babies are being named Karen because of the alleged stigma of being a "Karen."

How can we put this tactfully? These are the words of Bill "Spaceman" Lee, which at least in some small way, explain the earlier comments regarding "Karen," who called the Spaceman from Greenwich Village:

"Many years ago, Mickey Mantle was banging some chick (Karen) from the Commissioner's office. Well, to be truthful, so was I. She was that kind of girl. So, all these years later, she calls me from Greenwich Village (let's face it, she can no longer call Mantle), and she wants to hook up again! I couldn't come to the phone anyhow, I was in the fifth inning of pitching a shutout, but she left a message. There's no way I'm calling her back, and there's also no way she can find me up in the hills of Vermont. She's an urbanite. She's not finding my ass!"

CHAPTER THIRTY-SEVEN

John 3:16

"Reality is just a crutch for people who can't cope with drugs."
—*Robin Williams*

"A recent study found that humans eat more bananas than monkeys. I can't remember the last time I ate a monkey." —*Groucho Marx*

Those of a certain age may recall a man often referred to as "The Rainbow Man" or "Rock 'n' Rollen." The man's real name is/was Rollen Stewart and he became internationally famous for appearing at major sporting events throughout the world while wearing a trademark rainbow Afro-style wig and carrying a placard that read "John 3:16."

Stewart, a bizarre looking gentleman, seemed to be omnipresent, as he was front and center at the World Series, the Kentucky Derby, the Super Bowl, the NBA Finals, and at many major athletic events throughout Europe. The John 3:16 sign was obviously a reference to John 3:16 in the Scriptures, but the man's clownish countenance drew more scorn than admiration for the Holy Bible.

In truth, the Rainbow Man was mocked more than admired and the producers and directors of major sporting events often insisted to their camera crews that they avoid placing his image on the screen, and some networks threatened to fire any employees who crossed that line. Obviously, preventing Rainbow Man from being prominently displayed for all to see was virtually impossible. The guy was inventive. After all, how can a film crew prevent what amounted to the nation's initial "photobomber" from crashing the party? Rollen Stewart would strategically place himself directly behind home plate at major baseball games, and that is precisely the view from center field that is prevalent on all televised baseball games. It reached the point where broadcasters would joke, when asked about the meaning of John 3:16, that the number represented the great left-handed pitcher Tommy John's earned run average.

One might ask why the Rainbow Man was not simply prevented from entering the stadiums, but in truth, he was virtually unrecognizable until he suddenly donned his bizarre wig. The "born-again Christian," as he claimed to be, received his game tickets as donations from other "supportive" Christians. The Scripture "John 3:16" was going to be seen by all, detractors be damned, pun intended.

The reign of the Rainbow Man began in the late 1970s and lasted until the early '90s when predictable fate intervened. As Rainbow Man became even more pious and devout, his sanctimonious and ecclesiastical spirit would prove to be his downfall. It is written. "Rock 'n' Rollen" began to see himself as some sort of deity or Holy Spirit. As it was, the man was emotionally unstable, but he soon plummeted into a world of batshit craziness.

The Rainbow Man, who was reportedly homeless for a period, was involved in several stink bomb attacks. That is not a typo. However, in 1992, things got truly weird. In a Los Angeles hotel room, Rainbow Man, in his holy wrath, attempted to recruit two men he hardly knew, for a "job." When Rainbow Man attempted to kidnap a surprised maid, who locked herself in a bathroom to escape, the two men fled the scene. Police arrived and arrested Rollen Stewart, showing little or no respect for the Almighty demigod. Rainbow Man, of course, informed the arresting police officers that "The Rapture was due in six days." It is not known if they denoted that on their calendars.

During a standoff with the police, Rainbow Man threatened to shoot at airplanes landing at nearby Los Angeles Airport (LAX). My research did not avail information pertaining to his having a weapon on his person, but I digress. As the police searched the hotel room, they found numerous "John 3:16" placards.

Rainbow Man was arraigned and charged with three counts of kidnaping and hostage taking, and—I am not making this up!—he was sentenced to three concurrent life sentences for his transgressions against mankind. I should add that at the sentencing, Rainbow Man began a religious tirade and had to be restrained by bailiffs.

Incredibly, Rainbow Man became eligible for parole in 2002, but was denied. He was also denied in 2005, 2008, 2010, 2017, 2019, and most recently in 2020. Seriously, what is a holy man to do? Perhaps he should have merely murdered someone.

If you're wondering, Rainbow Man was married four times, most notably to a woman named Margaret Hockridge. Rock 'n' Rollen met Margaret in 1984, and like the Spaceman, John Steinbeck, and William Least Heat-Moon, they began traveling cross-country in 1985. The holy couple married in St. Louis in 1986, and of course, as was his wont, Rainbow Man decided to take in the World Series at Busch Stadium. As Margaret, his new bride stated, "He tried to strangle me for standing in the wrong spot with a John 3:16 placard." They were divorced in 1990, but apparently remained "friends," according to Mrs. Rainbow Woman.

So, what does all of this have to do with the earthling known as Bill "Spaceman" Lee's longtime Hall of Fame catcher, Carlton "Pudge" Fisk? Well, only Bill Lee could possibly explain the connection:

"I'm fairly convinced that Fisk and I are related. We're always fighting. Our mothers and grandmothers (The Hunts and the Fisks) were born on the Connecticut River. Scott, I want us to write a book called 'The Battery.' Maybe it's fiction, maybe not. 'The Battery' must be written in Louis Gates's style (*Finding Your Roots* by Henry Louis Gates, Jr.) based on genealogy, which would explain why Fisk and I fought so much. Think about our mothers and grandmothers bathing on opposite sides of the Connecticut River."

Note: Not to worry. The Spaceman was about to provide the Rainbow Man-Carlton Fisk analogy:

"Bernie Carbo, bless his little pointy head, would write 'John 3:16' on everything he would sign for me. I would always add 'Lee 3.37,' which is my name upside down and backwards. Bernie would always say to me, 'Bill, you've got to find Jesus!' I would answer, 'I didn't know he was missing.' What Bernie should have been signing was 'Fisk 3.75.' That was my ERA when Fisk caught me. With Tim Blackwell it was 3.30, with Gary Carter it was 3.34 and with Bob Montgomery it was 3.39. The next time Bernie signs something for me with 'John 3:16,' I'll just cross it out and write 'Monty 3.39' next to it."

The Spaceman further expressed his admiration for his dear, but often flaky friend, Bernie Carbo:

"Bernie is terrific, but he's a complete airhead. A couple of years ago, Bernie visited the Northeast Kingdom and was teaching at the River of Life Christian Center only twelve miles up the road from my home, but told me, 'I didn't know you lived here, Bill.' I'm afraid geography passed him by."

Upon the Spaceman being informed of the sad plight of Rainbow Man, Lee, thoughtful and empathetic as always, exclaimed, "Let me get this straight. The man travels all over the world and wears that rainbow wig, is constantly waving a John 3:16 placard around, and then he 'wigs out' in a California hotel and then they first claim that he just went nuts! And he's still in jail twenty-nine years later?! We've got to get him released!"

Note: It should be noted that Tommy John, who is famous for a surgery named after him, did not compile an earned run average of 3.16. But to once more prove there is some logic in our universe, a great Mexican American pitcher named Jesse Russell Orosco, who was born in Santa Barbara, California, and pitched for an incredible 24 major league seasons, finished his lengthy career with an earned run average of 3.16! Jesse saved 144 games during his illustrious career. Therefore, perhaps Rainbow Man, who remains jailed to this day, should have carried a placard which read, "JESSE SAVES!"

As a public service:

John 3:16 *"For God so loved the world that he gave his one and only Son, that whoever believes in him shall not perish but have eternal life."*

CHAPTER THIRTY-EIGHT

Illusion Versus Reality

A Tale of Two "Dreams" and an Inventive Geography Professor

Changing Speeds

"As much pot as I've smoked, the jury is still out as to what constitutes reality." —*Bill "Spaceman" Lee*

"What a long, strange trip it's been." —*Jerry Garcia*

"I read somewhere that 77 percent of the mentally ill live in poverty. Actually, I'm more intrigued by the 23 percent who are apparently doing quite well for themselves." —*Jerry Garcia*

"I don't believe in death." —*Bob Weir*

"You know why divorces are expensive? They're worth it!" —*Willie Nelson*

The earthling known as Bill "Spaceman" Lee was having a vivid dream, and it centered around "Vermont's most peaceful lake."

"An eagle made a kill on the Common. It wasn't actually the Common, it was on Lake Caspian. I walked out on the water to go for a swim. I had anticipated a front coming through as I walked down towards the water. It was there that I saw a young woman, maybe thirty to forty years old, and she was pontificating to a young man and a boy of perhaps twelve years old. The boy wasn't paying much attention to her as he was just staring at her tits. As I passed by, the woman said the most amazing thing. The woman said she had worked for the Peace Corps a long time ago and I heard her say that the key to life is having one thing you were good at and then expand it for the good of mankind.

"Despite my not entering the conversation, I stood facing the wind and I thought to myself, 'What am I good for?' I thought to myself that I'm either a politician, a lawyer, or a liar because I'm good at the art of deception, changing speeds and deceiving people. I'm from California. I could've been Richard Nixon."

The Spaceman continued:

"I stood facing the wind coming out of the west and I went out to my rock which very few know about. The rock is about two hundred yards out into the water, and as I stood atop the rock, the wind picked up and blew me off. The front came through and the temperature plummeted from seventy-four to sixty-three degrees within ten minutes. It was biblical. The eagle made the kill, but I couldn't see what he was grasping in his talons. I don't know what he had killed."

That was the first of two dreams the Spaceman had within a matter of hours, but the second one turned out not to be a dream. Bill Lee had just completed a podcast interview in which he was one of two legendary guests, the other being the legendary UCLA and professional basketball player, Bill Walton. Walton, of course, was not only a legendary athlete, but a controversial social activist and humanitarian. The podcast interview was called "Rivalries" and as is their wont, both the Spaceman and Bill Walton discussed much more than the mundane world of sports, despite both men having competed in championships.

As the interview progressed, the Spaceman informed the seven-foot Hall of Fame basketball star, "I've experienced this recurring dream that I met you in a Volkswagen Bus, and that your engine had caught fire. You were beneath a Eucalyptus Stand at UC Berkeley in San Anselmo, and you were telling me that you weren't mechanically inclined, and I dreamed that I helped you with your vehicle."

It was at that point that the seven-foot, two-inch giant Walton laughed and replied, "Bill, that wasn't a dream. It happened! I knew nothing about mechanical stuff and you just arrived out of the blue and rescued me."

During the one-hour program, Bill Lee and Bill Walton spoke about all the restaurants and the bars in San Rafael down on the waterfront, and the Spaceman wondered why, since they both hung out at the same places, they never ran into each other. Bill Walton explained, "Bill, you're that much older than me!" But the two men discussed Patty Hearst, Jack and Micki Scott and various other hot button topics, which confused the hosts of the show, since they had intended it to be less political and more about sports.

CHAPTER THIRTY-NINE

Toga! Toga!

USC's Answer to the Delta Tau Chi Fraternity

"Fat, drunk and stupid is no way to go through life, son."
—*Dean Vernon Wormer in* Animal House.

"Over? Did you say, over? Nothing is over until we decide it is!
Was it over when the Germans bombed Pearl Harbor? Hell, no!"
—*John "Bluto" Blutarsky in* Animal House.

"The catcher I've been grooming at Burlington High who is not very
bright, went down to a 'Future's Tryout Camp' and got twelve scholarship offers! He'll probably go to USC because they take dumb people."
—*Bill "Spaceman" Lee*

Imagine being a professor of geography at the University of Southern California and peering out at your class and seeing O.J. Simpson, Tim Rossovich, and the earthling known as Bill "Spaceman" Lee among your students.
This really occurred on Planet Earth in the year 1968. Life is rife with such
improbable events. So, who is or was Tim Rossovich? Many sports fans will
recall the name, but for those who are not familiar with the legend, we will
explain shortly.

As a geography major, the Spaceman was required to write a thesis in his
senior year. Even all-American athletes such as Bill Lee and O.J. Simpson
must follow protocol at such institutions. Said the Spaceman:

"My thesis was about the end of Route 66, which is Foothill Boulevard,
that extends out past the Cucamonga Alluvial Fan."*

> * Hey, you folks research the Alluvial Plain and the tallest peaks
> of the San Gabriel Mountains; I'm busy attempting to write this
> book.

The Spaceman continued:

"Tim Rossovich was one of my classmates in my geography class. Most people kept their distance from Rossovich, as he was apt to say or, even more threateningly, do some truly weird things. The man was nuts!"

Please keep in mind that when the Spaceman is impressed with someone's eccentricities, it is the equivalent of Stravinsky being captivated by another pianist. Not only was Rossovich an all-American linebacker on a terrific USC football team, and an equally successful player on the NFL's Philadelphia Eagles, his off-the-field exploits placed him in perhaps a singular category of lunacy. The Spaceman waxed ecstatic when describing the antics of his former classmate:

"Rossovich was a member of the KKG (the Kappa Kappa Gamma Sorority). He roomed with Tom Selleck. When he made it to the NFL with the Eagles, he was at a linebackers' meeting in Philadelphia and the coach asked Rossovich why he had been so quiet during the lengthy meeting. Rossovich opened his mouth, and a fucking bird flew out of it! Rossovich was also an actor. He had a cameo in a movie with Michael Keaton called *Night Shift*. He was naked except for a cowboy hat. He was with a hooker, and she told him, 'Hey, Tex, go back in there and play with your laureate.'"

Rossovich's idiosyncrasies were detailed by Philadelphia columnist Frank Fitzpatrick, who listed several of the linebacker's adventures. Fitzpatrick described him as having steel wool hair which added to his already bohemian reputation. Rossovich swallowed lit cigarettes and he drank motor oil. In a September 20, 1971 issue of *Sports Illustrated*, the great John Underwood mentioned to Rossovich that he'd never seen anyone eat glass. Rossovich immediately grabbed a piece of his wife's crystal ware and promptly consumed it.

As Fitzpatrick reported, "The Eagles defender liked to strip and cover himself with various substances—shaving cream, whipped cream, gasoline. He lived in a Rittenhouse Square apartment with teammate Gary Pettigrew and NFL Films executive Steve Sabol, and the three were invited to lots of parties. At one, Rossovich stripped and jumped into a birthday cake. Sometimes he arrived with his clothes aflame. Then, after friends would extinguish him, he would pop up and announce, 'Sorry, I'm in the wrong apartment.'"

It is likely that Rossovich suffered from CTE, but that simply awful disease was not yet diagnosed in the 1970s. Consider that Rossovich seemed to exult by ramming his head into his opponents when making tackles, and that even while in college, he often had to be dragged off the field after practices. He desired to keep hitting and be hit.

One night, according to Fitzpatrick, Rossovich leaped out of his future wife's second-floor dormitory window at USC. On another occasion, he climbed naked onto the lofty ledge of a campus building, allegedly to dry off more quickly. He once dove forty feet into a shallow river and cut his legs severely. A few days later, he plunged into a contaminated USC fishpond, infecting the wounds so badly that he fell into a coma for four days.

Get this: Tim Rossovich was often employed as a stuntman in various motion pictures. Hell, his entire life was lived as a stuntman, even on those occasions the camera was not on. At the Main Line Bar in Philadelphia, Rossovich once bit the bouncer's head.

After suffering a serious arm injury one season, Rossovich suddenly began repeatedly smashing the cast on his broken arm onto the bar, and upon removing the plastic shards he proudly shouted, "I'm cured!"

Tim Rossovich passed away on December 6, 2018. The Palo Alto, California native was only seventy-two.

It should be noted that folks like Tim Rossovich, although it's unlikely that anyone was zanier, were the people the earthling known as Bill "Spaceman" Lee associated with during his formative days on Planet Earth.

CHAPTER FORTY

All Who Wander Are Not Lost

Sticking It to the Man

The Real Bigots

> "Anyone who picks up this book and reads it will be hard-pressed to put it down. That's because I put some of that sticky substance on the pages to increase my spin-rate." —*Bill "Spaceman" Lee*

> "Ostentation is the signal flag of hypocrisy." —*Edwin Hubbel Chapin*

Launch angles, exit velocities, electronic sign-stealing, juiced baseballs, and a myriad of other allegedly inventive strategies implemented to further damage pitchers' effectiveness would, of course, eventually result in the pitchers' fraternity inventing methods attempting to even the score. "Eventually, though, all legislation goes against the hurlers. After all, we pitchers can think, and we adjust. In early 2021, hitters were striking out at a record rate and pitching dominated baseball. We can't have that, of course, since that would constitute real baseball, the way the game was intended," said the earthling known as Bill "Spaceman" Lee. "Having pitchers compete with a level playing field is entirely impermissible, at least according to Commissioner Rob Manfraud."

And then I, Scott Russell, had the audacity, the unmitigated gall and the brazen effrontery, to criticize a twenty-year-old athlete on the grossly misnamed "social" media, and in addition to my chutzpah, I copied my comments onto a respected site known as "The Baseball Reliquary," a LEGITIMATE collection of many learned individuals that truly love the game, as I do. All I had intended to do was to poke fun at a brash, but obviously gifted youngster named Wander Franco, who had been anointed as the numero uno prospect in all of minor league baseball by numerous experts, including the renowned publication, *Baseball America*.

Franco, a gregarious youth—and I was a nitwit (Peg claims I still am, but I digress)—for decades arrived for his major league debut at Tropicana Field

in St. Petersburg—or is it in Tampa Bay? I get confused—driving a brand
new, white $300,000 Rolls Royce. Willie Mays Aikens, eat your heart out.
The following is what I wrote, and I attempted to also "show off" my limited South Bronx Spanish-speaking skills. My high school Spanish teacher,
Charles Leiken, would no doubt have been impressed. Here are my words,
verbatim:

EL PATRON, MY ASS!
The much heralded "best prospect in baseball," Tampa Bay rookie,
Wander Franco, has been anointed "El Patron," and most likely, by him-
self. Humility, thy name is not Wander Franco.
Franco, modest to a fault, arrived for his major league debut at Trop-
icana Field in St. Petersburg last Tuesday, and he arrived in style. The
great Stan Musial once offered to give back some of his meager salary to
pay back for what he considered a subpar season. Not "El Jefe," however,
who arrived at the ballpark driving his $300,000 brand new white Rolls
Royce. Nothing like being inconspicuous.
Then Franco displayed why he was so ballyhooed, as he went 2-4
with a three-run home run. The Hall of Fame awaited. Since then, "the
subordinate," as I call him, has appeared overmatched and futile both at
the plate and in the field. Well, hey, after all, he's only 20 years old. Great-
ness no doubt awaits, however, but here is one youngster I will NOT be
rooting for.
To yours truly, Wander Franco is "El Mucamo," or "The Servant."
The Rolls Royce, I'm certain, has a nice warranty.
I wonder what Stan Musial drove.

Obviously, at least to most sentient people, I would have been equally
critical of ANY rookie arriving under such pompous circumstances, but
I would soon learn that I had stepped way over some imaginary line and
perhaps even forever branded myself as a racist. Honest. However, in these
oversensitive times, one must be extremely careful when questioning or
criticizing a "minority." Of course, it is getting more and more difficult to
identify who exactly qualifies as a minority. In the South Bronx of my youth,
we celebrated our differences. Today, we are denying our past and there are
those that deny our differences by emphasizing them.

Several of ESPN's "journalists," and I could not care less if any of them are offended, are infamous for finding racism where it doesn't exist and continually fail to see it where it does exist.

Regardless of how one feels about the subject, I was soon to be branded as a fool (no argument there) and perhaps even (gulp) a racist! I was quickly ducking the slings and arrows of self-righteous finger-pointers, who arrived at the conclusion that I was a bigot who at the very least required a thorough tongue-lashing or worse.

One of the offended individuals, and I am indeed naming him, was a Rich Ehisen whose name has a similarity to Rich Eisen, a former ESPN journalist (a good one, I might add). Well, the Ehisen fellow was apparently perturbed by what he perceived as racism. Dear God, I had criticized a minority athlete! During these contentious days, if you criticize a single Hispanic, African American, woman, Jew, or Bulgarian midget on roller skates, you are immediately accused of belittling all that fall under those categories.

Upon reading my comments regarding Wander Franco, the brash, attention-seeking "can't miss" superstar, Ehisen, as it were, wrote the following verbatim on "social" media:

"I have no idea what kind of person Wander Franco is, but you're sure giving us a pretty good idea what kind of person you are."

Well, Rich Ehisen was soon joined by other members of a pack of self-righteous indignant critics, many of whom were outraged, not by Wander Franco's hilarious antics, but the fact that I, Scott Russell, had the gumption to verbally abuse a non-Caucasian athlete. The judge and the jury had already found me guilty of racism.

I responded to Rich Ehisen as follows:

"There are folks such as 'Spaceman' Lee, Phil Mushnick, Jerry Remy and other notables that agree with my assessment (of Wander Franco). Some of us ridicule avarice, or blind devotion to what the great, late Pete Hamill referred to as 'acolytes of the religion of more,' so I feel I am in good company. Rich, I believe you are assuming far too much regarding my character. I have enjoyed your journalism, and this saddens me."

To his credit, Rich Ehisen offered this semi-apology:

"Your point to me is well taken in regard to your character. I shouldn't presume any more than anyone else should. But I'll add the caveat that making cultural references in this way is never going to be perceived in a positive light by most people these days. And especially not in an era now where overt bigotry has sadly been given a renewed acceptance in many circles."

The earthling known as Bill "Spaceman" Lee read the exchange and immediately came to my defense as follows:

"First of all, I've got your back, Scott. What people such as Rich Ehisen do not understand is that once a person is falsely accused of being racist, the STIGMA remains. By issuing an apology, and a rather lame one at that, the caveat and all, adds to the fact that some folks are no longer permitted to have an opinion that differs to theirs. It is a wolf pack mentality. What if you had died immediately following your conversation, and not having had the chance to respond? Those that didn't know you would be left believing that you were a racist, a stigma that would remain eternally."

The Spaceman was not through, however, as he continued:

"Is Rich Ehisen aware that you were the one who wrote the definitive analysis proving conclusively the superiority of black and Hispanic athletes, one that was heralded by the great Rod Carew? Of course not. His knee-jerk reaction was most likely the result of 'sensitivity training,' given to countless individuals. Of course, keep in mind that the sensitivity training is mandated. What these people do not understand is that in so many ways, it is really 'insensitivity training.' Assumptions are dangerous. This all harkens back to Kurt Vonnegut's 'Harrison Bergeron.' Rich Ehisen should read it because it is happening!"*

---

* "Harrison Bergeron" is one of a number of short stories in Kurt Vonnegut's *Welcome to the Monkey House*, written in 1961. The following is the premise of still another great work by the inimitable Kurt Vonnegut:

The year was 2081, and everybody was finally equal. They weren't only equal before God and the law. They were equal every which way. Nobody was smarter than anybody else. Nobody was better looking than anybody else. Nobody was stronger or quicker than anybody else. All this equality was due to the 211th, 212th, and 213th Amendments to the Constitution, and to the unceasing vigilance of agents of the United States Handicapper General.

In the year 1961, the great Kurt Vonnegut predicted what is occurring today in his short story, "Harrison Bergeron." Everyone must be equal, no one can be better looking or a better athlete, no one can be smarter than another person. There was a time when we celebrated our differences; now we deny them, and people find offense in everything that points out what they PERCEIVE as iniquities in our system. This is what partisan politics does to us, or what I define as racists accusing other racists of racism. Vonnegut's tale predicted this would occur in 2081. It is already happening. Look around you, it's happening. I am not on anyone's side. "Sides" are the problem, and those in the middle are victims.

In the year 2081, ballerinas are forced to attach heavy weights to their legs to counteract their gracefulness and to wear masks to hide their attractiveness.

It was the great Jackie Robinson who insisted that all of us should be given equal opportunity, but not advantages, and that we should all be judged by the same standards. By looking for and finding racism where it does not exist—and it most CERTAINLY EXISTS—we are doing more harm than good. There are enough racial iniquities around as it is, but to create additional that are not extant, merely divides us more deeply.

For yours truly to be even identified as a "possible racist," has a stigma which literally brought both anger and tears. I am among a frighteningly diminishing group of individuals who embrace our differences. As for young Rich Ehisen (if he is offended, so be it) I found his comments to be self-serving and pretentious.

Note: The author, Scott Russell, has literally lost two jobs for standing up for the rights of minorities.

CHAPTER FORTY-ONE

Bill & Diana's Excellent Adventure

Parasites, Pecking Orders

Possible Midlife Crisis

The White Man's Burden

"That's what you get for building a ballpark on the ocean."
—*Dennis "Oil Can" Boyd after seeing a game postponed at Municipal Stadium in Cleveland due to the fog above Lake Erie*

The first thing the earthling known as Bill "Spaceman" Lee saw as he drove off the ramp leading to the Maine Turnpike was his colorful colleague Dennis "Oil Can" Boyd's car pulled over on the side of the road with a state trooper's vehicle alongside it. Bill assumed that the officer had caught Oil Can speeding and was in the process of ticketing the ofttimes flaky right-hander. However, at closer inspection, Bill Lee came to the realization that the trooper was assisting Boyd in attempting to retrieve flying fifty-dollar bills. The Spaceman explained the circumstances surrounding still another bizarre incident:

"Oil Can and I were playing a legends game in Westbrook, Maine and he got paid $600 cash for his services. We were headed to Bangor to play the nightcap and I'm driving up the turnpike towards Augusta and the next thing I know I see a state trooper next to Boyd's Audi. Oil Can's car is pulled over and the lights are flashing, so I'm thinking he's getting ticketed for speeding, but then I see the Can, his wife, and the trooper out in the median and they're all chasing fifty-dollar bills that are flying around like green butterflies.

"I had told Boyd to not take cash, but to take a check from the Westbrook Fire Department, but he wouldn't listen. He had put the money in his glove compartment, but he was driving with the top down on his Audi, and suddenly he thought, 'Where did I put the cash?' So, he opens the glove box, a gust of wind blows through the car, and the fifty-dollar bills are blowing in the wind. Like I've always said, don't multitask on the turnpike."

The reminiscence regarding Oil Can Boyd's highway adventure had been aroused by a highly unusual weekend the Spaceman had just experienced. Boyd, a renowned eccentric much like Bill Lee, was a temperamental hurler who, also like Lee, often found himself in trouble. Boyd, who coauthored a terrific autobiography with the late, great Mike Shalin called, *They Call Me Oil Can: Baseball, Drugs and Life on the Edge*, admitted that he had often smoked cocaine and crack during his controversial career. The African American right-hander, a delightful character who had several relatives that had played in the Negro Leagues, was as colorful as anyone in the big leagues.

Bill and Diana had just appeared in a memorabilia show in Cranston, Rhode Island, during which he was told that Dennis Boyd had recently lost his two big toes to diabetes and would no longer be able to play Senior League Baseball. This, of course, saddened the Spaceman, who had already somehow found himself entangled in a strange weekend, not unusual for the southpaw. The Spaceman recalled:

"I was aboard a flight when a woman came over to me on the plane and asked for my autograph. I asked her if she knew who I was. She answered, 'Yes, you're Richard Branson.' I replied, 'Yeah, I'm Richard Branson, and I'm flying coach with you to Calgary!'"

I neglected to ask the Spaceman if he inked his John Hancock "Bill Lee" or "Richard Branson."

Bill continued with the peculiar events of the weekend of July 9 through July 11, 2021:

"I woke up in the morning to see that Richard Branson and his gang of industrialites were preparing to fly out to space, and that they were flying out of Truth or Consequences, New Mexico. Hey, at least I was out there and enjoyed the best Mexican breakfast I've ever had, but I don't think that's what you should eat before you board a rocket and you're weightless. Did you fart? Did you have the bean burrito?

"The entire weekend was a bad fucking dream. I attended a memorabilia show west of Warwick, Rhode Island, and I'm driving through the remnants of 'Elsa,' a tropical storm. There are torrential rains, and I came across at least five accidents with people sliding off the road. We arrived at the venue and somehow, I arrived on time. Diana and I had just spent the weekend with the 'Muldoons' (Mike and Dierdre Mulkern), and there were chickens in our bedroom. Poor Michael! Deirdre, apparently in the middle of a midlife crisis, is raising chickens in her house!"

The Spaceman was not done as he added:

"Diana woke up in the middle of the night and thinks that parasites had gotten into her throat. I told her, 'I guarantee that parasites have not gotten into your throat.' But these were gigantic fucking chickens. I'll tell you this: Deirdre's chicken coop is the most elegant chicken coop I've ever seen. The chicken coop is made entirely from scraps from her property. It's even got trap doors; she put all her energy into this project. It's right out of Lewis Carroll's *Alice in Wonderland*. Deirdre's chicken coop resembles the prison in Dannemora, New York.* It's either that or Stalag 17."

> * Note: Although a curious sort, I refrained from asking the Spaceman how he knew that fact. However, I did research the maximum-security Clinton Correctional Facility in Dannemora, New York, and was fascinated to learn that one can actually "Google" the "Nine Best Prisons in New York State." I mean, who knew? It even includes reviews and visiting hours, but there were no dining critiques. Peg and I are now considering Dannemora as our next vacation destination.

Bill Lee was not about to drop the subject of the chickens in the bedroom, however:

"Deirdre separates the chickens by their pecking order (I swear he said that). She cannot put the younger ones in the same coop because they would be pecked to death by the middle-aged chickens. But when Diana was fearful that parasites were crawling out from the cage, I asked, 'Why would they want to do that? Aren't they content where they are?' Diana, although from Western Canada, is an urbanite who has led a sheltered life. She requires an education on chickens and parasites."

The Spaceman was not through in describing the weird events of the weekend, however:

"On the way to the sports card show in Cranston, we had not eaten, so Diana suggested a stop at a nearby McDonald's. It was pouring rain and all the lights were against me, but I ran three red lights. Diana scolded, 'Hey, that was a red light,' but I answered, 'Who's going to care?' There was no traffic on the road. I yielded to humanity and not to the mechanical devices we created (see Richard Branson). We pull up to the McDonald's, but the sign reads 'No Dining In,' so we brought the food outside. We were eating outside of our car—I just wanted a muffin—but when I removed the wrapper, a gust of wind blew it out of my hand. It was God! Another gust blew the wrapper up into the truck. We got back into the car and my foot got stuck on the floor mat. I had stepped on a piece of gum and now my foot was stuck to the floor mat. I looked up to the sky and shouted, 'You are one funny son of a bitch!' I was thinking I was either possessed or that God was fucking with me."

Bill then reminded Diana that he had no use for Ray Kroc (McDonald's and the owner of the San Diego Padres), since he, Ballard Smith, and Jack McKean conspired to prevent him from pitching for the Padres. As Bill stated:

"The only time I stop at McDonald's is to take a shit because they have clean restrooms. They are nothing but a Kroc (sic) of shit."

Getting back to Oil Can Boyd apparently losing his toes to diabetes, Bill recounted:

"This kid comes up to me at the memorabilia show and told me that he had played vintage ball against Oil Can, but that he could not play anymore because of no longer being able to walk. Then I got home to Vermont, and I received a call from Josh Dixon, the guy who produced the documentary *A Baseball Odyssey*, about my trips to Cuba. Josh normally drives through Spokane on his way back to Seattle and he was wondering if I had stopped off to visit his son, but I hadn't. His son was out there because he had just married a Blackfoot Indian girl from Browning, Montana (his father-in-law is an elder in the tribe). Josh's son and his new bride had been arrested after their wedding in Glacier National Park. They ran out of stuff to build bonfires, so they dismantled tables to burn them up. That's what Indians do."

The Spaceman then lamented a few sad facts about the region:

"When you leave the property and hit the reservation, it is dead. There is no agriculture, and all the alfalfa is gone. Cars are overturned. It seems that all the money stops in the rich farmers' territory. Welcome to America."

Once more, the Spaceman's most recent journey ended strangely:

"When I returned home, I immediately turned on the television to see that *Field of Dreams* was on. The first thing I see is Ray Kinsella (Kevin

Costner) kidnapping Terence Mann (James Earl Jones) and within minutes, I hear 'Go the distance' being whispered. The scene switches to Fenway Park and who is on the mound? Yes, it's Oil Can Fucking Boyd! You can't make this shit up. I yelled out, 'No!' Moonlight Graham! It's all connected, I tell you. Read *Connections* by James Burke. It was really surreal."

CHAPTER FORTY-TWO

The Other Woman

Five-Step Programs to Avoid

> Two mafia hit men are walking through the forest late at night. One says, "I gotta admit, I'm scared out here." The other responds, "Whadd-aya mean you're scared? I gotta walk back alone!"

> "This is the best shit I've ever read since the days I was writing."
> —*de Tocqueville*

> "Ditto." —*Yogi Berra*

The earthling known as Bill "Spaceman" Lee was having a rough day, but perhaps not as bad as his beautiful wife, Diana. Bill awoke on a mid-July morning in 2021 in eager anticipation to "stretch" with his favorite Edmontonian, his limber "physical trainer," the celebrated host of the popular PBS program, *Classical Stretch: by Essentrics*, the bestselling author of *Aging Backwards*, Ms. Miranda Esmonde-White.*

> * It should be noted that Diana describes her husband's "stretching" as merely sitting atop a Pilates ball and wiggling his toes, but I digress.

As the Spaceman described the beginning of what would become an ordeal:

"I awoke and immediately became dismayed and slightly disoriented that Miranda, my exercise guru's show, had somehow been at least temporarily usurped by some frighteningly menacing woman named Kellyann Petrucci."*

> * Note: the author researched Ms. Petrucci and found her to be extremely attractive.

The Spaceman continued:

"This Kellyann person got stressed out on an airplane and the authorities removed her from the flight. She immediately began ranting that she
must get 'rebooted,' so she concocted a five-day plan to recover. I noticed
that my screen read DIRECTV, but there's an AT&T Earth logo on the left.
This was like being at Daisy Buchanan's at your own house. This Kellyann
Petrucci, at least that's who she claimed to be, was wearing a black dress,
like the one worn by Nurse Diesel (Linda Pizzuti Henry) on John Henry's
boat, the Iroquois. I assumed she is from Sicily and just came back from
attending Don Corleone's funeral. The Wicked Witch of the West was in a
black dress, too, but you're not in Kansas anymore, Dorothy! This Petrucci
woman was standing in front of a screen that showed all types of fruits that
would comprise a fruit diet. It's some sort of health-fad diet that's supposed
to be a five-step process to better health. I thought I saw dead flies off to the
side of the fruit."*

* Briefly afterwards, the Spaceman amended that remark that
the "dead flies" were most likely the little black seeds that you
grow a chia pet with.

The Spaceman made it clear that he was unhappy with PBS for removing
his beloved Miranda Esmonde-White with this blonde woman ("More than
likely Nurse Diesel with a blonde wig.")

"This Petrucci woman is a 'bone broth expert' and some sort of a weight-
loss lunatic, and she was railing on about the five things you have to eliminate
from your life, and it was a five-day program. Number four was to eliminate
stress. Stress," said the Spaceman, "is eliminated by Epsom salt which, of
course, has magnesium. The abbreviation of magnesium is 'MAG,' but that
also can stand for a .44-caliber handgun used by 'Dirty Harry.' Number
three are electronic devices; i.e. what is an electron? It is a negative force!
Keep in mind that this is a five-step program, but that it's a countdown from
five to one, but all I could see on the screen were five, four and three, but I
KNOW what numbers two and one are, Scotty," he told me. "Number two
is you, and number one is me, and we must eliminate the 'takers.'"

It suddenly dawned on me that I was the only one remaining on Planet
Earth capable of both understanding the Spaceman and writing this trilogy

with the Spaceman, and I am NOT boasting. This chapter proves conclusively, at least to me, that Bill Lee chose me because of my inherent insanity.

"You see," said Lee, "everyone else has an agenda when writing a memoir. They have a beginning and an ending. We have neither and we also don't have a middle. That's because we have no idea where the fuck we are going, and we won't know where we are until we get there, and maybe not even then."

Not surprisingly, but somewhat scarily, I again understood the Spaceman's comments. Somehow, inexplicably, the Spaceman then segued into telling me that I must watch the 1997 motion picture, *The Borrowers* starring John Goodman and Jim Broadbent. As I would learn, "The Borrowers" were a clandestine family of four-inch-tall people who lived inside the walls and beneath the floorboards of an old house that they had to save from evil real estate developers. These tiny folks live away from the "Beings," (meaning humans!) including a nefarious lawyer named Ocious P. Potter.

"Sounds realistic to me," I said in all honesty to the Spaceman.

Bill Lee concluded his critique of Ms. Kellyann Petrucci with the following:

"The entire program consisted of extremely bad imagery. I wasn't about to hang around to find out what numbers one and two were, because I knew they were you and me! This Petrucci woman is an Italian who dyes her hair blonde. She wears this belt that is way too tight around her waist, and it cuts her in half and prevents circulation. She was raving like fucking Elmer Gantry! She had the crowd mesmerized and there was something going on that is very scary. I was afraid to walk near my TV after that. She scared the shit out of me!"

I must warn you that the Spaceman's day was about to get even worse!

"I left the house after watching this wretched woman on television. It was hotter than hell, so I drank half a beer. Scott Reed's hay got all wet, so we restacked it and then I went and got Diana who had a rough day yesterday. She was in the truck, and she finished the second half of my beer. I put some fuel in the car and we headed up to North Troy to see Durwood and Lorraine. Durwood was in his chair and the volume was loud on his TV because he doesn't hear too well. Diana staggered in. She only had half a beer! She literally falls into Durwood's chair and she remained there. Durwood's wife, Lorraine, comes down and I go into the pool for a swim."

The Spaceman's nightmare day was about to get even more bizarre:

"Diana always tells me to bring a bottle of wine when we visit, so I gave them a bottle of wine before I jumped into the pool. We were aware that Durwood and Lorraine had to leave shortly for a charity event, but Diana cannot stand up! I had to hold her up by the back of her pants, but she fell onto the lawn. She was just sitting there, and I realized it was reminiscent of one of Andrew Wyeth's paintings!* I had always wondered what that painting really was, and now I finally knew! That girl was hammered!"

> * The iconic 1948 Wyeth painting the Spaceman was referring to, was of course, called *Christina's World*. The actual model for the painting was a young woman named Christina Olsen, who was a neighbor of Andrew Wyeth in South Cushing, Maine, one of the two locations where Wyatt created all his amazing etchings. Christina Olsen was the inspiration for Wyeth's masterpiece, which came about when Wyeth peered out from his window and saw the young woman crawling outside in the grass. Christina had lost the use of her legs in her early thirties, due to a degenerative muscular condition. In the painting, Christina can be seen from behind. She is wearing a pink dress and is lying in a grassy field. Although she appears to be in a position of repose with her torso propped up by her arms, she is apparently fixed to the ground. It is one of the most known paintings of the twentieth century.

In "Diana's World," however, the Spaceman offered:

"Diana had also lost the use of her legs, but for far different reasons. I got Diana up, but she went down again. She looked like Archie Moore trying to get up after getting battered by Diana's Canadian countryman, Yvon Durelle, except that Moore got up. First, I thought she was attempting to crawl back into Canada, but she was headed in the wrong direction, and she was only one mile from the Canadian border. If she had turned around, she would be in Canada by now. We were in the town of North Troy, right on the Canadian border. In high school, I was on the Terra Linda Trojans, and at Southern Cal, I was a USC Trojan. Now I was in North Troy! The men of Troy!"

The Spaceman's description of his wife's ordeal may not have been the most sympathetic, but it was beyond hilarious, as he continued:

"Now she was crawling across the gravel road in Durwood and Lorraine's driveway. They've got to get into their Mercedes to go to their charity event, but Diana is blocking their path. Strange things happen up here in the Northeast Kingdom. If I put Diana in the Missisquoi (River) in North Troy, they'd never find her. The day began with John Henry's wife (Nurse Diesel) in a blonde wig telling me I had to learn about a five-step program to better health, but she was taking an awful fucking long time to get to that fifth step. It almost took as long as it took Diana to crawl across that gravel road. When we finally got home, I paced in front of my TV for an hour. It was so fucking scary, I was afraid to turn it on!"

CHAPTER FORTY-THREE

Huevos y Nom Noms

Ariverderci Romo

What Came First, the Stewardess or the Egg?

Happiness Is Awakening One Morning and Seeing That Your Grape Juice Has Fermented

The earthling known as Bill "Spaceman" Lee awoke on a July morning, not in the greatest of shape. It seems that lovely Diana had drank half a glass of Casamigos Añejo (tequila) but left the other half where the Spaceman soon found it. "What do you expect when actor George Clooney, and a baby food guy, Rande Gerber, get together to promote a tequila? You know it's time to go into the other bedroom when you find your wife lying in bed fully clothed."

"You do realize," I responded, "that just because you find a remaining half glass of tequila that you are not obligated to drink it."

As the Spaceman elaborated:

"The manufacturers of Casamigos Añejo are justifiably proud of their product. Their tequila is aged seven to nine years from the rich soil of Jalisco, Mexico. They brag that their agave piñas are roasted in traditional brick ovens for over seventy-two hours, when most others steam theirs for only seven hours. However, it takes Diana far less time to get roasted."

The day had begun bizarrely enough. As the Spaceman explained:

"Diana had just returned from Willey's Store. They carry bear traps, women's clothing, alcohol, and dynamite. I see her getting out of the car. She's got a beer in her hand, and I'm looking out of the window pretending to be filming her as if I'm cranking an old-time camera. I tapped on the window, she looks up and staggers, but she doesn't go down. It reminded me of an old Irish joke."

The joke in question: An inebriated Irishman is returning home after purchasing a pint of scotch from his liquor store, but he trips on the curb and falls to the ground. As he struggles to get to his feet, he notices liquid pouring down the sewer two feet from him, and he cries out, "Please, dear Jesus, I hope that's my blood!"

The day, however, was about to take a turn for the worse. As he explained:

"I picked up my mail and I see a letter from Gallup, New Mexico. I figured it was just some more fan mail for me to sign and return. I immediately thought that the only people in Gallup, New Mexico were either Native Americans or people in the Witness Protection Program. These two women had Italian names, and all the bars in Kansas City are run by the mob. I open the envelope and there's a returned stamped envelope inside. The letter from this woman read, 'My friend and I picked you up in a bar in Kansas City and took you back to my house.'

"The woman went on to claim that I didn't have a hotel room because the Red Sox traveling secretary (Jack Rogers) forgot to book one for me. That didn't sound right. The woman then said I was with Carl Yastrzemski in the bar. Again, this didn't sound right unless it was the Muehlebach Hotel in downtown KC. Besides, what the fuck would I be doing drinking with Yaz anyhow? So, this woman said that I allegedly went to her house, but that I told her I had to get back to the hotel before curfew."

The Spaceman was not done as he followed:

"The entire thing sounded fishy, but who knows? This girl claims she's down in Gallup, New Mexico which is near East Bumfuck in the middle of nowhere. All there is in Gallup are gas stations, hookers, and Mexican food. The place is just off '40 near the Arizona line, but I felt obligated to write back to her since she had sent me a self-addressed stamped envelope. I refolded her letter, and wrote on the back of it, 'Sometimes a ballplayer will do anything to get away from Carl.'"

Wait, there's more. Since the woman claimed she had met Bill at the historic Muehlebach Hotel in Kansas City, the Spaceman thought it was time to regale me with a story about his former Red Sox teammate and fellow hurler, Vicente "Huevo" Romo.

For the record, Vicente Romo y Navarro hailed from Santa Rosalía, Mexico, and had a good major league career. Over eight years, "Huevo," which is egg in Spanish (Romo had a round face, the shape of an egg), Romo compiled a 32-33 mark with an excellent 3.36 ERA. He also saved 52 games. Romo, like the Spaceman, was a great character.

"There was this bar in Kansas City called 'The Apartment,' and that is where Romo jumped out of a fucking cake, and he was wearing a Mexican general's uniform. It was the final day of the season. This happened at a TWA flight attendants school down from the Muehlebach Hotel, and everyone was hooking up with the stewardesses. Would you like some TWA coffee, some TWA milk, or some TWA-T?"

If that tale at the Muehlebach Hotel wasn't intriguing enough, the one the Spaceman told of his great, late teammate Tony Conigliaro was even more hilarious. As Bill Lee expanded:

"We were staying at the Muehlenbach Hotel, but Tony C. was late for curfew. Kasko, the most anal-retentive manager in history, asked Tony why he had been late the following day in the dugout as the game was going on. Tony C. told Kasko he was late because there was a mouse eating spinach on his chest. Kasko just stared incredulously at him. We couldn't stop laughing for two innings!"

It should be noted that Vicente "Huevo" Romo arrived in a trade from the Cleveland Indians along with Sonny Siebert and Joe Azcue, for Ken "Hawk" Harrelson, Dick Ellsworth, and Juan Pizarro on April 19, 1969.

The Spaceman continued to receive bizarre phone calls and letters, however:

"I received one call from Oregon threatening Diana with extortion and another from Chicago. I called the one in Chicago to bust their balls, and the guy answered in French, but the guy had no idea I had a rudimentary knowledge of French since my days in Montreal. I busted his chops so bad in French that he wound up hanging up on me. It was hilarious. Then a landscaper woke me up by butt-dialing me from Oklahoma."

The Spaceman informed me that he listens to a radio show every night, and that the show is aimed at kids. It's supposed to address the youngsters' concerns about various topics, but Bill decided to answer the questions aloud.

"I thought that I could start a new career as a talk show radio host for kids," said the Spaceman. "One of the questions was why there were so many F-35s in Burlington. I answered, 'Well, Bobby (Bill decided the kid's name was "Bobby."), that's where the fucking airport is!' Another kid asked, 'Why are the planes so loud?'"

"'Well, Bobby, that's so that the engines can keep the nuclear devices up in the air so they don't fall on your heads in Burlington.'"

The Spaceman concluded with, "I soon realized I was not cut out to host a children's podcast."

SPEAKING OF MEMORABLE PHONE CALLS, THE AUTHOR IS PROUD OF THIS ONE:

DOUGIE'S GOIN' DOWN & HE'S TAKING ZOLTOC WITH HIM!
Subtitled - I NEVER LIKED THE LITTLE BASTARD ANYHOW

Well, I received one of those dreaded phone calls we all fear. It wasn't the standard "You're in trouble with the IRS, so send $$$ to this address or risk being incarcerated." This was even better. Here it is, practically verbatim:

SR: Hello

Caller: Mr. Russell, I'm calling you to tell you that we've got your grandson, and if you don't give us ten thousand dollars within two hours we're going to kill him.
(Note: Peg and I have no grandchildren, incidentally).

SR: Which grandson do you have? Is it Dougie or Phil?
(There was a brief hesitation)

Caller: It's Dougie. Yeah, we've got Dougie!

SR: Thank God it's not Phil! I knew that little putz, Dougie, was going to get himself in a lot of trouble someday. Now, what did he do?

Caller: Never mind what he did. If you don't give us ten grand we're going to kill Dougie. Do you understand?

SR: How can I be sure you really have Dougie?

Caller: Yeah, we've got him all right. But if you ever want to see him alive again, you have to give us ten grand. Time is running out. Two hours for the cash or Dougie is dead! Understand?

SR: Calm down, please, sir. Listen, ten thousand is a reasonable price for a life.

Caller: Now, you're getting smart. Listen, it's got to be cash. You got that? And in two hours. I'll tell you where to meet us. But if you call the cops, we'll kill Dougie immediately. So, get your ass to the bank.

SR: Calm down, sir. No problem, but can you do me a huge favor?

Caller: What's that?

SR: I've got this Bulgarian midget living in my basement. For an extra two thousand, can you whack him, too?

Caller: What are you sayin'?

SR: Can you do two for the price of one? You know, first whack Dougie. I can't stand the little prick, but can you come over and whack this Bulgarian midget while you're at it? We tried to get a mafia guy to whack him three years ago, but the guy chickened out. Oh, and he wanted twenty grand, so you guys are reasonably priced. What do you say pal, do we have a deal? (Brief silence.)

Caller: You WANT us to kill your grandson?

SR: Yeah, of course. So, do we have a deal or not? But no deal if you don't do the midget, too.
(Brief silence once more.)

Caller: You know, you're a sick motherfucker!

(I heard a dial tone.)

I wonder if they offed Dougie.

CHAPTER FORTY-FOUR

Ten Biggest Assholes

In the *Spaceman Chronicles*, Bill Lee named the ten biggest assholes he had encountered during his lengthy pitching career. We even added an honorary mention list of those that didn't quite "make the grade." Well, this time, and we realize we're sounding like Casey Kasem's countdown to the number one song in the country, the Spaceman has achieved immortality. You see, he has placed himself atop the list of ignominious bastards. Bill Lee leaves little doubt that he has reached the "pinnacle," or perhaps the depths of depravity.

Please consider:

#1 through 10 – BILL "SPACEMAN" LEE

Regardless if this incident occurred during Bill Lee's first, second, or current marriage, the event definitively places the earthling known as Bill "Spaceman" Lee at the summit of "Asshole Mountain." Allegedly, Bill's wife was in the process of attempting to read *The Exorcist*, the frightening novel by William Peter Blatty, which was adapted into an equally terrifying motion picture.

"Oh, my God," said the wife of the Spaceman, "this book is so scary that I cannot even finish reading it. It's giving me nightmares. I refuse to read another word!"

With that, Mrs. Lee put the unfinished book in her car, drove it to the beach, and threw it into the ocean. There would be no more nightmares.

The following day, the Spaceman traveled to a bookstore, purchased another copy of *The Exorcist*, soaked it in the sink as his wife slept, and placed it on the nightstand next to her bed.

CHAPTER FORTY-FIVE

Since there existed no human being elected as the forty-fifth president of the United States, this chapter is not included in this book.

CHAPTER FORTY-SIX

Unavoidable Engagements

"Sandy Koufax and Bill Bradley are two of the most brilliant men I've ever met. I place Bill Lee on that list, but in a different category."
—*Jane Leavy*

"Scott Russell is a gem." —*Jane Leavy*

"I think she meant 'germ.'" —*Peg Russell*

Note: Author Jane Leavy is an award-winning former sports journalist and feature writer for the Washington Post, *and is the author of* New York Times *bestsellers* Sandy Koufax: A Lefty's Legacy, The Last Boy: Mickey Mantle and the End of America's Childhood, *and* The Big Fella: Babe Ruth and the World He Created. *Ms. Leavy is, in our opinion, the greatest biographer in journalistic history.*

In the world of the earthling known as Bill "Spaceman" Lee, some convergences are pre-destined. The initial meeting between Bill Lee and renowned author Jane Leavy really took place several years ago outside of the Country Store in Craftsbury, Vermont; however, the Spaceman had no clue as to the identity of the attractive, tiny, albeit formidable woman he was speaking with. However, Ms. Leavy, as is her wont, did not exclaim like many of her prominence would, "Hey, look at me, I'm Jane Leavy!"

If Jane did make mention of her name on that occasion, it didn't register in the mind of the inimitable Spaceman. What I find so endearing about Jane Leavy, is that for one of the most brilliant women on Planet Earth, she has little or no ego. There exists a preponderance of attention-seeking nitwits these days, but not Jane Leavy, and I'm not certain if her modest upbringing in her native Bronx, New York, helped formulate her humility, but if so, that would not astonish me. Jane writes. Jane's words are her legacy, and her legacy is astounding.

Having Bill Lee and Jane Leavy meet and discuss the ills of the world, therefore, was imperative. The encounter was thereupon arranged in early

August in the summer of 2021, and the venue chosen was a Cape Cod League game in Orleans, near Ms. Leavy's home. I should add that Jane's dog, "Betty," is the mascot of the Orleans team, and an adorable one at that. I made mention that Betty was not quite as attractive as Jessica Biel, who starred in the outstanding motion picture, *Summer Catch*, which subject is the Cape Cod League, and Jane, of course, got the inference.

Bill and Diana were driving down from Vermont to meet Jane behind home plate at 3:15 p.m., but Jane was having difficulty reaching Bill on her iPhone, so she alerted me. I told her not to worry, and that Bill would be there and that he doesn't do anything conventionally. Jane, of course, strongly suspected that.

Shortly after Bill and Diana arrived at the ballpark, the Spaceman was already in the process of being interviewed by WEEI and by another broadcast intern who had graduated from USC, and Bill had already met the coaches of both teams and all the players, but had not yet met Jane Leavy, who was sitting in the dugout with her pooch. Shortly thereafter, the paths of both Bill and Jane Leavy finally crossed.

The following several days were a delightful blur, at least to the Spaceman. In a matter of several deliciously delirious hours, Bill and Jane deliberated in regard to baseball, politics, the sorry state of our planet and species, and knowing Bill, most likely the overabundance of cicadas earlier this spring.

"I KILLED JANE LEAVY'S DOG!" —BILL "SPACEMAN" LEE

Upon Bill Lee's return to his home in Vermont after his sojourn to the Cape to see the great Jane Leavy, I was greeted with the Spaceman's blunt admission. However, before you put this book down to call your local ASPCA, I suggest you read his "confession."

"I didn't find Jane at the ball field until the game had begun. She was in the dugout, and I was holding court with the media. Jane plays catch with that dog (Betty) all day. By the time I met Jane I had met everyone at the ballpark. Even Al Leiter (former major league hurler and ESPN analyst) was at the park. The guy is QAnon.* I'm convinced that these people watch Fox News all day. They went to bed and half their brains were sucked out by Fox News. Al Leiter is one of those guys that looks good and says nothing. His entire goal in life is to say nothing wrong. When I was speaking with

Leiter, we could've been Nicolai Levin and John Birch! Leiter is a fucking left-handed Curt Schilling!"

* Note: Bill's comments regarding Al Leiter are merely his opinions.

Now for the startling admission that the Spaceman had killed Jane Leavy's beloved dog, Betty:

"Betty had the misfortune of hearing me speak for three hours nonstop on Jane Leavy's couch. The dog eventually rolled over and lied on her back with her stomach completely exposed with its feet up in the air like a dead horse. I killed the poor dog. I apologized to Jane for killing her dog. It had to be the sound of my voice—I have that effect on all women. I anesthetize them with my words. We went over the hitters."

The Spaceman had somehow either mesmerized the dog, or perhaps pulverized its brain.

"Jane told me that Betty had never behaved like this. The dog hid in a hedge with her tail sticking out just to get away from me."

Betty the Dog was obviously all right, at least physically. The Spaceman was soon to learn that upon visiting Jane Leavy's home later that evening, he had entered the world of an almost exclusive registry. Please allow Bill Lee to explain:

"Jane told me that the first person to have visited her property before she even built the house was the incomparable Sandy Koufax! Sandy had stood on the same hill atop what would eventually be the location of Jane's home! I was in select company."

The Spaceman continued to expound on his excellent adventure to Jane Leavy's beautiful home:

"Diana and Jane hit it off beautifully. Jane is so gracious. While at the ballpark and her home, Jane made lobster rolls and we got to meet her friends. I got to throw out the first pitch and I threw a perfect strike right down the middle. Then I got the ball back and threw an 'eephus pitch,' but this was unlike the one I threw to Tony Perez in 1975. I didn't hang it, and Tony could've never blasted this one. I asked Jane lots of questions about Sandy Koufax."

While at the ballpark, the Spaceman paused to do some stretching.

"I was stretching with my back to the playing field. There were about five hundred people in attendance. Jane said that I was mooning the crowd and had my ass in the sunset. Jane asked if I did that intentionally. I told her I didn't, but that they deserved it."

How impressed was Bill Lee with Jane Leavy? Bill's comment regarding Jane Leavy spoke volumes:

"Jane Leavy would be the perfect Commissioner of Major League Baseball."

Also present at the ballpark with the Spaceman and Jane Leavy was veteran sportscaster Lesley Visser, who was the first female NFL analyst on television. Lesley is also the former wife of former Red Sox play-by-play man Dick Stockton, a man yours truly, the Spaceman, Mike Mulkern, and the great, late George Kimball, got into a food fight with at a restaurant on US 17 in Winter Haven back in 1977. Well, truthfully, we initiated it, and we were acting like petulant children, but I digress. The Spaceman laughed as he recalled that Ms. Visser was present for a memorable game at Olympic Stadium on October 19, 1981, a game that still sticks in the craw of Montreal fans some forty years later. As the Spaceman recalls:

"In game five of the NLCS, we were tied 1-1 in the ninth, but Dick Williams decided to pitch Steve Rogers in relief. Steve was a terrific starting pitcher, but an established relief pitcher should have been used instead. Rick Monday took Rogers deep over the center field fence with two out, and it cost us our shot at the World Series. So now, forty years later, I'm with Jane Leavy and Lesley Visser at this Cape League game, and both women were in the clubhouse after the game in 1981. Lesley denied ever seeing anyone naked in the clubhouse, but Jane told her she was full of shit! Jane recalled that Warren Cromartie was wearing nothing but a friggin' towel and that he scurried under the food table when he saw Visser approaching. Jane correctly recalled that 'Cro' toppled the entire table, and that food was flying all over the place. Visser saw more swinging cocks than at some damned chain gang at a Louisiana penitentiary!"

Back at Jane's home, Bill was treated to a beautiful sunset.

"Here I was, standing at the same spot that Sandy Koufax had stood years ago, and the sun was going down. I looked out at the sinking sun and realized it was the same scenario as when I was looking out at the sunset in Malibu many years ago. Back then I was with my uncle, Grover Sowder, and this was the same type of venue. In Malibu, we were staring out towards Anacapa Island, and we were in Grover's home with Pat Riley, the basketball coach.* The name 'Anacapa' derived from the Chumash Native American name 'Anypakh.' There are three islands that make up the Channel Islands, and they are part of Channel Islands National Park. My grandma Hazel would sit out on the cliffs, and she would paint portraits of the rocks. She drew two paintings of one of the rocks, a large painting and a small one. I have the smaller one, but my former sister-in-law sold one out on the street, the cocksucker! She sold it outside of my Aunt Annabelle's home. I should have killed her. If I had killed her in Canada, I'd be out on parole by now."

* Pat Riley rented the house and then bought it.

So here was the Spaceman, watching the sunset in Truro down on the Cape, and he was transported back in time:

"So here I am watching the sun go down, and the sun reached the point where I knew what was going to happen next. This was the exact point of view I had in Malibu, and I instinctively knew what the sunset would look like. It got to a point where I told Jane, 'Wait for it, watch this!' When Jane saw the amazing sunset that I had described, she asked breathlessly, 'How did you know that?!' I told her about the sunsets in Malibu and of my meteorology background at USC. I knew from my vantage point that a front had stalled over Boston, and I saw the 'lining,' and when the sun peeked out and finally reached the horizon, it lit up the sky."

Jane Leavy—Skee-Ball Wizard

The Spaceman filled me in regarding one of Jane's hobbies:

"Jane plays this 'Skee-Ball Game,' but I'm not sure what it's about. It's about getting rings. You roll a ball up a ramp and try to get numbers. Jane holds the record with five 100s in a row. The game belongs in arcades; it's sort of like pinball.* I've never met Sandy Koufax, Mickey Mantle or Babe Ruth, but I've now met Jane Leavy!"

* Note: This greatly confused the author, who is normally confused as it is. I was afraid to ask if this is the Jewish version of Bocce.

"I KILLED JANE LEAVY'S DOG, AND APPARENTLY I'VE ALSO KILLED JANE LEAVY!" —BILL "SPACEMAN" LEE

"I explained to Jane that I awake in Craftsbury before the sun comes up, and I'm usually watching the sunset, too. I told her that nothing good happens other than on the first forty minutes of the morning or beyond the last forty minutes of the day. The rest belongs to the hitter. There are no timelines in baseball, there are just impatient people. Games aren't too long; people, especially hitters, are just impatient."

The Spaceman concluded by adding:

"I killed Jane Leavy's dog yesterday, and I think I killed her, too. I attempted to call her this morning, but she didn't answer her phone."

CHAPTER FORTY-SEVEN

Close Encounters of the Weird Kind #2

"Television is where you watch people in your living room that you would not want near your house." —*Groucho Marx*

The inevitable get-together between the earthling known as Bill "Spaceman" Lee and Ms. Jane Leavy evoked thoughts about other exceptional and perhaps even abnormal pairings in history. Consider that in September of 1959, after removing and banging his shoe atop a table at the United Nations in New York City, as part of his itinerary, Soviet Premier Nikita Khrushchev insisted on traveling to Hollywood, California to visit 20th Century Fox. However, the lone celebrity he wanted to meet—and can you blame him?—was Marilyn Monroe.

In 1953, playwright Samuel Beckett, who had just written *Waiting for Godot*, purchased land in a French commune forty miles north of Paris, and with the help of a Bulgarian-born farmer named Boris Rousimoff, he built a cottage on the property. Beckett (not to be confused with former Red Sox hurler, Josh Beckett, a renowned asshole) had a twelve-year-old son at the time, and the famous playwright befriended the youngster. The twelve-year-old child turned out to be the humongous professional wrestler known as "Andre the Giant."

In the early 1960s, Groucho Marx met T.S. Eliot, and that may be as close of a similarity as Jane Leavy meeting the Spaceman.

In 1904, Charles Stewart Rolls met Frederick Henry Royce. I believe you can figure out what transpired.

In March 1842, Charles Dickens met Edgar Allan Poe. Nevermore, however.

In October 1984, Steve Jobs met Andy Warhol!

In 1865, Ulysses Grant met General Robert E. Lee.

Then there was a truly unique meeting between the great actor and filmmaker Orson Welles and one of his early mentors. Welles was a teenager studying in both Germany and Austria in the 1930s, when he accompanied one of his teachers on a hike. The "educator" was a young aspiring fascist. His name was Adolph Hitler.................Rosebud!

My very favorite, however, was the curious meeting between Albert Einstein and Charlie Chaplin, the great actor of silent motion pictures. Einstein was still a German citizen when he traveled to Los Angeles, but the lone Hollywood star he wanted to meet was Charlie Chaplin. The following was a conversation between the two geniuses:

"Mr. Chaplin, what I most admire about your art, is your universality. You don't say a word, yet the world understands you!"

Charlie Chaplin responded as follows:

"True, Professor Einstein, but your glory is even greater! The whole world admires you, even though they don't understand a word of what you say."

Jane Leavy meets "Spaceman" Lee. It all makes sense, in some way.

CHAPTER FORTY-EIGHT

Memories of Hyannis

B ill Lee's visit with Jane Leavy awakened recollections of past trips to the Cape:

"I've known Dave Colombo for over twenty-five years," said the Spaceman. "Dave's father, Lou, was one of the greatest musicians of all time, but few know that he was also a legendary baseball player." And that he was.

Louis Bernard Colombo played baseball for Brockton High School for four years and NEVER struck out! Lou Colombo won a Silver Bat in American Legion ball and after graduating from Brockton High, he inked a contract to play professional baseball for the Brooklyn Dodgers. While playing in the minor leagues, incredibly, Lou Colombo struck out a mere 91 times in 2,774 at bats, but he suffered a devastating ankle injury that ended his baseball career. At the age of eighteen, Lou joined the army where he played trumpet in the army band during World War II, but Lou was not your average run-of-the-mill trumpet player. In fact, his musical career remains legendary to this day.

Bill Lee described Lou's genius as follows:

"Lou played trumpet with one hand! He played the valves with his right hand, but he didn't hold the horn with his left. He would play to capacity crowds at Colombo's Bistro on Main Street in Hyannis. Lou lived then in South Yarmouth. Lou was so renowned in the music business that he played with legends such as Charlie Spivak, Artie Shaw, and Prez Prado. He played jazz, swing, and even rag. He was a musical force on Cape Cod. Lou raised six children, one of them being my friend, Dave Colombo."

To prove once again the Spaceman's firm belief in connections, Lou moved to Fort Myers, Florida, the current spring training home of the Boston Red Sox, and even at his advanced age, Lou still entertained throngs with his musical wizardry. On March 3, 2012, moments after leaving the bandstand where he had just concluded another magnificent performance, Lou left a club and immediately got into a fatal car accident. Lou was eighty-four years of age and died just after doing what he so loved.

"So while I was visiting Jane Leavy, I was walking around Hyannis, when a complete stranger called out to me, 'You look familiar.' We got to talking, and the guy told me he was a friend of Dave Colombo! What are the odds? Dave also has a bar down in the area, and he had a bartender who could forge anyone's signature, including Ted Williams's! The guy was a renowned counterfeiter. Then again, so was Ted's son, John Henry, who would forge his own father's signature. I think that Dave Colombo owns 'The Black Cat,' a great bar down in Hyannis. It's down by the harbor where the ferries go out. I think that Dave also ran 'The Roadhouse Café' in Hyannis, and that was probably originally his dad's 'Colombo's Bistro.' It's near the carousel near the rotary."

CHAPTER FORTY-NINE

A Memory by the Author

The Dumbing of America

I Blame the Vietnam War & Evelyn Wood

Irwin was a childhood friend of mine in the South Bronx. The blonde-haired youth was a popular youngster with a great sense of humor. Irwin was a close friend and I recall his mom being perhaps the most beautiful young woman in our area.

Irwin was a classmate of mine at both PS 61 and at JHS 98, aka "Herman Ridder Junior High School." Irwin and I hung out together with numerous other friends and spent entire summers playing baseball, stickball and basketball and other sports in Crotona Park and often atop "the Plateau" overlooking the apartment buildings on Crotona Park East and Boston Road.

I recall playing in a pickup game one fine spring day with Irwin as my teammate. I managed to line a hit to right-center field with Irwin the runner at first base. As I rounded first, I was running with my head down, much in the manner I went through the early years of my life, oblivious to what was in front of me. In this instance, what was in front of me was Irwin, who had stumbled rounding second base, and as he scrambled back to the base, I was headed to that very same base, which of course, was already occupied by Irwin.

We youngsters in the South Bronx weren't exactly affluent, and our bases at that time were linoleum squares. Even home plate consisted of a chalk drawn creation. As the opposing team's shortstop hesitated as he attempted to figure out which one he should tag out, since both Irwin and yours truly were both standing on second base, Irwin, as I said, a youngster blessed with a quick wit, suddenly reached down, and shouted at me, "Quick! Grab this!" With that, Irwin tore the linoleum square (second base) in half and handed me one of the portions. With that, we both occupied separate second bases!

I immediately doubled over in laughter, as did the entire opposing ball club. However, their shortstop was reduced to tears, and he was laughing so hard that he couldn't move! He was frozen in place. Irwin immediately took off towards third base with no one in pursuit. We were both safe.........

As I recall, the game didn't even continue. None of us could cease laughing hysterically. Therefore, there was no need to resume playing.......................

I was an average student in those days, as was Irwin. I suppose we both fared well in those subjects that interested us. Life, as you are all aware, gets in the way of friendships, even close friendships. Irwin and his family moved away, presumably out of the Bronx, and we lost contact.

Many years later, a mutual friend of ours reported that Irwin had become a teacher at JHS 98. My first reaction was, "Irwin is a teacher? What could he possibly teach?"

Listen, I do not intend this as an insult to my childhood friend, but trust me, neither of us were qualified to teach ANYTHING.

Irwin became a teacher, as I learned, to avoid "the Draft," and therefore, having to serve in the US Army during the war in Vietnam. Countless other young men took the same nonviolent route to avoid being shipped overseas and participate in a controversial and unpopular conflict. I fault no one who exercised this option, and certainly none that served. Those were unusual and unique times. I avoid judging others religiously. That was, is, and will continue to be my wont.

My point is that the war in Vietnam contributed greatly to the dumbing down of America. There were literally thousands of "Irwins" who chose to alter the entire direction of their lives because of reasons I didn't, do not, nor will ever attempt to comprehend. However, just as the Second World War affected major league baseball, wherein the vast majority of big leaguers were called to serve, too often ineffectual "teachers" became the byproduct of the awful conflict in Southeast Asia.

By the late 1950s, America began its inexorable slide into the abyss of stupidity by its proclivity to heed to and adopt absurd theories, in my opinion. One such proposition was offered by a misguided woman named Evelyn Wood, who decided that inventing "speed-reading" would benefit students. Ms. Wood suggested that gathering and absorbing more information at a faster rate would assist us in education.......................Seriously.

Incredibly, many, and presumably my old and dear friend, Irwin, espoused these very practices. Unfortunately, this is still in effect, and I find the exercise senseless.

Upon sitting down to read a book, I want to inhale it, embrace it and drink in every word. Hell, to this moment, when reading a book, I keep a pad and pen handy to take notes and perhaps have an opportunity to ask questions of the author, or to question the historical facts within. I want the likes of the John Thorns and Jane Leavys to provide me with as much education as I can absorb.

Speed-reading? Sorry, folks. If I truly love a book, I do not want it to end, and when it does, I'll look forward to the day that I can revisit its magnificence. Words on paper. There is nothing greater on this planet.

I fear for our future.

I know for a fact, that only "Spaceman" Lee could have possibly been involved in such a play.

I wonder how Angel Hernandez would have ruled Irwin's "linoleum play."

Alas Poor Yorick, I Knew Him Well

And a Compendium of Short Stories

December 2020

The day I dreaded finally arrived. Annually, at this time of year, my long-suffering bride, Peg, saddles me with the responsibility of writing Xmas cards to people I hardly know and perhaps communicate with as often as the New York Jets win a football game.

Peg, of course, tosses a few boxes of these holiday greetings at me, as well as an address book, a book or three of colorful Christmas stamps, and return address stickers. I am instructed to add a banal comment or two beneath the lame unimaginative garble created by Hallmark or whomever, regarding our latest endeavor or situation.

Peg, of course, has zero intention of even perusing my scribblings before I send them off to our mailbox; this yearly accountability belonging to yours truly. Well, I decided to liven things up a bit this year and embellish, as it were, our messages to those eagerly awaiting our missives, or more than likely asking, "Who TF are the Russells?" I believe you see where this is going.

Having a vague idea as to the identity of some of these people and seeming to recall the fact that there existed zero likelihood that any of them were anticipating their Oxford scholarship acceptances in the mail, since I was burdened with this task, I thought I'd at least add some mirthfulness to the drab obliga-tion. Therefore, rather than include my name at the bottom of the card, I inked a "Season's Greetings, Peg and Kilgore Trout." I then grabbed Peg's iPhone and awaited the inevitable. Five days hence, I finally struck pay dirt.

Enthusiastically, I read the text message being transmitted onto Peg's iPhone. My affixation of "Season's Greetings from Peg and Kilgore Trout" had apparently and implausibly activated the brainwaves in the unlikeliest of sources.

"If I'm not being too personal," the communique read, "is Scott all right?"

Of course, being a thoughtful sort, I clumsily typed my response onto the screen. The brief exchange between "Peg" and the originator of the message, suddenly transformed my prior chore of penning Xmas cards into something truly worthwhile. Here it is verbatim:

Q: Is Scott all right?

Peg: I'm afraid he is gone.

Q: Gone?

Peg: Gone. Gone for good. Perished.

Q: Scott is dead?

Peg: Deader than you can imagine. Deader than Bruce Jenner's schlong. Deader than a plump rat who wandered into a marketplace in Wuhan, China. Dustier than a bookshelf in John Rocker's house.

Q: OMG, I had no idea. Was he ill?

Peg: Mentally, of course. But I had to rid myself of him.

Q: What? I'm not sure what you mean.

Peg: I contracted one of my Italian relatives from the North Shore. They'll never find his sorry ass.

Q: You had him killed? I thought he was a good guy.

Peg: He was an imbecile. Besides, he was a lousy lay.

Q: I'm not sure what to say.

Peg: You'll really like Kilgore Trout. You must visit us sometime.

Q: Well, Merry Xmas.

Peg soon asked me where her iPhone was, telling me she believes she misplaced it, and asked, "Did you mail all of those Xmas cards out the other day?"

"Yes, dear," I responded.

CHAPTER FIFTY

The Mind of the Spaceman

"Never let the truth get in the way of a good story."
Note: Mark Twain is generally given credit for this quote, but that might not be the truth.

The visitor's clubhouse at Tiger Stadium in Detroit had a sign that read: "No Visitors Allowed."

The following are random thoughts (not that he has any other kind) of "Spaceman" Lee:

"I played in the great Bob Feller's last game. It was one of those Hall of Fame games in Cooperstown. Feller was ninety years old at the time, and he was on the bump. I played right field in the last game 'Rapid Robert' pitched. Paul Molitor hit a BB right past Feller's head and he didn't even see it. It would've killed him. The next hitter was Steve Finley who had just retired. Finley hit a topspin line drive over my head that short-hopped the wall in right. I played it perfectly and held Finley to a single. The next hitter bounced into a force play. Finley was out at second and Molitor scored. They came out and took Feller out of the game. When I came into the dugout, Feller yelled at me, 'You've got to catch that fucking ball, Lee!' Feller was tough as nails, but he was a great guy. He was an entrepreneur minimalist. He was walking up and down Main Street in Cooperstown and selling books. I loved him!"

"My wife Diana is always yelling at me to clean up the house. She hates clutter. She told me if I cleaned up the house that I'd find things, but I told her it's better this way because each day is a treasure hunt!"

"I played great golf yesterday on the first five holes, but then I sobered up and the wheels fell off."

"I just watched the slowest animal in the world (a slug) crawling through my grass. He was climbing up a leaf at a forty-five-degree angle. He looked like Shrek."

"Bernie (Carbo) was stoned out of his gourd. He once had drugs shipped to him at the ballpark in Cleveland. He was so wasted he thought he was invisible."

"Bernie is precious. If Bernie was a flower, he'd be a peony. The peony is the most fragile flower I've ever seen. They spend so long in the bulb that ants must climb over them. I watch every flower from the moment it springs out of the ground to the moment it dies. I've watched groundhog holes for over two hours."

"I've had it with these 'Siris' giving you advice. These electronic devices are taking over. It's becoming a Danny Kahneman-type psychiatrist. I'm worried about 'voice recognition' to the extent it will be telling you by just hearing your voice that you may be having a stroke in four minutes and twenty-seven seconds."

"Me and my old friend Dr. Zoom (Gordy Grayburn) were thrown out of a Christian bookstore for asking if they had any nonfiction books."

"I once asked my old teammate Gary Peters why he always pushed himself to do torturous stretching exercises, and he answered, 'So someday I can blow myself.'"

The Spaceman admitted to the author that he truly loves watching the sport of "curling," at least when the young women on the Swedish team are yelling, "Hurry, hurry, hard!"

The Spaceman also admitted that it was understandable, at least to him, when the women's Norwegian volleyball team was fined for doing a photo shoot in bathing suits rather than in their tradition bikinis. "Hell," said Lee, "that's why we watch!"

CHAPTER FIFTY-ONE

Mudcat: The Kid and an Insubordinate in Need of a Life Lesson

"Jim 'Mudcat' Grant, who passed away on Saturday, June 13, 2021 at the age of eighty-five was a sweetheart of a man. He was a great guy, a terrific pitcher, and he had a heart of gold." —*Bill "Spaceman" Lee*

One of seven children born to hardworking parents born in the deeply segregated South, Jim "Mudcat" Grant was no stranger to racism. Grant, an African American, first saw the light of day in a town called Lacoochee, Florida in 1935, forty miles north of Tampa, in a place where blacks had little or no rights.

Jim Grant became an outstanding athlete and signed a meager deal with the Cleveland Indians in the hope he would become a major league pitcher one day. However, he knew that the road would not be easy.

In the spring of 1958, a year that would herald Grant's arrival in the major leagues, spring training in the South was still completely segregated. While white players enjoyed the privileges of luxury hotels and fine dining, black players were housed "across the tracks," so to speak, far away from the benefits of big league life.

Upon Jim Grant's arrival in Sarasota where his Cleveland team had arrived to play an exhibition game against the Boston Red Sox, Grant was advised that his luggage had mistakenly been delivered to the "white hotel." Therefore, Grant arrived at the hotel to retrieve his bag.

Jim "Mudcat" Grant, now an aspiring twenty-two-year-old "major league athlete," was stopped in his tracks by an equally young white employee of the hotel.

"Where you goin', boy?" the officious young man demanded.

"My bags were delivered here in error. I'm just here to pick them up."

The young white racist shouted, "Stop right there, boy. You ain't goin' nowhere. Leave right now!" With that, the angry young man pointed sternly towards the door.

Unseen by either Jim Grant or the decidedly unfriendly hotel employee, the great Ted Williams had entered the lobby of the hotel and had witnessed the hostility spewed by the hotel employee.

As Ted Williams approached the two young men, he inquired, "What seems to be the problem?"

The angry youngster, of course, recognized Teddy Ballgame, as did, of course, Jim Grant.

"I told the negro to leave. He ain't allowed in here!"

Jim Grant explained, "I just came to pick up my suitcase, Ted. They delivered it here by accident." Ted Williams glared at the hotel employee and asked, "Do you want to continue working here?"

"Yes, sir," was the response.

Ted Williams immediately instructed the obstinate hotel employee, "Then this is what you MUST do. You go get *Mister* Grant's luggage and you PERSONALLY deliver it to where Mister Grant is staying. Do you understand?!"

The young racist, now humiliated by the great Ted Williams, replied sheepishly, "Yes, sir."

With that, Ted Williams put his arm around the shoulder of Jim "Mudcat" Grant and said softly, but loud enough for the hotel employee to hear, "Jim, please let me know if you have any problem."

In a fourteen-year career, Jim "Mudcat" Grant, compiled a record of 145-119 in 571 games and also totaled 53 saves and 89 complete games! In 1965, Grant finished sixth in the AL MVP voting in compiling a 21-7 record and leading the Minnesota Twins to the World Series.

In February 2007, during an event to honor Black History Month, President George W. Bush honored Grant, Ferguson Jenkins, Dontrelle Willis, and Mike Norris at the White House.

In 2012, Jim Grant entered the "Baseball Reliquary Shrine of the Eternals," honoring the history of blacks in baseball.

Throughout his life, Jim "Mudcat" Grant was quick to pay homage to the history of blacks in baseball.

As I recall, the Ted Williams fellow wasn't too shabby of a hitter, either.

BEGINNINGS

In Which the Author, "Scott Russell" or Whomever, Receives a New Career Opportunity

SCOTT RUSSELL, ORATOR, AMERICAN PATRIOT, DEFENDER OF THE FLAG, BON VIVANT & FUTURE OF OUR GREAT NATION

"I HAVE NOT COME TO PRAISE CAESAR"

The lovely young woman's timing could not have been more precise. She had arrived at our door at the very moment two "Jehovah's Witnesses" went scurrying back to the safety of their foreign automobile. Little did this young woman realize at the time that she had perhaps hatched a new career for the aging nitwit known as "Scott Russell." Such is life. It is written.

"Leave this instant, you un-circumcised Philistines! I shall smite you with my mighty sword!"

My brief, but powerful oration had been delivered with a bombast and an elocution that would have impressed even the lowliest of citizens. It was prescience (now I must repair to look up the word "prescience," but I digress) at its utmost dominion.

As the two acolytes of Charles Taze Russell, who I falsely claimed was my "Uncle Charlie," drove off in fear, Peg, my long-suffering bride, looked on in both bemusement and horror. The poor woman removed the half-empty bottle of Grey Goose vodka I had been waving around as if it were an ancient artifact, perhaps an old American League chest protector.

The conversation with the Jehovah's Witnesses had ended abruptly when I frustrated the male of the pair by proclaiming that if it were not for infusions, my wife and I would be deceased. I will not go into his retort, but it was then that I launched into my tirade, a response that would have impressed the great, late Dr. Hunter S. Thompson. As I waved my fist at the panic-stricken "clergyman," he quickly entered the driver's side of his escape vehicle. He did not hold the door open for his "fellow" clergywoman. Chivalry apparently perished on the cross. Such is the price of salvation.

It was then that the aforementioned young woman smiled at us and asked if we had a moment or two to speak with her. We immediately acquiesced, although I immediately regretted not having an American flag draped around my shoulders at that moment.

Note: As many of you are aware, I ABHOR partisan politics, and that goes for the countless nitwits on BOTH sides of the aisle. However, this brave young attractive woman really represented one of those sides............ But I adamantly refuse to identify which one. Speculate to your heart's content. You will only get my name, rank, and serial number.

What began as a conversation on our front steps, soon evolved into a blessed event that (gulp) saw yours truly invite, as God is my judge, a young politician into our home!!!! I soon learned that this young woman, who shall remain nameless, is the chairman (chairwoman?) of our town, a delegate at our state conventions, and had twenty-plus years as a pharmaceutical industry professional with a focus on cancer therapy. For the next thirty minutes—she was on her way to five o'clock mass at our local church—we discussed the sorry state of partisan politics.

Incredibly, I was impressed. The mere fact that she witnessed an aging fool threatening a pair of Bible-waving imbeciles, somehow avoiding their imminent death, and was not at all intimidated, told me that this was a true woman of God. She had won me over. Peg looked on in what I assume was some form of shock. Her crazed husband was in the middle of engaging in civil discourse with a politician! Oh, the hypocritical ramifications of such an unlikely meeting.

All right, now it gets crazier: This young woman will be appearing at a fundraiser later this month............Do you see where this is going? This fine lady, and I testify that she appeared to be both sane and sentient, informed me that she does not have a "keynote speaker" for the event..........She asked if I were interested................Honest. Peg witnessed the entire conversation.

I, of course, answered—and truthfully—to this brilliant young woman that I would strongly consider it, but informed her that, in the event I did appear, that my oration would not be kindly to either of our two unfortunate partisan political parties. Implausibly, she stated that she would still desire me to speak.

Well, there you have it. I am considerably younger than Bernie, and much better looking (and modest to a fault) than all of the other male candidates. Who knows, this may be the very beginning of a new career for your humble servant.

Oh, I did not mention the Bulgarian midget in the basement and the fourteen Dominican nuns at the nearby convent. The young politician, thankfully, did not notice the yak grazing in our backyard.

I look forward to my own oratory. There will be no notes. I will "wing it," so to speak. Oh, and I am bringing the earthling known as Bill "Spaceman" Lee to the gathering. A man has got to eat.

Somewhere, I suspect, Dr. Hunter S. Thompson is beaming..........or perhaps threatening to rip my lungs out while referring to me as a "mutant pigfucker." Nevertheless, I eagerly await the next step in my improbable and maudlin existence.

I wonder if the Jehovah's Witnesses will return. I want to offer them my plasma.

IN ADDITION

The following conversation took place between yours truly (a nitwit) and a priest (Father Thomas) at a local church. I wrote this over two and a half years ago. However, I am still a nitwit.

SR: Forgive me Father, for I have sinned.

FT: What sins have you committed, my son?

SR: For the past several years I've been living in sin with fourteen Dominican nuns, a pet yak, and a Bulgarian midget.

FT: Surely you jest, my son, and yes I'll call you "Shirley" if I choose to; it's my rectory.

SR: Yes, Father.

FT: Oh, and fourteen Dominican nuns? That's absurd.

SR: All right, perhaps there were merely three Dominican nuns, and there may have been a Franciscan nun mixed in, too.

FT: The yak is somewhat disturbing, too.

SR: Well, Father, I'm not an expert on yaks. Perhaps it's an emu. How does one tell the difference?

FT: I've been to your home on several occasions, Scott. I can assure you I've never seen a farm animal, just cats. I fear you're delusional.

SR: Speaking of my home, Father, I suspect that Peg is having an affair with Donald Duck.

FT: Scott, that photograph of your lovely wife is over thirty years old, and that duck happened to be a young woman.

SR: My wife is a lesbian?

FT: Seriously, Scott. I cannot have you sit in the confessional booth all morning. And besides, you're Jewish.

SR: You discriminate?

FT: You are exasperating, my son.

SR: I can no longer be Jewish, Father. Natalie Portman rejected me. I want to convert.

FT: You don't even know Natalie Portman, Scott, and she certainly does not even know who you are. Once more, you are delusional. Have you ever considered professional help?

SR: Yes, Father, but I was told not to come back. Something about me discouraging the other patients.

FT: If you do decide to convert, Scott, I suggest the Catholic Church in Wrentham.

SR: What? Don't you love me any longer, Father? Besides, what do you have against the church in Wrentham?

FT: That's a valid point, Scott. However, God does love you. He has a wonderful sense of humor. After all, He created you.

SR: Father, if I converted, do you think I'd stand a chance with Jen Bricker?

FT: Scott, my son, you're old enough to be Jen Bricker's father. It's not a realistic quest. Besides, you're happily married.

SR: Thank you, Father. I'll see you next Sunday.

FT: I was afraid of that. Oh, and if you do come, please leave that Bulgarian midget home. Zoltoc is annoying my other parishioners.

SR: Father, do you think Emily Ratajkowski would like me?

FT: Surely you jest.

SR: Please don't call me "Shirley," Father.

FT: I'll light a candle for you, my son.

Scott Russell, Aspiring Viking

At the tender age of nineteen, the author was informed, in no uncertain terms, that it was imperative that he seek full-time employment. In my day, unfortunately, rather than show gratitude for allowing youngsters to sponge off them for nearly two decades, ungrateful parents would insist that their offspring earn their keep, as it were. Therefore, young Scott Russell was summarily removed from his comfortable surroundings and ordered out into the frightening world of adulthood.

My first stop was Snelling & Snelling, an employment agency in the heart of Manhattan. I was immediately impressed with the offices of the prospective employment agency and even more impressed with the shapely legs of my interviewer, a lovely middle-aged (most likely in her thirties, which for a nineteen-year-old thug from the South Bronx seemed somewhat ancient, but I digress) woman named "Adele Joyce." Most employment "recruiters" in those ancient times went under assumed names.

Adele summoned me to her cubicle (she apparently did not have an office) and pointed to a seat. I immediately ascertained that I was to sit down at that point. The attractive brunette then inquired as to my job preference.

"What type of work do you wish to pursue?" she asked.

"Viking," I responded.

"Pardon?" The poor woman looked a bit confused.

"Viking," I repeated. "I would like to rape, pillage and plunder, although truthfully, I have absolutely no idea what plundering entails."

Surprisingly, Ms. Joyce laughed and smiled at me. I must have appeared to be a lost pup of some sort.

"How are you with math?" she asked.

"Fairly good," I replied, although at the time I was more interested in Ms. Joyce's measurements. Those numbers intrigued me.

Within minutes, Ms. Joyce sent me on my way to Columbia University, an institution of higher learning, a prestigious Ivy League college at 116th Street and Broadway. I was interviewed by a gentleman named Ross Hendricks of Spokane, Washington. For some reason unknown to mankind, he took a liking to the young hoodlum from da Bronx. I was hired and within a year, Ross provided me with a title. I was promoted to the position of "Assistant Property Supervisor of the Government Contract Division of Columbia University."..............Ross said it would look good on my résumé.

I had sought and successfully achieved gainful employment. I was on my way. To what, I still have no idea. My days as a prospective Viking were never attained. If only Ms. Adele Joyce had shared my vision..........She sure had nice legs, though.

CHAPTER FIFTY-THREE

Welcome to "Big Dick's Halfway Inn."

We Put the "Ho" in Hotel!

Our slogan is – "Because you deserve better than the backseat of a car."

"If we knew you were staying all night, we'd have changed the sheets."

The earthling known as Bill "Spaceman" Lee and his Canadian bride, the lovely Diana, were en route to their dear departed friend Rheal Cormier's memorial tribute (see chapter thirty-two) in Moncton, New Brunswick, Canada, but first they'd have to somehow make it past United States Customs in Waterville, hard by the Canadian border. In past years before the bizarre age of Covid, this was no picnic to begin with, but now the "regulations" imposed by the US government made such a trip even more daunting.

What began as an anticipated delay became the human version of a surrealistic painting by Van Gogh. As the Spaceman explained in describing his mid-August 2021 foray into Canada:

"They stopped to question us for half an hour. Four people jabbering at us as they looked in our backseat. I basically told them, 'Listen—these are not the Covid tests you're looking for,' but they kept on. This is how screwed up our healthcare system is. They tested us for Covid and told us it would take up to seventy-two hours for us to be allowed into Canada, the information was put into a portal of some sort. But then AFTER they let us in, they told us the results would not be available for another forty-eight hours! They called it an 'RT,' whatever the hell that is. Does that stand for 'rapid test' or 'rat turd?' There is no logic to our system. But somehow I pulled an 'Obi-Wan Kenobi' and we made it into Canada."

In the life of "Spaceman" Lee, however, seldom does anything go entirely smooth, and this would be no exception:

"We were so happy crossing into New Brunswick. It was foggier than shit—'Nightmare on Elm Street' foggy. We had arrived at the Algonquin Inn at St. Andrews by-the-Sea. We immediately see a beautiful little cottage with a vacancy sign. I told Diana I was hungry, so I figured we'd eat and stay there tonight. So, we pulled into the first parking spot right in front of the lobby of the Algonquin Manor. We had just had a great meal, the best halibut, the best drinks, the best dessert, the best waiter, everything was perfect, but when we went back to the hotel, the sign no read, 'No Vacancy.' We're back in the car, driving around, but we can't find a room, we're approaching St. John, New Brunswick, it's dripping fog, my lights are faltering, and we end up at the fucking Bates Motel!"*

| * Listen, this is the Spaceman, so please indulge him/us:

"We turn off the highway, and there it is! Through the fog, in all its ominous glory, is the fucking Bates Motel! This godforsaken place is in Lorneville, just west of St. John. There's an Indian (East Indian) in the lobby (he's apparently the proprietor), and he's wearing a 'kurta.' * He's talking on the phone, he's speaking in English to some other East Indian calling him from either India or perhaps Canada, and he's telling the woman, 'No, you cannot barbeque a goat in your hotel room. We don't allow it.' (For the record, the Spaceman effects a perfect East Indian accent). The guy turns to me during his phone conversation and apologizes for the wait. I told him I was fine."

| * A "kurta" is the traditional East Indian garb for men, although in recent years, it has become a unisex clothing item. And you thought Americans were the lone progressives.

The tale of "The Bates Motel,"—and that, of course, is not its actual name—was not over as the Spaceman further expounded:
"In the morning, I woke up and walked out to my car. On the way back up to my room, a fucking scraggly girl with a cigarette dangling from her lips walks up to me and asked, 'Excuse me, do you have a condom?' She was 'methed' out of her mind. I answered, 'Excuse me, I'm a bit hard of hearing, did you just ask if I had a condom?' She replied, 'Yes.' I responded, 'Do I look like the kind of guy who would wear a condom?' She walked down to the lower level of the motel where there were about seven other guys. She then walked over to the Indian (the proprietor) and repeated the question to him. He reached into his pocket and handed her a condom."

Once you stop spitting up your coffee, please allow the Spaceman to end this segment with, "Apparently, she was 'working' the floors, but she was definitely not a chambermaid."

Bill and Diana then got into their vehicle and proceeded on their journey to honor Rheal Cormier in Moncton, New Brunswick. Things were about to get considerably better.

"We went from a leper colony to Room 410 at the Canvas Hotel on Queen Street in Moncton. The place is great. We're in a balcony that has two Adirondack chairs overlooking the Petitcodiac River at the headwaters of the Bay of Fundy's Tidal Bore. There is a king-sized bed and two additional rooms and a tub and a shower. I've got two IPAs on ice and two bottles of wine. And a huge flat-screen TV. Plus there's no broad asking me for a condom and no one is trying to barbeque a goat.

"Earlier, I had attended a clinic. I was the only one in uniform. I go out to the stations and wander around while I do my stretching exercises. I can't teach the kids until I do my stretching. I wound up going over to the pitching station and I wound up throwing to every girl who came through the station. The girls' fathers all told me, 'Mr. Lee, that was the greatest experience of my daughter's life.' I replied, 'You know what? If they want to play baseball, you're right!' Afterwards, I told their fathers what each had to work on to improve. I then signed lots of autographs, including baseballs. It was a beautiful day."

CHAPTER FIFTY-FOUR

Flashbacks

REALLY BAD IDEAS—NEW WINNER ANNOUNCED!

#3—In 1940, bandleader Tommy Dorsey had his orchestra enter the monkey house of the Philadelphia Zoo to perform a concert for the apes.

#2—In 1949, a Nobel Prize in Medicine was awarded to the man who perfected the lobotomy.

Speaking of lobotomies, we have a new leader atop the summit of "REALLY BAD IDEAS."

#1—On May 3, 2021, the New York Mets fired hitting coach Chili Davis and replaced him with a former screenwriter and bartender named ....Hugh Quattlebaum!

In the immortal words of Casey Stengel, "You can look it up."

The harrowing experience at the "Bates Motel" brought back memories of other close calls incurred by the Spaceman during his various sojourns across Canada. Once during an unfortunate trip (see chapters fourteen & fifteen) back from western Canada, Bill Lee had a close encounter with a raging bull. As the Spaceman recalled:

"Somehow my license blew across a field and each time I attempted to pick it up, this jersey bull was running up my ass, but every time I stopped, he stopped. Once the bull almost caught me, but I managed to jump over a barbwire fence just before he was about to gore me."

The Spaceman had also had a less than auspicious day in a Senior League game recently, and his hapless team was to blame for the defeat. As Lee explained:

"I threw the shit out of the ball today, but my team was throwing the damned ball all over the lot. I had a premonition about this game, and sadly, it was realized. My team unfortunately is all academics. There was a filmographer from California videoing our game for a movie he's making called 'Eephus,' although this movie has already been made. It should be called 'The Spirit of Paul Blair.' It was mystical. I got fucked in this entire game. I wound up throwing twelve eephus pitches, and all but one was excellent. The kid was working with Brett Rapkin, who produced some of my other videos. I gave up two runs in the first inning, thanks to some lousy fielding. I knew before the game even began that something was amiss. A black dog ran out onto the field, and it said hello to every one of the opposing players. He must have been delivering genes and gloves. The dog was homeless, but I know that dog was the reincarnation of someone significant."

The Spaceman drew a deep breath and continued:

"You'd have to read W.P. Kinsella's short story 'Distances,' to fully understand. We were down two runs because of lousy fielding, and then I led off the third inning with a perfect bunt, but their third baseman made a great play and threw me out by a half-step. Meanwhile their left fielder was making every play possible. He was like a gazelle, and he was better than Freddie Lynn! This kid, and he was thin, covered so much ground! He caught every ball but one, and on that one he made a great play and held our hitter to a single. I got two hits, but when I led off the ninth inning, I told my team that if I walked, we would come back and win (we were down by two runs). I didn't walk, but got a base hit and my team got all pumped. When we lost, I told them, 'No! I said we'd win if I got a walk! I didn't get a walk; I got a hit!'

"I kept the game close, but my fielders were just awful. Three unearned runs bled me to death. The first two runs I allowed were both earned, but mental mistakes prevented me from getting them out. The last three runs were definitely unearned runs. My second baseman looked like he was doing an imitation of Denny Doyle in the 1975 World Series, when the little SOB was doing everything in his power to avoid contact with Pete Rose, who was ready to knock him into 1976. On that play Doyle looked like Mary Martin (the girl who played Peter Pan in the movie)."

The bizarre scenario extended beyond the field of play, however:

"I looked up on the hill (overlooking the field) where Diana had been sitting in our truck, but she's gone. I knew she wouldn't be hard to find, though. I just drove out through the cornfields just like in *Field of Dreams*, and Diana was in the parking lot down by the Utopia Brewing Company.

She was going to pick me up and we were going to have a beer, but I couldn't find her in the parking lot. She was hidden by the dumpster and could no longer speak English."

The Spaceman continued with some additional hilarity:

"After the game, Rodney Scott called from Indianapolis, and he also was having some problems. I told Breeze that we should run away together. Of all the people to call me after a rough day it was the second baseman who SHOULD have been behind me. Breeze was the best defensive infielder I ever played with, and we were BOTH blackballed from baseball. I told Breeze that we should film a remake of *The Defiant Ones*, an African American and a white guy chained together. We could make a lot of money filming a motion picture about two blackballed ballplayers running away in chains!"*

> * *The Defiant Ones* starred Sidney Poitier and Tony Curtis, who escaped from a prison while shackled to each other.

So how was your day?

CHAPTER FIFTY-FIVE

Up On Cripple Creek

"Some days you eat the bear. Some days the bear eats you."
—*Anonymous*

"Up on Cripple Creek, she sends me
If I spring a leak, she mends me
I don't have to speak, she defends me
A drunkard's dream if I ever did see one."
—*Jaime "Robbie" Robertson of the Band.*

The very first thing the earthling known as Bill "Spaceman" Lee told me on the morning of Tuesday, August 17, 2021 was "I want to see a black bear today." The Spaceman made that wish during breakfast that morning, and although there are indeed black bears roaming around the Catskill Mountains in and around Big Indian, New York, they tend to mostly avoid what passes for civilization. But this is Bill Lee we're talking about.

When we awoke the following morning, Peg had already brewed coffee for me, the Spaceman, and his bride, Diana. Bill Lee beckoned us to the kitchen window of the cottage we were sharing and pointed out the location his truck sat after experiencing what was most certainly an eventful night.

"Holy crap!" I exclaimed as I immediately became aware of the debris surrounding the Spaceman's truck. After surmising the significant mess encircling Bill Lee's vehicle, Peg, recalling Bill's wish of desiring to see a black bear that day, cautioned, "Be careful what you wish for." However, the Spaceman, being the Spaceman, was not at all dismayed at seeing what a black bear had wrought.

Upon walking out to the vehicle, we noticed that unopened beer cans were strewn all over the gravel parking area, but that the huge black bear, whom we never actually saw, had indeed made off with the bottled Lite beer that the Spaceman had stored in his cooler.

The Spaceman, truly pleased at what he had discovered, opined, "I guess the bear was on a diet. He only made off with the Lite beer bottles." However, I responded, "Bill, I believe the reason for his choice was merely not having opposable thumbs, that the beast was incapable of opening the beer cans." Nevertheless, the bear no doubt threw a rather private bash for himself as we slept, and in fact, attempted to make off with his largesse, as we spotted the Spaceman's cooler some seventy-five feet into the woods. Then it got even better, at least for the bear. We became aware that there were several wrappers scattered around the vehicle, capsules which once contained brownies. Since these brownies were indeed baked by the Spaceman, I advise you to use your imagination as to their ingredients.

Peg took her iPhone out and began taking photographs of the destruction the bear had left in his wake, and this included the discarded empty wrappers and what once was a significant amount of beer. Suffice to say that there was no doubt a black bear was staggering around the woods of the Catskill Mountains smiling and stoned out of its gourd. There is no word if the bear has since entered a rehab facility.

I want you to keep in mind there were no more than seventy-five to eighty folks at this campsite, but ONLY one truck was broken into by a black bear. Such incidents are countless when examining the life of the Spaceman.

The reason we had all congregated in the charming little hamlet of Big Indian, New York, was to hang out with the enormously great "The Weight Band," a group of some of the most legendary singers and musicians in rock 'n' roll history. "Camp Cripple Creek," as it is renowned, hosts an annual gathering some thirty miles out of the iconic Woodstock, New York, and also near the town of Saugerties, where the music of "Big Pink" (the Band) was recorded. The history of that place is synonymous with Bob Dylan and many other musical giants of the industry.

The original band included the following: Levon Helm, Garth Hudson, Rick Danko, Richard Manuel, and Jaime "Robbie" Robertson. Levon, who passed in 2012, anointed several members of the Weight Band to replace the originals after they became ill or deceased. Therefore, the Weight Band is NOT a tribute or cover band, they are the Band, and in the author's opinion, just as great, if not greater than the original.

Levon Helm, the heart and soul of the Band, was one of the truly great musicians in the annals of rock 'n' roll history, as well as a wonderfully eccentric character. As for The Weight Band, its members have transitioned from one to another for a myriad of reasons, sadly including the unexpected and tragic death of Marty Grebb and the departure of Randy Ciarlante, who, although he joined us at Camp Cripple Creek, no longer wished to endure life on the road.

As for Levon and the highlight of our stay at Camp Cripple Creek, other than the visitation by the huge black bear (see the photograph of the Spaceman examining its formidable paw prints on the back of his truck), seeing Levon's lovely widow, Sandy, enjoying the music, was beyond heartwarming. Levon, a lead vocalist and extraordinary drummer for the Band, was also a terrific actor. The hilarious Levon Helm tales told by many of those present at Camp Cripple Creek would fill an entire book, especially the stories told by Levon's lovely road manager, Barbara O'Brien.

The current members of the musically gifted Weight Band include alphabetically, Michael Bram, Brian Mitchell, Albert Rogers, Jim Weider, and Matt Zeiner. There can easily be an analogy drawn between a baseball team and a rock 'n' roll band. People from all walks of life and backgrounds joining together to create harmony and cohesion. Oh, and ALL members of the Weight Band bonded with the Spaceman almost immediately, all of them being aware of Bill's successful pitching career and wonderful eccentricities (See the photo section for several examples of their interaction).

In addition to the legendary singers and musicians, also performing were the incredible "Sisters of Slide," two of the greatest slide guitarists in history, Cindy Cashdollar and Rory Block, who is also an authentic blues singer. Also present were legends Dave Bromberg, a man whose vocals and guitar playing are unsurpassed in the industry, as well as the great Larry Packer, and Larry Campbell, who served as Bob Dylan's lead guitarist for a decade. Campbell, who can seemingly play any instrument known to mankind, hit it off with the Spaceman, who immediately noted Larry's amazing facial resemblance to Lee's former pitching teammate, Dennis Eckersley. There is a photo in this book, in fact, of the Spaceman lecturing Larry Campbell in utilizing the proper technique to relieve stress in his shoulder! It turns out that Larry Campbell is also an athlete!

CHAPTER FIFTY-SIX

A Piece of the Action

Coquetry 101

When Mail-Order Brides Go Awry

> Hooker: It's ten dollars on the grass, thirty on the sofa, and fifty in bed.
> John: I'll pay fifty.
> Hooker: You're a man of class.
> John: Class my ass; I want it five times on the grass.

Trevor Bauer is perhaps the Spaceman's favorite current major league pitcher. Bauer, much like Bill Lee, is an eccentric, delightfully off-the-wall character and like his predecessor, the Spaceman, Bauer marches to the beat of his own drummer. It stands to reason then, that young Trevor Bauer often finds himself "over the old proverbial line."

I recall an old joke—its origin escapes me, but it goes like this: A man approaches a lovely stranger and asks, "Would you sleep with me for a thousand dollars?" The woman, although taken aback, hesitates before responding, "Yes, for a thousand dollars, I would sleep with you." The man then counters with, "How about sleeping with me for fifty dollars?" Insulted and infuriated, the woman angrily replies, "How dare you?! What kind of woman do you think I am?!" The man, fully composed, answers, "We've already established what kind of woman you are. We're merely negotiating a price."

Listen, Trevor Bauer was a fool for getting himself into a world of trouble early in the 2021 baseball season, but as the Spaceman often exclaims, "Boys will be boys." Oh, and long before a Los Angeles judge issued her verdict on the assault charges filed against the former Cy Young Award winner, Bill Lee offered to represent him in court, once more quoting his colorful former Red Sox hurler friend, Dick Radatz, who has inscribed on his tombstone, "Can't a Man Unwind?"

Upon seeing that Trevor Bauer had been charged by a young nameless woman on June 28, 2021, and placed on paid leave by his employer, the Los Angeles Dodgers, the earthling known as Bill "Spaceman" Lee immediately smelled a rat, and his name was not Trevor Bauer. In a sixty-seven-page ex-parte document, whatever the hell that is, the young woman plaintiff claimed that the colorful and ofttimes unconventional Bauer assaulted her on two different occasions. The document is quite vivid, and it includes graphic vice as the accuser and the defendant apparently engaged in wild sexual encounters which included various barbaric acts of a depraved nature.

The Spaceman, a renowned skeptic, as is the author, immediately suspected that perhaps the young "lady" was merely attempting to "shake-down" a wealthy athlete for wads of cash. At the time the story hit the news, the Spaceman stated, "I want to be Bauer's defense lawyer. Two people engaging in kinky sex, this is a normal occurrence in the world of athletes and performers. My opening statement would be, 'Never bite off more than you can chew.'"

Before you believe that the Spaceman is a typical member of the species, and you'd be at least partially correct, please allow him to continue:

"This could've happened to me at least seventeen times. Somewhere Mickey Mantle is smiling. If the prosecution says, 'I object,' I will counter with, 'Exactly!' I feel badly for Trevor, even if he was a fool for getting involved with this woman. This type of thing happened in Milwaukee, in Kansas City. It happened everywhere."

I want you to consider that she initiated contact with Bauer through an Instagram direct message and that she claimed that Bauer "assaulted" her during the sexual encounters at his Pasadena home on April 21 and May 16, but that what began as a consensual relationship that included AGREED-UPON rough sex, led to, well, rougher sex! Oh, and get this: The woman admitted to the judge that the "choking part was consensual." The judge, a superior court judge named Dianna Gould-Saltman, ruled the following: "The woman said 'she wanted all the pain.' Those were her own words."

Judge Gould-Saltman, God bless her, also stated:

"We consider that, in the context of a sexual encounter, when a woman says 'No,' she should be believed, so what about when she says 'Yes'?"

In denying the young "lady's" civil domestic restraining order, Judge Gould-Saltman also ruled, "The defendant, Trevor Bauer, honored her boundaries." The superior court judge also stated that Bauer did not pose a threat to the twenty-seven-year-old woman, and therefore, denied the restraining order.

Of course, in such instances, the accusations make headlines, but the retractions are too often on page ninety-six in a small box in the back of a newspaper.

This reminded the Spaceman of an occasion when a man offered to pay his buddy, Red Sox reliever Dick "The Monster" Radatz, to "throw oranges at his bare ass."

Listen, supplication can be a tricky thing. We apologize for bringing religion into this; however, supplication is the action of asking or begging for something earnestly or humbly, a prayer asking God's help as part of a religious service, invocation, divine service, a reverent petition to a deity.

The Spaceman has a suggestion for young Trevor Bauer which goes as follows:

"Bauer should seek a job doing pornos in the San Fernando Valley. He can be the new 'Long John Holmes.'"

Only the Spaceman can conclude with, "Both Trevor Bauer and Jackie Robinson have something in common. Neither were allowed to cross into Glendale."

As for the superior court judge who denied the plaintiff's restraining order, the Spaceman noted that Bauer fulfilled the requests made by the young "lady," but that Dick Radatz should have been sued by the gentleman who wanted Radatz to throw oranges at his bare ass, because Radatz was so wild, he failed to connect! At least the guy had a case against Radatz.

Said the Spaceman, "Trevor Bauer will never be convicted by a jury of his pears (sic). .....All right, orange you going to laugh?"

Thus concludes this chapter on responding to inducements and/or enticements on Instagram. Oh, and Trevor Bauer remains the Spaceman's very favorite modern-day hurler.

CHAPTER FIFTY-SEVEN

A First Glanz (*sic*) Can Be Deceiving

Dear Mr. Postman

"There are three side effects of acid: enhanced long-term memory, decreased short-term memory, and I forget the third."
—*Dr. Timothy Leary*

"LSD is a psychedelic drug which occasionally causes psychotic behavior in people who have not taken it." —*Dr. Timothy Leary*

"In the information age, you don't teach philosophy as they did after feudalism. You perform it. If Aristotle were alive today, he'd have a talk show." —*Dr. Timothy Leary*

"I hung a curve ball to José Canseco, and he hit the shit out of it."
—*Pitcher Timothy James Leary, New York Yankees, 1990*

"The Big Guy in the sky that everyone worships is a jester. He's dancing. He's like 'Pan' in *A Midsummer Night's Dream*. It's like Shakespeare on acid. Why else would I receive this letter? Is this a coincidence? I think not." —*Bill "Spaceman" Lee*

Like most former major league baseball players, the earthling known as Bill "Spaceman" Lee receives a great deal of fan mail. However, 99.9 percent of the time, the fan mail was intended for him. The following is not one of those times.

In the late summer of 2021, perhaps the most bizarre year in history, the Spaceman retrieved his mail and read a request addressed to "Tim Leary," however the envelope contained Bill's address in Vermont. Is this some sort of joke? thought the Spaceman. After all, Dr. Timothy Leary was a controversial counterculture professor at Harvard University from 1960-62, and he lectured on the "Harvard Psilocybin Project," a fact that raised both eyebrows and a significant amount of ire from his fellow faculty members.

Dr. Timothy Leary, in fact, encouraged his students to use drugs and was summarily fired by the university in 1963. Oh, and Dr. Leary was also incarcerated in thirty-six different prisons worldwide. Dr. Leary believed in what he referred to as "mind expansion." However, the "Tim Leary" that the Spaceman received fan mail for was not the psilocybin advocate, but a retired veteran right-handed pitcher who toiled for seven major league teams during the period from 1981-1994.

As best we can, we will attempt to explain why we believe (one can never be certain as Daniel Kahneman attempted to teach us) Bill Lee received an autograph request for Tim Leary, at his home in Craftsbury, Vermont, despite the fact that Tim Leary, pitcher, resides in Santa Monica, California.

To begin with, a fifteen-year-old boy was the author of the letter intended for Tim Leary but mailed to the Spaceman. The boy's name is Anthony Glanz and he resides in South Hampton, New York. As with most youngsters seeking major league autographs, the youngster wrote politely and thoughtfully. He informed the Spaceman that he loved the game of baseball, and that Tim Leary was his hero. Please note how it's unlikely that a fifteen-year-old boy would have a rather obscure hero who had pitched in the majors long before he was born. However, that is a ploy that can prove to be effective when soliciting autographs.

In the well-written letter, Anthony Glanz informed "Tim Leary" that he had been struck above the eye by a batted ball and that it required six stitches, and it was "very scary," and after recovering, he was hesitant about returning to the field of play. The boy stated, "I was worried I might get hit and hurt again."

Okay, now you're thinking about why his letter was sent to the Spaceman's address in Vermont and not Tim Leary's home in California. Being a sleuth, the erstwhile southpaw, the Spaceman, offered his thoughts:

"There is a publication that lists the addresses of former major league players, and it is, of course, alphabetical. Well, it's likely that the kid saw the name 'Leary' just above 'Lee' and copied the wrong address. Or maybe that ball that struck him in the eye affected his horizontal eyesight and he just read the wrong line."

Being a curious sort, I asked the Spaceman what he intended to do with the autograph request. The youngster had indeed placed a 1991 Topps fortieth anniversary card of Tim Leary in a Yankee uniform for the player to sign.

The response I received from the Spaceman was predictable in an unpredictable manner:

"I signed the card 'Tim Leary,' and added, 'guess again.' I also advised him not to field balls with his face. I included my name and address, and we'll see if he can figure it out. He seems like a smart kid."

The Spaceman said that this was one of the "magical letters" he occasionally receives. He also noted that major league baseball recently failed to renew its contract with Topps, and that constitutes "A sure sign of the Apocalypse. It's a sign. It's cosmic. It's a sign to sell all of your shit. I mean, Timothy Leary?"

Leary, as the Spaceman ascertained from the back of the 1991 Topps card the youngster had enclosed in the envelope was, like him, a Capricorn and a fellow Californian. The Spaceman also noted that Leary had gone 9-19 for the 1990 Yankees, a subpar team, and that Leary's lifetime record was 78-105 with a 4.36 ERA.

Anthony Glanz, the autograph seeker, also mentioned that Tim Leary had always inspired him. He signed the letter, "Anthony Glanz, your biggest fan."

The Spaceman added, "This Anthony Glanz kid unknowingly has experienced a psychological fucking breakthrough! He's not really a Yankee fan, but a Red Sox fan, and he's probably been dropping acid since he's twelve years old! Dr. Timothy Leary is dead, but no, no. He's on the outside looking in!"

For those in need of a history lesson, the aforementioned Dr. Timothy Leary (not the pitcher) was a disciple of a Swiss chemist named Albert Hoffman, not to be confused with 1960's counterculture hero Abbie Hoffman, an American political and social activist, who was a member of "The Chicago Seven" and a proponent of the "Flower Power Movement." Albert Hoffman (1936-1989) was the inventor of the psychedelic drug known as "Lysergic Acid Diethylamide," also known as "LSD." The drug was first synthesized on November 16, 1936, by the Swiss chemist.

CHAPTER FIFTY-EIGHT

Miramichi Blues

The Legend of Sleepy Hollow

The Headless Horseman

This Chapter Opens Up a Whole New Can of Tuna

"When logic and proportion
Have fallen sloppy dead
And the White Knight is talking backwards
And the Red Queen's off with her head
Remember what the dormouse said
Feed your head
Feed your head."
—*Grace Slick*
Myoxidae & Muscardinidae

"The more you know, the more you know you don't know, and the more you know that you don't know."
—*David Byrne of the Talking Heads*

The earthling known as Bill "Spaceman" Lee received an impassioned plea from Maureen Cronin, the daughter of the legendary Joe Cronin, a Hall of Famer and a teammate of the immortal Ted Williams, the last major league player to have hit .400. Ted, a war hero and arguably the greatest batsman of all time, had been unceremoniously jettisoned to a "cryonics lab" in Scottsdale, Arizona shortly after his death at the age of eighty-three on July 5, 2002, in Inverness, Florida.

John Henry Williams, the mutant son of the legendary Teddy Samuel Williams, who batted .406 in 1941, a mark that most likely will never be equaled, decided on his own to have his father's remains transferred to the Alcor Life Extension Foundation in Scottsdale, Arizona, a godforsaken place far away from Ted's beloved Florida Keys, the place where Williams had written in his will that he be cremated and have his ashes scattered in that deepest part of the Atlantic Ocean. However, Ted's full remains were sent to Alcor at the direction of the nefarious John Henry Williams, a lout who often made poor decisions during his brief time on Planet Earth.

As the Spaceman stated eloquently, "John Henry was living proof that talent skips a generation."

For many years, the author and his wife, Peg, were benefactors of a major charity event known as "An Evening with Champions," an annual figure skating event that raised hundreds of thousands of dollars for the Dana-Farber Children's Cancer Institute, aka "The Jimmy Fund," a favorite charity of the great Ted Williams. The event, which was attended by many sports legends which included "Spaceman" Lee and former New England Patriots quarterback Steve Grogan, included a silent auction. Over two decades ago, Peg and I attended a memorabilia show in Woburn, Massachusetts, hoping to purchase autographed sports items for the event, when we came upon a beautiful young blonde standing in front of some extraordinary Ted Williams sixteen-by-twenty framed photographs.

The young woman was named Anita Lovely and she was representing a company known as "Green Diamond Sports." In my naiveté, I was not aware that the enterprise was owned and operated by both Ted Williams and his less than popular son, John Henry. We informed Ms. Anita Lovely of our affiliation with the Jimmy Fund, and she graciously offered to sell us two magnificent autographed sixteen-by-twenties at a reduced price for our auction.

Upon purchasing the wonderful photos, one showing Ted standing in front of his fighter jet, and the other depicting Williams crouched in the dugout with Babe Ruth, I foolishly offered, "Thank you, Ms. Lovely. We love Ted even if we cannot stand John Henry."

Anita Lovely, and that she was, smiled and responded, "I hear that from a lot of people, but I'm going to marry him anyway."

If I could have crawled beneath the rug at that moment, I would have. However, Anita Lovely immediately sensed my embarrassment, and sweetly grabbed my hand and said thoughtfully, "Please don't apologize. You are among a legion of people that have had less than good experiences with John Henry."

Note: Ms. Lovely never did marry John Henry Williams, incidentally.

Shortly thereafter, I met a noble gentleman named Dave McCarthy. If the name sounds familiar, well, it should. Dave, although at the time I met him I was not aware, is the executive director of the Ted Williams Museum and Hitters Hall of Fame located inside Tropicana Field in St. Petersburg, Florida. Dave is also the executive director of the Ted Williams Foundation! And that's not all: Dave is a retired New Hampshire state trooper, who not only was the commander of the Bureau of Enforcement overseeing uniformed New Hampshire state troopers on patrol statewide, but also commanded the Executive Protection Unit serving as a bodyguard to the governor of New Hampshire. Oh, and Dave was also Ted Williams's bodyguard. Dave is an imposing man, but one with an enormously wonderful sense of humor.

Upon Peg and me meeting Dave McCarthy, he peered at one of my sixteen-by-twenty framed and autographed photos of Ted Williams. He had not yet introduced himself. However, he asked, "Did Ted really sign that?"

I immediately and truthfully answered, "Well, either Ted signed it or his prodigal son, John Henry signed it. One can never be certain."

Dave McCarthy responded by laughing uproariously as he replied, "Yes, John Henry has developed a proficiency at forging his dad's signature." I would soon learn that John Henry would often prod his illustrious father into inking various items, even after his elderly dad was tired due to his age and failing health. John Henry was all about the almighty dollar, and little else.

Dave McCarthy, who was also representing Green Diamond Sports in those days, regaled Peg and yours truly with a story that did not surprise us considering John Henry's reputation. He told of an occasion when Dave was in a remote town in northern Wisconsin, a place where McCarthy noticed a small sports memorabilia store. Dave McCarthy figured he'd see if the proprietor would be interested in purchasing an autographed Ted Williams item or two, and therefore, introduced himself as follows:

"Hi, I'm Dave McCarthy, and I'm with Green Diamond Sports." He no sooner got those words out of his mouth when he was assailed with, "The outfit operated by John Henry Williams?! That SOB owes us money and he misrepresented his company!"

Dave McCarthy immediately got on his cell phone, dialed John Henry and scolded, "John, is there ANYWHERE in the United States that you haven't as yet pissed EVERYONE off?!"

John Henry Williams was renowned for arriving unexpectedly at sports shops, immediately peering at allegedly autographed memorabilia signed by his dad, and spewing loudly, "This is a fake! This is NOT Ted Williams's autograph!" John Henry made that mistake once too often, when he came upon an enraged dealer who countered, "I bought it from you, you prick!" And that he had. The vendor turned the item over to show John Henry the useless "Certificate of Authenticity" that had been signed by………….. John Henry Williams!

So now you know all you have to know about Ted Williams's less than admirable son. Consider that on July 13, 1999, Ted Williams was being honored on the field at Fenway Park prior to the All-Star Game. Each player on both teams gathered around Ted, who was seated in his wheelchair, and everyone basked in Ted's limelight. It was a magnificent and spontaneous meeting of the minds, especially when the great San Diego Padres star, Tony Gwynn, who was amid making a run at Williams's magical .400 batting average, initiated a conversation with his hero, the immortal Splendid Splinter. Everyone within earshot listened intently as Williams and Gwynn discussed the art of hitting…………

And then John Henry happened.

Commandeering his father's wheelchair, he quickly and decisively wheeled his father away from the historic meeting for still another photo op. Both Ted and Tony Gwynn, who died way too young, are gone now, but I suspect that discussion is now taking place on higher ground.

With John Henry's insistence that his father's body be sent to the Alcor Life Extension Foundation in Scottsdale, Arizona, a major amount of publicity resulted from the decision, and John Henry was all about publicity. The controversy surrounding this bizarre and relatively unknown practice became national news because the great Ted Williams's remains were involved, and that elicited both shock and anger, especially by friends and some family members of the great slugger.

The premise, for lack of a better word, for such storage of one's remains is the hope that the deceased are suspended in liquid nitrogen in the event future generations learn how to revive them. Oh, and get this: The heads are decapitated (or is the body decapitated? See Michael Lewis's *The Undoing Project*) and stored in separate steel tanks, hopefully to be reunited. You can't make this shit up. Are you infuriated? Hell, I am. But here's where the

Spaceman, hopefully, comes to the rescue, and despite the morbidity of this ongoing situation, leave it to Bill Lee to provide us with some comic relief.

"When Maureen Cronin approached me in Centerville on Cape Cod a few years ago and asked if I would consider interceding on Ted's behalf, and attempt to retrieve Ted's head and body from the cryonics facility in Arizona, I replied I couldn't possibly place Ted's head in the front seat of my car, because it would be yapping at me for the entire cross-country trip, but I am reconsidering it today," said the Spaceman. "After all, with his head in the front seat, it would allow me to drive in the HOV lane. Maureen Cronin wanted to give Ted a proper burial at sea. I wonder if she meant a 'Viking burial?' You know, when they put the ship out, they burn it and place three virgins aboard, but where are we going to find three virgins on Cape Cod? Listen, I hear they have Ted's head and body stored in two separate containers in two separate buildings at the cryonics facility, and that there are rumors they've been bowling with it."

Once you stop laughing, the Spaceman continued, "I'm a locksmith. I can break into the facility to retrieve Ted, but I'll need a blueprint for the building. I would like to find out what type of security they have."

As absurd as the Spaceman's proposal sounds, it is not that farfetched upon learning the REAL scenario behind the Alcor Life Extension Facility. Truth is way stranger than fiction. Please allow us to explain the FACTS surrounding this beyond extraordinary and grotesque improbable scenario, a screenplay Ray Bradbury would have classified as too weird.

Larry Johnson, an Albuquerque-born former chief operating officer at the Alcor facility, became a whistleblower in 2003, and detailed his admissions by writing a book titled, *Frozen: My Journey into the World of Cryonics, Deception, and Death,* in which he graphically describes what took place beyond the doors of the now infamous indoor graveyard. Hang on tight; you're not going to believe this stuff.

In *Frozen,* published by Vanguard Press, Larry Johnson vividly described how Williams was beheaded and how his mutilated head was repeatedly abused and even used in a bizarre form of "batting practice." Ted Williams's "identification number" at the facility was "Alcorian A-1949," to which the Spaceman wondered "Why not 1941, the year he batted .406?" but I digress.

Larry Johnson also wrote in *Frozen,* (sounds like the name of a children's book, said the Spaceman) that technicians with no medical certification "gleefully" photographed and used crude equipment to decapitate Williams. Larry Johnson reportedly wrote his book while in hiding, fearful for his life.

In 2003, in an article by Nathaniel Vinton, the *New York Daily News* reported that a reporter named Buzz Hamon, a close friend of Williams and a former director of the Ted Williams Museum in Hernando, Florida, sneaked into the Alcor facility with the help of a mortician friend, and was appalled by the conditions there, where Ted Williams's body and more than fifty others were stored in steel tanks alongside cardboard boxes and assorted other junk. Hamon reportedly committed suicide in 2004, if this wasn't already eerie enough. Johnson wrote that Ted's head was balanced on an empty can of Bumble Bee Tuna. The Spaceman added that Ted loved fishing, but that he loved line-fishing and this crap was caught in nets, and that Ted would've been extremely upset to learn his head was placed atop a can of the cheap shit.

Author Larry Johnson also accused Alcor of joking morbidly about returning Williams's thawing remains back to the family if John Henry (what a surprise!) did not pay his outstanding debt to Alcor.

It's about to get even more intriguing. Obviously, Alcor Life Extension Facility called Larry Johnson's book, *Frozen*, a complete pack of lies, and filed a defamation lawsuit versus Johnson and his publisher in 2010. However, on May 19, 2014, the defamation complaint against Johnson and Vanguard Press was dismissed! No judge or jury has ruled on the veracity of the contents of the book! Holy crap, it's apparently true!

Lest you think that Larry Johnson is a bastion of integrity, this gets even more delicious. I will now list the names of SOME of the numerous books written by Larry Johnson, the esteemed author of *Frozen: My Journey into the World of Cryonics, Deception, and Death*. Please keep in mind that Larry Johnson REALLY wrote these books! Here are the titles:

EMUTATE - Emutate is a shocking, futuristic look at what could/might/would happen on Earth when the planet is infiltrated by flesh-eating aliens. The aliens operate in subtle ways so they can slowly take over the government and stay under the radar of the authorities. Or as the Spaceman exclaimed, "Add it to my reading list."

YOGA ALCHEMY

ABSOLUTE HONESTY: Building a Corporate Culture that Values Straight Talk and Rewards Integrity.

FUCKING MY BEST FRIEND'S WIFE—the Spaceman has yet to

mention adding this to his reading list, although he claims to have read the sequel, the harrowing discovery of finding his best friend in bed with his wife and.........."My Best Friend, My Wife, My Baseball Glove!"

SHOW CATS: Portraits of Fine Felines.

HORNY GIRLS SEX STORIES: Hot, Horny Girl gets Fucked Hard.

Sounds like good beach reading for the summer.

There you have it. Larry Johnson is to be mentioned in the same breath with the immortal Philip K. Dick, who penned forty-four novels and 121 short stories, a hero of mine, and since I am the real Kilgore Trout, well, I take these things seriously.*

The Spaceman would also like to remind you that in addition to writing his now legendary "The Legend of Sleepy Hollow – the Headless Horseman," Washington Irving also wrote "Rip Van Winkle." Once more, Bill Lee draws an analogy to his own life, which of course, includes his own headless horseman, his old friend, Ted Williams.

"Everything is connected," says the Spaceman. "Read James Burke's *Connections*. The connection here is Truett Banks "Rip" Sewell. You see, Rip invented the eephus pitch, and only one player blasted it for a home run. That player was Ted Williams! It happened in the 1946 All-Star Game. Just like me, only one of my eephus lobs was ever hit for a home run, and that was by Tony Perez in the 1975 World Series. Rip invented the eephus pitch. It's cosmic."

If the Spaceman is successful in retrieving the head and body of Ted Williams, he plans on bringing it to the Splendid Splinter's favorite fishing spot, the Miramichi, and propping it up with a fishing pole in his hands.

---

* Regarding prolific author, Philip K. Dick: On February 20, 1974, while recovering from the effects of sodium pentothal administered for the extraction of an impacted wisdom tooth, Dick received a home delivery of Darvon from a young woman. When he opened the door, he was struck by the dark-haired girl's beauty, and was especially drawn to her golden necklace. He asked her about its curious fish-shaped design. As she was leaving, she replied: "This is a sign used by the early Christians." Dick called the symbol the "vesicle pisces." This name seems to have been based on his conflation of two related symbols, the

Christian ichthys symbol (two intersecting arcs delineating a fish in profile), which the woman was wearing, and the vesica pisces.

After the woman's departure, Dick began experiencing strange hallucinations. Although initially attributing them to side effects from medication, he considered this explanation implausible after weeks of continued hallucination. Dick stated:

"I experienced an invasion of my mind by a transcendentally rational mind, as if I had been insane all my life and suddenly had become sane."

The life of John Henry Williams, Ted's only son, remains an enigma to this day. John Henry, who attempted to exploit, and sadly, perhaps somewhat successfully, his father's fame, especially during the early 1990s during the height of the sports memorabilia craze, sadly died of leukemia in March of 2004 at the tender age of thirty-five. It is still rumored that John Henry was scheming to literally sell his father's DNA! Can anyone possibly get lower than that?!

It has also been reported that upon John Henry Williams's death, he too was sent to the Alcor Facility in Scottsdale. If this is true, the Spaceman offered to drive his body home, as well:

"I'll take it to Fenway Park and suggest the Red Sox reinstitute those old troth urinals they had in the men's bathrooms. I'd place his head at one end of the urinal, and his body at the other side, and everyone can piss between the two."

POSTSCRIPT

William Least Heat-Moon's writing had provided me with a map. Not a literal map, but a map of the soul. Upon reading and rereading Heat-Moon's epic prose, I become instinctively aware how to approach writing Bill Lee's journey, which is not a story of harmony, but perhaps a lesson in why seeking harmony, although too often fruitless, is the proper way to coexist with fellow members of our questionable species. Bill "Spaceman" Lee has learned this, and often the hard way. In many ways, Bill Lee is much like the unidentified elderly man who took down Heat-Moon's license plate, in what was an apparent attempt to prevent him from discovering truth; and yet by asking Heat-Moon if he had ever met someone from the future, he learned an invaluable history lesson. Bill Lee, I believe, is indeed from the past and therefore, the future. They are interchangeable.

Bill Lee is perhaps the most improbable world-class sports competitor of my lifetime. By that, I mean that other than perhaps former basketball star and US senator Bill Bradley, and Bill Russell the former Celtics great, Bill is the most erudite, well-read, and educated athlete of modern times. Despite the Spaceman's eccentricities, and those are indeed, numerous, I never imagined that a significant portion of collaborating with him would require an enormous amount of reading. Bill Lee suggested—no, change that to INSISTED—that I read and reread a large volume of books and essays to fully complete this written and tangible journey. I will admit that initially, I thought to myself that I was once more in high school or college, and that my teachers and professors had gone completely daft.

Being "required" to reread Kurt Vonnegut, in truth, was something I had planned to do anyhow, and that in itself was a pleasure, but each day as my "assignments" were meted out, I began wondering if I would be able to ace the course, or at the very least, retain enough information to receive a passing grade. However, before long, I realized that the Spaceman was literally attempting to not only explain himself, but the human condition as well. I began to see the world, at least partially, through his eyes, and soon I realized I was communicating closely with, well, a genius, as well as a madman. Oh, and those two are often not inconsistent.

Vonnegut, and then *Connections* by James Burke. The Spaceman, and James Burke, of course, convinced me that everything was indeed, "connected."

There was *Behaviorism* by B.F. Skinner (all animal behavior was driven not by thoughts and feelings, but by external rewards and punishments).

Perhaps my favorite required reading assignment was the great Michael Lewis's *The Undoing Project*, a mind-boggling volume I turn to on a consistent basis. Bill Lee nearly invariably quotes conversations between the two main subjects in the book, Israeli psychologists Daniel Kahneman and Amos Tversky. Kahneman, in fact, shared a Nobel Prize in economics in 2002, but sadly Tversky had passed.

Much of what is written regarding the theories of the two Israeli geniuses revolved around false pretenses and accepted beliefs that were basically pure bullshit. Michael Lewis explains that generally what you are doing and saying is total bullshit, without any discernible effect on the behavior of psychologists.

The Spaceman often references "Gestalt Psychology," which offers that our perceptions are best not trusted, i.e. "A light appeared brighter when it emerged from total darkness. The color gray looked green when surrounded by blue. If you said to a person, 'Don't step on that banana eel,' he'd be sure that you had said 'peel' and not 'eel.'"

Michael Lewis, the author, even included sports into the equations. Analyzing former NBA executive, Daryl Morey, he observed, "A person who knows his own mind well enough to mistrust it." Morey, an innovator, was interested in "studying things that had previously gone unmeasured," in scouting the strengths and weaknesses of basketball players. Many form opinions that never change. Morey referred to this as "confirmation bias." A scout would settle on an opinion about a player and then arrange the evidence to support that specific opinion.*

| * This is also a basis for partisan political opinions.

"Spaceman" Lee constantly reminds me of Daniel Kahneman's philosophy, which was, "Of Kahneman's many doubts, the most curious were the ones he had about his own memory." As Michael Lewis explained, "His defining moment was doubt."

Incredibly, the Spaceman offered a somewhat hilarious incident regarding his own pitching career. Bill was selected for the 1973 All-Star Game, a prestigious honor given to the greatest players in baseball. Before the game, National League manager Dick Williams, who was also Bill's first manager in the majors and then again in Montreal, gathered his pitchers in the locker room before the game and asked, "Is there anyone here who is not certain he can get these American League All-Stars out?"

The Spaceman raised his hand. As Bill exclaimed, "How the fuck can you be certain about anything?!" Postscript: Bill did not appear in the game. Bill Lee was Daniel Kahneman way before Daniel Kahneman.

Speaking of Michael Lewis's mind-numbing *The Undoing Project*, the Spaceman conveyed that it is interesting to note that Daniel Kahneman, the pessimist, is still living, while Amos Tversky, the optimist, is deceased. Bill Lee also categorized Amos Tversky as "the Jewish Audie Murphy, another pint-sized war hero," because he lived in the moment.*

> * Audie Murphy, who also became an actor and songwriter, was one of the most decorated soldiers in American history, and due to his heroics in World War II, Murphy was awarded every military combat award for valor available.

The Spaceman believes strongly that those of the ilk of Sergeant York and Audie Murphy understood the principles of Mark Manson's *Everything is F*cked*, because the two men "lived in the moment," and realized that the thinking brain does not run the show. "It doesn't."

"Why do you think there's an eraser on the cover of Michael Lewis's *The Undoing Project*?" the Spaceman asked. "Why did they make the eraser two colors? That's because your brain is fucked. It's split down the middle. Like my coach (Rod Dedeaux) taught at USC, 'You have no chance if you think.' Dedeaux would say, 'You can think BEFORE the action, but when the battle begins, you had better cut your fucking head off.' Dedeaux told me to cut my head off when I was a sophomore at USC. It was a great lesson."

To this moment, the Spaceman, a disciple of both Daniel Kahneman and Amos Tversky, often states, "Do not rely on human judgment." As Kahneman lectured his students, "When someone says something, don't ask yourself if it is true. Ask what it might be true of."

Somehow the Spaceman transitioned into a lecture regarding "The Coriolis Effect." Hold on tight for this one:

"People attempt to eliminate prejudice, but they create prejudice because we're dealing with a binary system. When you flush a toilet, does it spin faster? Does it spin faster at the beginning, or when the turd goes down the fucking drain? The answer is the Coriolis Effect.*

* Just think of all the money you saved by not having to learn this in college! The Coriolis Effect, as I would soon learn, is named after French mathematician Gaspard-Gustave de Coriolis, and it affects weather patterns, ocean currents, air travel, and the brain of the author. Despite its importance, many have not heard of it and even fewer understand it. Count me among the classification "fewer." "The key to the Coriolis Effect," said the Spaceman, "lies in the Earth's rotation, and influences the deflection of an object." *

* Note: At the time of the Spaceman explaining this phenomenon, he was in the process of reading the great Leigh Montville's epic *Tall Men, Short Shorts*, and the only "deflection of an object" that entered my mind, was one of the countless blocked shots performed by the legendary Bill Russell.

Perhaps the most intriguing "homework assignment" given to me by the Spaceman was the spellbinding *The Power of Myth* by the late Joseph Campbell (1904-1987), as told to journalist Bill Moyers. The book is based on the six-hour 1988 PBS documentary which featured six hours of simply enchanting conversation between the two men. There are religious ramifications involved, and both the television program and the book are rife with controversy and provide an amazing tour through mythological and religious history, which many propose are indeed synonymous.

Included in my other reading "responsibilities" were the WONDERFUL works of William Least Heat-Moon (*Blue Highways*), the Jack Reacher novels written by Lee Child, and many other wonderful volumes I am still attempting to absorb.

As the Spaceman teaches, "Take whatever someone says to you, and try not to tear it down, but to make sense of it. When gut feelings are removed, judgments improve."

Those of you that read this book in its entirety, well, God bless you. Just know this: The earthling known as Bill "Spaceman" Lee is as authentic as anyone I've ever known. Never in my life did I anticipate ever knowing a combination of some of the great philosophers in history and Mel Brooks.

Victory Is Mine!

The following is the lone listing of each of Bill "Spaceman" Lee's 119 victories before he was forever blackballed by major league baseball

It should be noted that the Spaceman never lost any of the games he won, nor did he win any that he lost.

#1 in relief on September 20, 1969 @ Detroit—Red Sox 6 Tigers 3
   Losing pitcher—Gary Taylor

#2 Starting pitcher—on April 28, 1970 vs. Oakland—Red Sox 2 Athletics 1
   Losing pitcher—Al Downing

#3 Starting pitcher—on May 23, 1970 vs. Washington—Red Sox 5 Senators 3
   Losing pitcher—Dick Bosman

#4 in relief on April 30, 1971 vs. Minnesota—Red Sox 4 Twins 3
   Losing pitcher—Jim Kaat

#5 in relief on May 4, 1971 @ Chicago—Red Sox 4 White Sox 3
   Losing pitcher—Tom Bradley

#6 in relief on May 7, 1971 @ Milwaukee—Red Sox 5 Brewers 4
   Losing pitcher—Ken Sanders

#7 Starting pitcher—on May 20, 1971—Red Sox 5 Yankees 2
   Losing pitcher—Stan Bahnsen

#8 in relief on July 1, 1971 @ Detroit—Red Sox 8 Tigers 7
   Losing pitcher—Fred Scherman

#9 in relief of Jim Lonborg on July 4, 1971 vs. New York—Red Sox 7 Yankees 4
   Losing pitcher—Steve Kline

#10 in relief of Jim Lonborg on July 8, 1971 @ Cleveland—Red Sox 5 Indians 3
　　Losing pitcher—Vince Colbert

#11 in relief on July 15, 1971 vs. Minnesota—Red Sox 3 Twins 0
　　Losing pitcher—Stan Williams

#12 in relief of Luis Tiant (8.1 innings!) on August 2, 1971 @ Baltimore—Red Sox 7 Orioles 4
　　Bill pitched 8.1 innings of two hit shutout ball! Red Sox 7 Orioles 4
　　Losing pitcher—Tom Dukes

#13 in relief on May 9, 1972 @ California—Red Sox 4 Angels 3
　　Losing pitcher—Lloyd Allen

#14 in relief on May 12, 1972 @ Oakland—Red Sox 7 Athletics 6
　　Losing pitcher—Rollie Fingers

#15 in relief on May 23, 1972 vs. Baltimore—Red Sox 6 Baltimore 5
　　Losing pitcher—Doyle Alexander

#16 in relief on May 26, 1972 vs. Milwaukee—Red Sox 5 Brewers 4
　　Losing pitcher—Doyle Alexander

#17 in relief on June 17, 1972 vs. Chicago—Red Sox 10 White Sox 8
　　Losing pitcher—Phil Regan

#18 in relief on July 12, 1972 @ Oakland—Red Sox 7 Athletics 6
　　Losing pitcher—Rollie Fingers

#19 in relief on September 27, 1972 vs. Milwaukee—Red Sox 7 Brewers 5
　　Losing pitcher—Ken Brett

#20 in relief on April 25, 1973 vs. Minnesota—Red Sox 4 Twins 3
　　Losing pitcher—Ray Corbin

#21 Starting pitcher on May 5, 1973 @ Minnesota—Red Sox 5 Twins 1
Losing pitcher—Bert Blyleven

#22 Starting pitcher on May 10, 1973 vs. Cleveland—Red Sox 4 Indians 3
Losing pitcher—Jerry Johnson

#23 Starting pitcher on May 24, 1973 vs. Milwaukee—Red Sox 10 Brewers 1
Losing pitcher—Bill Champion

#24 Starting pitcher on May 29, 1973 vs. California—Red Sox 2 Angels 1
Losing pitcher—Nolan Ryan

#25 Starting pitcher on June 6, 1973 vs. Kansas City—Red Sox 5 Royals 4
Losing pitcher—Doug Bird

#26 Starting pitcher on June 10, 1973 @ Texas—Red Sox 10 Rangers 1
Losing pitcher—Sonny Siebert

#27 Starting pitcher on June 20, 1973 @ Milwaukee—Red Sox 3 Brewers 2
Losing pitcher—Bill Parsons

#28 Starting pitcher on June 25, 1973 vs. Detroit—Red Sox 2 Tigers 1
Losing pitcher—Jim Perry

#29 Starting pitcher on July 5, 1973 @ New York—Red Sox 9 Yankees 4
Losing pitcher—Pat Dobson

#30 Starting pitcher on July 9, 1973 @ Minnesota—Red Sox 2 Twins 0
Losing pitcher—Joe Decker

#31 Starting pitcher on July 18, 1973 vs. Chicago—Red Sox 6 White Sox 1
Losing pitcher—Steve Stone

#32 Starting pitcher on August 19, 1973 vs. Kansas City—Red Sox 4
Royals 3
Losing pitcher—Al Fitzmorris

#33 Starting pitcher on August 24, 1973 @ California—Red Sox 3 Angels 2
Losing pitcher—Dick Lange

#34 Starting pitcher on August 29, 1973 @ Oakland—Red Sox 6 Athletics 4
Losing pitcher—Vida Blue

#35 Starting pitcher on September 2, 1973 @ Milwaukee—Red Sox 10
Brewers 4
Losing pitcher—Jim Colborn

#36 Starting pitcher on September 18, 1973 vs. New York—Red Sox 4
Yankees 2
Losing pitcher—Doc Medich

#37 Starting pitcher on April 12, 1974 vs. Detroit—Red Sox 6 Tigers 3
Losing pitcher—Lerrin LaGrow

#38 Starting pitcher on April 17, 1974 @ New York—Red Sox 4 Yankees 3
Losing pitcher—Pat Dobson

#39 Starting pitcher on May 8, 1974 vs. New York—Red Sox 4 Yankees 0
Losing pitcher—Mel Stottlemyre

#40 Starting pitcher on May 12, 1974 @ Detroit—Red Sox 4 Tigers 3
Losing pitcher—John Hiller

#41 Starting pitcher on May 21, 1974 vs. New York—Red Sox 14 Yankees 6
Losing pitcher—Dick Tidrow

#42 Starting pitcher on May 26, 1974 vs. Milwaukee—Red Sox 4 Brewers 1
Losing pitcher—Ed Sprague

#43 Starting pitcher on June 9, 1974 @ Chicago—Red Sox 10 White Sox 6
Losing pitcher—Skip Pitlock

#44 Starting pitcher on June 15, 1974 @ California—Red Sox 5 Angels 3
  Losing pitcher—Bill Stoneman

#45 Starting pitcher on July 1, 1974 @ Baltimore—Red Sox 6 Orioles 4
  Losing pitcher—Doyle Alexander

#46 Starting pitcher on July 11, 1974 vs. Texas—Red Sox 12 Rangers 3
  Losing pitcher—Steve Hargan

#47 Starting pitcher on July 28, 1974 vs. New York—Red Sox 8 Yankees 3
  Losing pitcher—Dave Pagan

#48 Starting pitcher on August 1, 1974 vs. Baltimore—Red Sox 11 Orioles 3
  Losing pitcher—Wayne Garland

#49 Starting pitcher on August 9, 1974 @ Oakland—Red Sox 6 Athletics 2
  Losing pitcher—Ken Holtzman

#50 Starting pitcher on August 19, 1974 vs. Chicago—Red Sox 6
White Sox 1
  Losing pitcher—Jim Kaat

#51 Starting pitcher on August 29, 1974 @ Chicago—Red Sox 3
White Sox 2
  Losing pitcher—Wilbur Wood

#52 Starting pitcher on September 12, 1974 @ Cleveland—Red Sox 3
Indians 2
  Losing pitcher—Jim Perry

#53 Starting pitcher on September 21, 1974 vs. Baltimore—Red Sox 6
Orioles 5
  Losing pitcher—Dave Johnson

#54 Starting pitcher on April 15, 1975 @ New York—Red Sox 5 Yankees 3
  Losing pitcher—Catfish Hunter

#55 Starting pitcher on May 1, 1975 vs. Cleveland—Red Sox 7 Indians 6
Losing pitcher—Jim Perry

#56 Starting pitcher on May 6, 1975 @ Cleveland—Red Sox 4 Indians 1
Losing pitcher—Dick Bosman

#57 Starting pitcher on May 11, 1975 @ California—Red Sox 5 Angels 2
Losing pitcher—Bill Singer

#58 Starting pitcher on May 20, 1975 vs. Oakland—Red Sox 7 Athletics 0
Losing pitcher—Vida Blue

#59 Starting pitcher on May 24, 1975 vs. California—Red Sox 6 Angels 0
Losing pitcher—Andy Hassler

#60 Starting pitcher on May 28, 1975 @ Texas—Red Sox 4 Rangers 1
Losing pitcher—Fergie Jenkins

#61 Starting pitcher on June 7, 1975 vs. Minnesota—Red Sox 3 Twins 1
Losing pitcher—Ray Corbin

#62 Starting pitcher on June 15, 1975 @ Kansas City—Red Sox 8 Royals 7
Losing pitcher—Lindy McDaniel

#63 Starting pitcher on July 6, 1975 @ Cleveland—Red Sox 5 Indians 3
Losing pitcher—Jim Bibby

#64 Starting pitcher on July 18, 1975 vs. Kansas City—Red Sox 9 Royals 3
Losing pitcher—Steve Busby

#65 Starting pitcher on July 22, 1975 @ Minnesota—Red Sox 5 Twins 4
Losing pitcher—Dave Goltz

#66 Starting pitcher on July 27, 1975 @ New York—Red Sox 1 Yankees 0
Losing pitcher—Catfish Hunter

#67 Starting pitcher on July 31, 1975 vs. Detroit—Red Sox 3 Tigers 2
  Losing pitcher—Bob Reynolds

#68 Starting pitcher on August 9, 1975 @ Oakland—Red Sox 7 Athletics 2
  Losing pitcher—Sonny Siebert

#69 Starting pitcher on August 19, 1975 @ Kansas City—Red Sox 5
Royals 0
  Losing pitcher—Al Fitzmorris

#70 Starting pitcher on September 24, 1975 vs. Chicago—Red Sox 6
White Sox 1
  Losing pitcher—Wilbur Wood

#71 in relief on August 1, 1976 vs. New York—Red Sox 5 Yankees 4
  Losing pitcher—Dick Tidrow

#72 Starting pitcher on August 23, 1976 vs. California—Red Sox 7 Angels 3
  Losing pitcher—Nolan Ryan

#73 Starting pitcher on September 8, 1976 vs. Detroit—Red Sox 4 Tigers 3
  Losing pitcher—Dave Lemanczyk

#74 Starting pitcher on September 18 @ Detroit—Red Sox 5 Tigers 4
  Losing pitcher—Vern Ruhle

#75 Starting pitcher on September 23, 1976 vs. Milwaukee—Red Sox 10
Brewers 3
  Losing pitcher—Bill Travers

#76 Starting pitcher on May 15, 1977 @ Seattle—Red Sox 5 Mariners 4
  Losing pitcher—Rick Jones

#77 Starting pitcher on May 23, 1977 @ New York—Red Sox 4 Yankees 3
  Losing pitcher—Ed Figueroa

#78 Starting pitcher on June 4, 1977 @ Minnesota—Red Sox 5 Twins 2
    Losing pitcher—Paul Thormodsgard (no matter how many times I look at this surname, I cannot get over the nagging feeling that I somehow misspelled it. Or perhaps Paul has misspelled his own name).

#79 Starting pitcher on June 9, 1977 vs. Baltimore—Red Sox 7 Orioles 3
    Losing pitcher—Jim Palmer

#80 Starting pitcher on August 27, 1977 vs. Minnesota—Red Sox 7 Twins 5
    Losing pitcher—Ron Schueler

#81 Starting pitcher on September 1, 1977 vs. Cleveland—Red Sox 3 Indians 1
    Losing pitcher—Dennis Eckersley

#82 Starting pitcher on September 6, 1977 @ Toronto—Red Sox 11 Blue Jays 2
    Losing pitcher—Mike Darr

#83 Starting pitcher on September 11, 1977 vs. Detroit—Red Sox 6 Tigers 2
    Losing pitcher—Fernando Arroyo

#84 Starting pitcher on September 23, 1977 @ Detroit—Red Sox 5 Tigers 1
    Losing pitcher—Bob Sykes

#85 Starting pitcher on April 9, 1978 @ Chicago—Red Sox 5 White Sox 0
    Losing pitcher—Wilbur Wood

#86 Starting pitcher on April 15, 1978 vs. Texas—Red Sox 12 Rangers 4
    Losing pitcher—Dock Ellis

#87 Starting pitcher on April 20, 1978 vs. Milwaukee—Red Sox 10 Brewers 4
    Losing pitcher—Moose Haas

#88 Starting pitcher on April 25, 1978 @ Milwaukee—Red Sox 4 Brewers 3
    Losing pitcher—Jerry Augustine

#89 Starting pitcher on May 11, 1978 @ Baltimore—Red Sox 5 Orioles 4
    Losing pitcher—Dennis Martinez

#90 Starting pitcher on May 16, 1978 @ Kansas City—Red Sox 3 Royals 2
    Losing pitcher—Paul Splittorff

#91 Starting pitcher on May 26, 1978 vs. Detroit—Red Sox 6 Tigers 3
    Losing pitcher—Milt Wilcox

#92 Starting pitcher on June 23, 1978 vs. Baltimore—Red Sox 5 Orioles 2
    Losing pitcher—Jim Palmer

#93 Starting pitcher on July 5, 1978 @ Chicago—Red Sox 9 White Sox 2
    Losing pitcher—Steve Stone

#94 Starting pitcher on July 15, 1978 vs. Minnesota—Red Sox 5 Twins 4
    Losing pitcher—Darrell Jackson

#95 Starting pitcher on April 16, 1979 @ Chicago—Expos 2 Cubs 0
    Losing pitcher—Mike Krukow

#96 Starting pitcher on April 27, 1979 vs. San Francisco—Expos 14 Giants 8
    Losing pitcher—Bob Knepper

#97 Starting pitcher on May 1, 1979 vs. Los Angeles—Expos 7 Dodgers 3
    Losing pitcher—Bob Welch

#98 Starting pitcher on May 6, 1979 @ San Diego—Expos 7 Padres 5
    Losing pitcher—Gaylord Perry

#99 Starting pitcher on May 30, 1979 vs. Philadelphia—Expos 2 Phillies 0
    Losing pitcher—Nino Espinosa

THE FINAL ODYSSEY OF THE SWEET RIDE

#100 Starting pitcher on June 4, 1979 @ Atlanta—Expos 8 Braves 1
Losing pitcher—Tony Brizzolara

#101 Starting pitcher on June 19, 1979 @ Cincinnati—Expos 3 Reds 2
Losing pitcher—Mike LaCoss

#102 Starting pitcher on July 4, 1979 @ Chicago—Expos 2 Cubs 1
Losing pitcher—Bill Caudill

#103 Starting pitcher on July 9, 1979 vs. Los Angeles—Expos 3 Dodgers 0
Losing pitcher—Don Sutton

#104 Starting pitcher on July 21, 1979 @ Los Angeles—Expos 3 Dodgers 0
Losing pitcher—Don Sutton

#105 Starting pitcher on August 19, 1979 vs. Atlanta—Expos 5 Braves 1
Losing pitcher—Tony Brizzolara

#106 Starting pitcher on August 24, 1979 @ Atlanta—Expos 2 Braves 0

#107 Starting pitcher on August 29, 1979 vs. Houston—Expos 5 Astros 3
Losing pitcher—Joe Niekro

#108 Starting pitcher on September 3, 1979 vs. New York—Expos 7 Mets 2
Losing pitcher—Ray Burris

#109 Starting pitcher on September 8, 1979 @ St. Louis—Expos 7
Cardinals 2
Losing pitcher—John Fulgham

#110 Starting pitcher on September 23, 1979 @ Philadelphia—Expos 7
Phillies 4
Losing pitcher—Nino Espinosa

#111 Starting pitcher on May 10, 1980 vs. New York—Expos 5 Mets 3
Losing pitcher—Kevin Kobel

#112 Starting pitcher on May 23, 1980 @ Cincinnati—Expos 7 Reds 4
Losing pitcher—Mike LaCoss

#113 Starting pitcher on June 6, 1980 vs. St. Louis—Expos 7 Cardinals 2
Losing pitcher—Bob Forsch

#114 in relief on September 20, 1980 @ St. Louis—Expos 5 Cardinals 4
Losing pitcher—John Littlefield

#115 in relief on May 1, 1981 vs. Los Angeles—Expos 9 Dodgers 8
Losing pitcher—Bobby Castillo

#116 in relief on August 10, 1981 vs. Pittsburgh—Expos 3 Pirates 1
Losing pitcher—Pascual Perez

#117 Starting pitcher on September 15, 1981 vs. St. Louis—Expos 4
Cardinals 3
Losing pitcher—Mark Littell

#118 Starting pitcher on September 24, 1981 vs. Pittsburgh—Expos 7
Pirates 1
Losing pitcher—Odell Jones

#119 in relief on October 3, 1981 @ New York—Expos 5 Mets 4
Losing pitcher—Neil Allen

POSTSCRIPT TO THE POSTSRIPT

"Consistency is the most overrated of all human virtues. I'm someone who changes his mind all the time." —Malcolm Gladwell

Reacting to a commotion taking place in the Legends Suite at Fenway Park, Tom Werner, the legendary television producer and the chairman of the Liverpool soccer club and the Boston Red Sox, arrived, albeit sans cutie Katie Couric, to see the earthling known as Bill "Spaceman" Lee waving a New York Yankees cap and saluting the fans below by waving his middle finger in derision at the capacity crowd who were happily singing along to Neil Diamond's "Sweet Caroline," long a tradition in the middle of the eighth inning.

"What are you doing, Bill, and why are you hoisting a Yankees cap to the Fenway Faithful?" asked the longtime successful Hollywood mogul, who no doubt was entirely aware of the Spaceman's countless eccentricities.

The date of this historic event was Saturday, September 25, 2021, and the hated New York Yankees were in the process of sweeping a three-game series versus the Olde Towne Team. Giancarlo Stanton, a Yankee villain of epic proportion, had just absolutely pulverized a first-pitch fastball hurled by Red Sox lefthander Darwinzon Hernandez, and the fact that Bill Lee had accurately predicted it a mere ten seconds before it occurred, and there are numerous witnesses to validate that fact, made the blow even more memorable and noteworthy.

"Darwinzon!" muttered the Spaceman in disgust, "That's evolution for you!"

Now for a little backdrop as to why the Spaceman at one time had donned the Yankees cap during his "Nostradamus foretelling."

The Spaceman and his beautiful wife, Diana, believe in "paying it forward." Therefore, after spending a full week at Camp Cripple Creek with the legendary "Weight Band" in Big Indian, New York in August, Diana thought it would be a wonderful reciprocal gesture to have the Spaceman, and the Red Sox, of course, host the great musicians, Michael Bram, Brian Mitchell, Albert Rogers, Jim Weider, Matt Zeiner and their enormously great sound engineer, Mark Rudzinski, the Weight Band's "babysitter." The Spaceman stated unequivocally that the band members wouldn't have even found

Fenway park without Mark at Fenway Park. The fact that Brian Mitchell, a Bronx native, is a huge Yankees fan, did not get in the way of the invitation. Friendship is friendship, even if the three-game series was critical for both ballclubs.

Please note that the Spaceman is devoutly opposed to the playing of Neil Diamond's "Sweet Caroline" during the eighth inning, and the fact that Bill had literally locked Diamond out of his home in Malibu (as you've read, Bill was a locksmith) did not factor into his disdain for the song. The Spaceman also strongly dislikes the chant, "Yankees Suck," but adds, "They should add Pondh20 to it." It should be noted that the Spaceman also loathes "the wave."

Brian Mitchell, who is one of the greatest musicians on planet Earth, and whose girlfriend Lela is a Greek goddess, was hoping for a Yankee comeback as his team was batting in the top of the eighth inning, was amazed, as was his bandmate, Albert Rogers, a great bass player and singer, that the Spaceman seemed to be calling each pitch in advance, and incredibly, accurately so. Therefore, with the Red Sox leading 2-1, upon seeing that Boston Manager Alex Cora had summoned his erratic lefthander, Darwinzon Hernandez from the bullpen, the Spaceman winced. Bill Lee had strongly suggested that the Red Sox leave right-hander Tanner Houck in the game and elaborated, "Houck may have walked a few guys, but they weren't going to hit him."

Within moments, Hernandez had plunked the Yankees left-handed hitter, Anthony Rizzo with a pitch that loaded the bases. The Spaceman immediately became apoplectic when he saw Manager Cora walk to the mound, an unusual occurrence, considering that most managers send their pitching coach out to calm their embattled hurlers.

"No!" cried the Spaceman, "Cora's telling him to throw strikes! He's chastising him rather than giving him the proper instruction. Giancarlo Stanton has enormous power, and he KNOWS that Darwinzon is going to groove a first-pitch fastball right down the middle and Stanton's going to crush it! I know what Cora told his pitcher. He scolded him by yelling, 'Throw strikes!' This won't end well."

No sooner than Alex Cora reentered the dugout, the Spaceman proved prophetic. As Darwinzon Hernandez came to the belt a split second before delivering his fateful pitch, the Spaceman shouted, "Watch this!"

There is a sickening sound familiar to all pitchers that just tossed a horrible meatball. It is the sound of a baseball being obliterated. The Spaceman described what transpired as follows:

482 fucking feet, and Stanton hit it down near the handle! If he had hit it slightly more towards the barrel, the baseball would need flight attendants on it!"

Albert Rogers of the Weight Band, who Bill described as "a terrific person, a sweetheart," shouted, "Bill, I can't believe how honest you are. You were telling it like it is. You called the pitch and the grand-slam home run!"

Of course, Yankees fan, Brian Mitchell, was ecstatic. However, in his graciousness, for the first time in his life, he accepted the Spaceman's Red Sox cap and placed it on his head! He then offered his Yankees cap to the Spaceman, and now you know why Bill was waving it around when Red Sox chairman Tom Werner entered the suite!

With the Yankees now up 5-2 as Neil Diamond's "Sweet Caroline" seemed to rub dirt in the Spaceman's wound, Bill noticed that many of the Fenway faithful had begun their inexorable pilgrimage out of the ballpark. Therefore, the Spaceman began waving the Yankees cap around and flipping off the fans beneath the Legend's Suite. Bill shouted, "You fucking fair-weather Red Sox fans! You fucking anal-retentive motherfuckers!" The Spaceman described his actions and words a "Hunter S. Thompson moment."

Drastic Times Call for Drastic Measures and Other Undesirable Idioms

Bill Lee, the renowned Yankee-killer, who has the third best winning percentage of any pitcher in history versus the Yankees, one of them being Babe Ruth, had plans for his newly acquired Yankees cap, however. Upon returning to his home in Vermont after the Yankees had swept the three-game series, and the Red Sox had lost two games to the lowly Baltimore Orioles, the Spaceman planned to exorcise the demons. As he explained:

"I'm going to hang it on the cottonwood tree and set it up 60' and 6" away. I'm going to blast it with #5 steel duck load. If that doesn't work, I'm going to shoot it with BB steel goose shot ammo! But that may not be enough," cried the Spaceman. "I shot the cap twice, but now I think I've got to give it a 'booster shot' to kill the Yankee virus. I don't know how long the initial anti-viral shot will be effective. I plan to speak with Dr. Fauci at the CDC."

Within a week, as Diana Lee reported, Bill indeed shot the crap out of the Yankees cap and then he planned to wear it as he danced to every song (at the Weight Band concert in Peterborough (New Hampshire) "as if I were a succubus. I will spin my hands backwards, and if that doesn't work, I'm going to go to Salem to see Laurie Cabot. I'll go to Salem to get a recharge for my succubus outfit, or whatever they call it."

As it evolved, the earthling known as Bill "Spaceman" Lee wound up receiving "life-saving" advice and instruction from an unlikely source. With the Red Sox in desperate straits, having to face the powerful New York Yankees in a one-game "wildcard playoff game" at Fenway Park on Tuesday, Oct. 5, 2021, and with the behemoths Giancarlo Stanton and Aaron Judge waving their bats menacingly at the left field wall, Bill received a phone call from his friend and wine-partner, Jeff Whitman in California. He instructed the Spaceman to shoot the offending Yankees cap to indeed, disMANTLE, pun intended, the Yankee menace. But first.

The Spaceman indeed, blasted the Weight Band's Yankees cap as it clung desperately to life from his cottonwood tree, and then Bill retreated into his home to watch the proceedings. In the first inning, the initial effect of the Spaceman's noble venture was felt by the powerful Giancarlo Stanton of the Yankees. The huge Yankees slugger ripped into Red Sox starter Nathan Eovaldi's offering, and there was little doubt that the baseball would leave Fenway Park in search of another stratosphere. The call by longtime Yankee's radio broadcaster John Sterling, would be perhaps the most memorable of his career, although in this instance, an embarrassing one.

As the baseball soared towards the heavens, Sterling issued his signature call, the one he had made famous for countless seasons. Sterling shouted, "That ball is high, it is far, it is gone out of the ballpark—a Stantonian home run!" John Sterling then hesitated for a moment before continuing with:

"What did I do wrong? What did I see wrong? Stanton is at first base!"

And that he was. As the Spaceman explained:

"As Stanton's drive was leaving the ballpark, a hand reached out of the sky and gently pushed it back. It was Stephen King's 'Under the Dome!'"

Even with the Spaceman's intervention, dangers still lurked as the dying

Yankees cap somehow managed to threaten Boston's tenuous hold on the outcome of the critical game. With the Red Sox ahead 3-1 in the sixth inning, and Nathan Eovaldi on the ropes, Bill Lee's phone rang. It was indeed Jeff Whitman calling from the west coast. Eovaldi had just allowed a home run to the Yankees Anthony Rizzo and Aaron Judge had reached on an infield single. Red Sox manager summoned righthander Ryan Brazier to face the fearsome Giancarlo Stanton who represented the tying run. The Red Sox season was hanging in the balance as Jeff Whitman hurriedly advised the Spaceman as follows:

"Bill, do you have the gun loaded?"

"Yes," Bill Lee responded.

"Good," said Jeff Whitman, a direct descendent of Walt Whitman, "You must go out and shoot the Yankees cap again. It will serve as a 'booster' to the vaccine. Hurry!"

With that, the Spaceman, clad only in his civvies, grabbed the 410 loaded gun ("Not the 12 gauge," he added), put the cell phone down and rushed outside at 9:49 PM.

"You'll wake the neighbors!" shouted Diana.

"I don't care!" was the Spaceman's retort. "The Yankees must die!"

Spaceman Lee took careful aim at the wounded Yankees cap and did not heed his friend, the great Luis Tiant's advice.

"Don't you do that Santeria, Bill. That shit works! You do Santeria, you'll get fucked!"

Literally moments after Bill had finally given the Yankees cap its "booster shot," Giancarlo Stanton drove a ball so hard it nearly knocked down the left-field wall! The ball was clocked at 116 miles per hour! However, the ball was hit so hard that it ricocheted to Kike Hernandez, who relayed the ball to shortstop Xander Bogaerts, who in turn threw the ball to catcher Kevin Plawecki, who decisively tagged out the sliding Aaron Judge at home plate! End of rally! End of the Yankees! The Spaceman had killed the dastardly cap!

"The cap had a Blue Jays feather in it, "chirped Bill Lee. "Now the Blue Jays and Yankees are in the rear-view mirror. Stephen King (Under the Dome) and Laurie Cabot (the Salem witch) were involved in this."

The following morning, the Spaceman received a call from a gentleman named Robert (Rob) L. Brennan, an award-winning real estate developer with a background in law, politics, and commercial development. Rob is the president of the CapeBuilt Companies. Rob is one of the most beloved people down at the Cape. "There is a film festival on Saturday, September 16, and Rob told me they're going to show "High and Outside." "High and Outside" is a terrific documentary and is perhaps the best explanation of Bill Lee's persona ever filmed.

Rob Brennan attended the one-game wildcard battle at Fenway Park and told the Spaceman, "It was the most beautiful experience. I had to park my car at South Station and walked all the way to Fenway and back after the game. I didn't return home until nearly 2:00 AM, but it was worth it. The crowd was so great and positive."

It should be noted that the Spaceman did NOT watch the game on television! As Bill explained:

"When I tuned in and saw ARod and all of those other fucking Yankee blowhards in the booth and the fucking video they played before the game, I said, 'I ain't watchin' this bullshit!' I turned on the Red Sox radio feed and it worked fine for me. Jerry Remy threw out the first ball. Nothing could have possibly gone wrong! Hey, John Sterling couldn't even see the ball scrape the paint. It was magic!"

The Spaceman was not through as he entertained the possibility of meeting the Weight Band up in Lewiston, Maine:

"I'll go up to Lewiston, Maine, the place where Muhammad Ali landed his phantom punch. The last time I pitched in Lewiston, I took a backroad and drove in past a cemetery. I recall having to take a shit before the ballgame. So, I was in the cemetery and I was hiding behind a tree. I heard this huffing and puffing and I see that there's a guy copulating with a girl atop a gravestone."*

> * The author then replied, "I hope it was the guy and girl huffing and puffing." The Spaceman responded as follows:

"I don't know if it was or not, and I wasn't going to check on it! It was something out of a Stephen King novel."

A week after being the gracious guest of Bill and Diana Lee at Fenway Park, Yankees fan and the Weight Band's great Brian Mitchell offered:

"I waited a full week to admit that the sausage at Fenway Park was better than any I've eaten at Yankee Stadium."

I then responded to Brian with, "I hope it didn't take a full week to digest it." This reminded the Spaceman of the time he had taken his second grandson, Kazden out to Fenway Park:

"Kazden is my son, Michael's second boy, after Hunter. Kazden was about four years-old, and we took him to the Legends Suite at Fenway. To be contrary, Kasten decided he was a Yankees fan because everyone was pushing the Red Sox down his throat. Well, Kazden was in the process of stuffing Fenway franks down his throat when he suddenly blew his lunch down onto the people seated below in section 14. Which proves you should never give a Fenway frank to a Yankees fan."

INDEX

ABOUT THE AUTHOR

Scott Russell was born in the Bronx, New York in the year 1945. "His high school yearbook photograph is adorned with the words: "The Strong Mind Knows the Power of Gentleness." The words were not his idea. So be it.

Russell loves baseball, at least the way it was played prior to the abomination it has evolved into, and absolutely adores all animals. Scott grew up in a city where as he describes, "We did not believe in political correctness, and in fact, never even once heard that term. We lived in a marvelous melting pot, we insulted each other frequently, and yes, even ethnically, but we had each others backs and ate in each others homes."

Author Russell seldom uses the word "hate," and often quotes the inspirational motivational speaker and athlete Jen Bricker-Bauer, whose comment is "I hate hate." However, Russell loathes partisan politics and anything that divides us. Not too long ago, Russell stated, "I'm not on your side. 'Sides' are the problem." Scott also is a strong believer that we are victims of our environment.

Scott Russell resides in "The Cliffs" of North Attleboro, Massachusetts with Peg, his long-suffering bride of 37 years and their assorted deranged felines.

Other books by Scott Russell include:
Too Much Time on His Hands
Still Too Much Time on His Hands
Joey
Prophet's End
The Scorekeeper
The Spaceman Chronicles

Made in the USA
Middletown, DE
15 February 2022